JUSTICE LEAGUE OF AMERICA
SECOND COMING

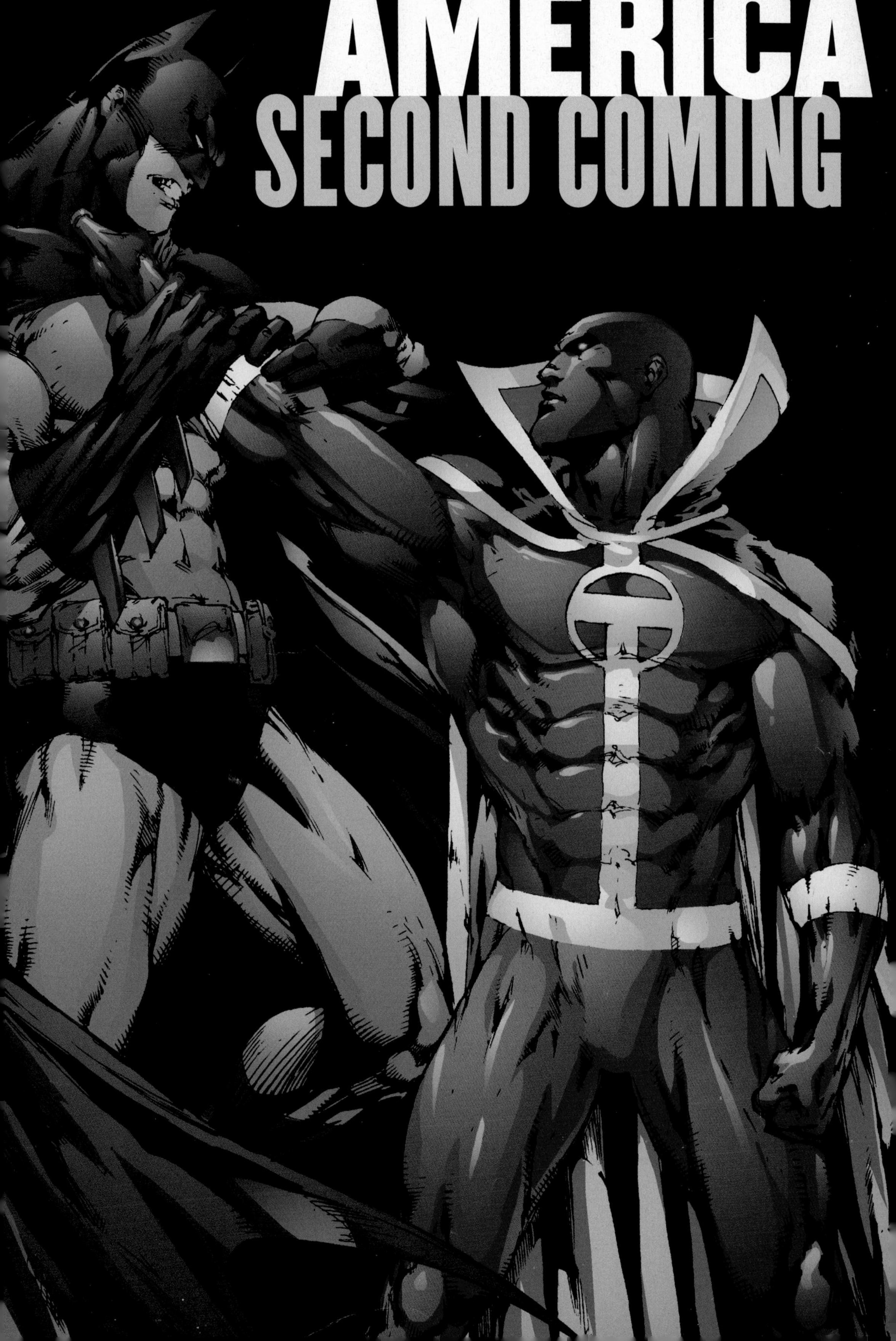

Dan DiDio Senior VP-Executive Editor
Eddie Berganza Editor-original series
Adam Schlagman Associate Editor-original series
Bob Joy Editor-collected edition
Robbin Brosterman Senior Art Director
Paul Levitz President & Publisher
Georg Brewer VP-Design & DC Direct Creative
Richard Bruning Senior VP-Creative Director
Patrick Caldon Executive VP-Finance & Operations
Chris Caramalis VP-Finance
John Cunningham VP-Marketing
Terri Cunningham VP-Managing Editor
Amy Genkins Senior VP-Business & Legal Affairs
Alison Gill VP-Manufacturing
David Hyde VP-Publicity
Hank Kanalz VP-General Manager, WildStorm
Jim Lee Editorial Director-WildStorm
Gregory Noveck Senior VP-Creative Affairs
Sue Pohja VP-Book Trade Sales
Steve Rotterdam Senior VP-Sales & Marketing
Cheryl Rubin Senior VP-Brand Management
Alysse Soll VP-Advertising & Custom Publishing
Jeff Trojan VP-Business Development, DC Direct
Bob Wayne VP-Sales

Cover by **Ed Benes**
with **Hi-Fi**

Justice League of America: Second Coming

DC Comics, 1700 Broadway, New York, NY 10019
A Warner Bros. Entertainment Company
Printed in USA. First Printing.
HC ISBN: 978-1-4012-2252-9
SC ISBN: 978-1-4012-2253-6

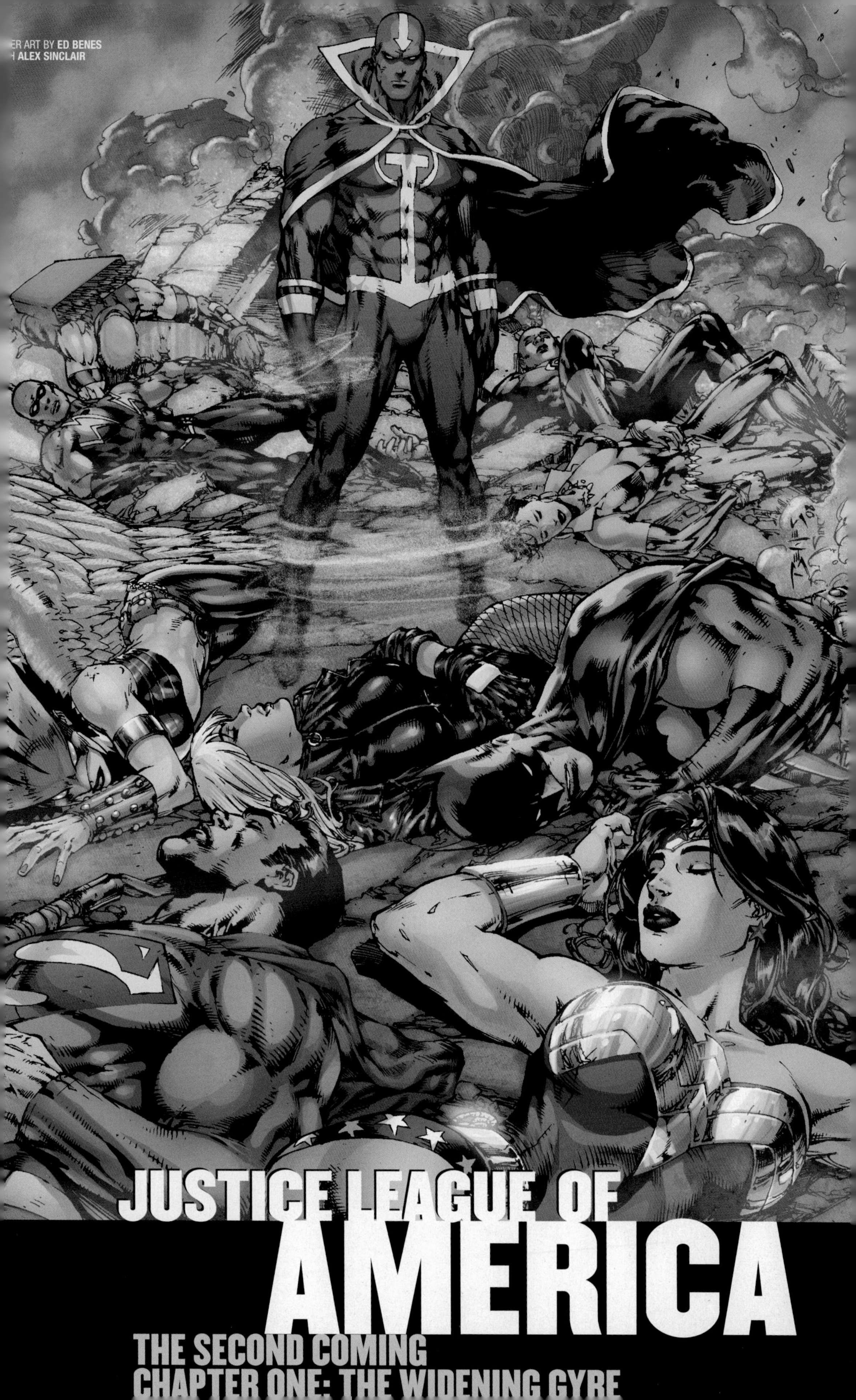
ER ART BY ED BENES
H ALEX SINCLAIR
JUSTICE LEAGUE OF
AMERICA
THE SECOND COMING
CHAPTER ONE: THE WIDENING GYRE

THE SECOND COMING
Chapter One: The Widening Gyre

Dwayne McDuffie
Writer

Ed Benes
Artist

Rob Leigh
Letterer

Pete Pantazis
Colorist

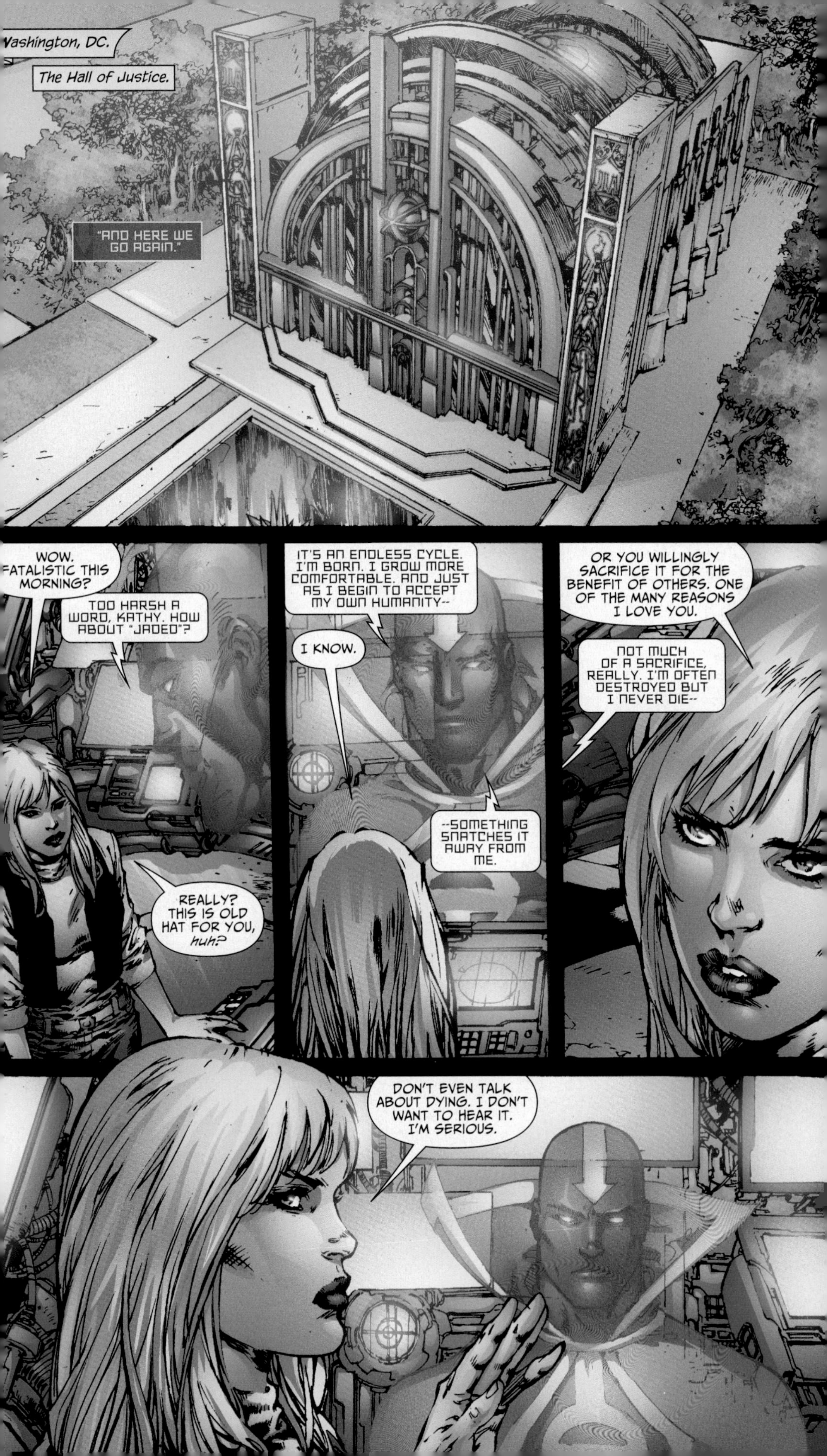
Washington, DC.
The Hall of Justice.
"AND HERE WE GO AGAIN."
WOW. FATALISTIC THIS MORNING?
TOO HARSH A WORD, KATHY. HOW ABOUT "JADED"?
REALLY? THIS IS OLD HAT FOR YOU, *huh?*
IT'S AN ENDLESS CYCLE. I'M BORN. I GROW MORE COMFORTABLE. AND JUST AS I BEGIN TO ACCEPT MY OWN HUMANITY--
I KNOW.
--SOMETHING SNATCHES IT AWAY FROM ME.
OR YOU WILLINGLY SACRIFICE IT FOR THE BENEFIT OF OTHERS. ONE OF THE MANY REASONS I LOVE YOU.
NOT MUCH OF A SACRIFICE, REALLY. I'M OFTEN DESTROYED BUT I NEVER DIE--
DON'T EVEN TALK ABOUT DYING. I DON'T WANT TO HEAR IT. I'M SERIOUS.

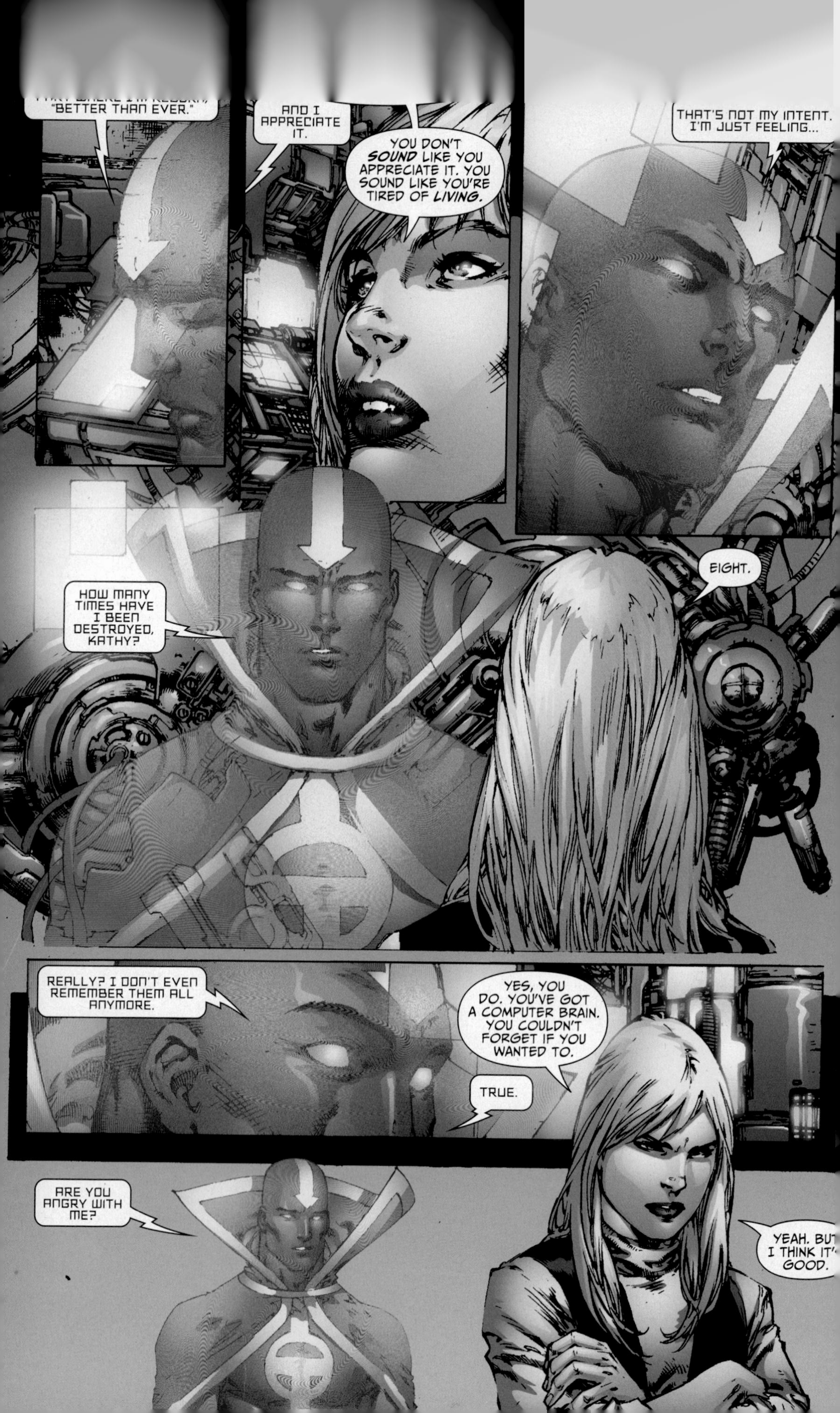
"BETTER THAN EVER."
AND I APPRECIATE IT.
YOU DON'T *SOUND* LIKE YOU APPRECIATE IT. YOU SOUND LIKE YOU'RE TIRED OF *LIVING.*
THAT'S NOT MY INTENT. I'M JUST FEELING...
HOW MANY TIMES HAVE I BEEN DESTROYED, KATHY?
EIGHT.
REALLY? I DON'T EVEN REMEMBER THEM ALL ANYMORE.
YES, YOU DO. YOU'VE GOT A COMPUTER BRAIN. YOU COULDN'T FORGET IF YOU WANTED TO.
TRUE.
ARE YOU ANGRY WITH ME?
YEAH. BU I THINK IT' GOOD.

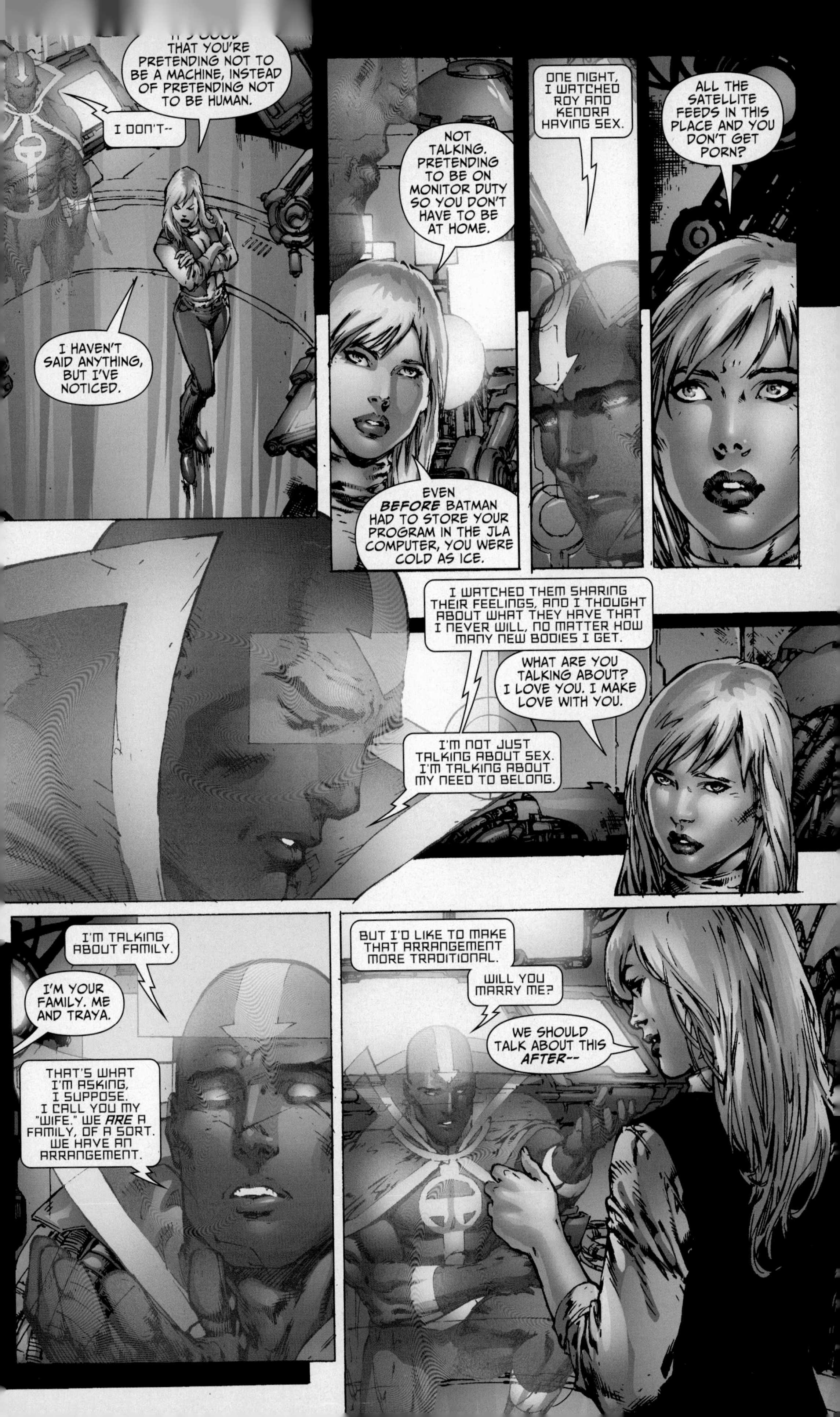
IT'S GOOD THAT YOU'RE PRETENDING NOT TO BE A MACHINE, INSTEAD OF PRETENDING NOT TO BE HUMAN.
I DON'T--
I HAVEN'T SAID ANYTHING, BUT I'VE NOTICED.
NOT TALKING. PRETENDING TO BE ON MONITOR DUTY SO YOU DON'T HAVE TO BE AT HOME.
EVEN *BEFORE* BATMAN HAD TO STORE YOUR PROGRAM IN THE JLA COMPUTER, YOU WERE COLD AS ICE.
ONE NIGHT, I WATCHED ROY AND KENDRA HAVING SEX.
ALL THE SATELLITE FEEDS IN THIS PLACE AND YOU DON'T GET PORN?
I WATCHED THEM SHARING THEIR FEELINGS, AND I THOUGHT ABOUT WHAT THEY HAVE THAT I NEVER WILL, NO MATTER HOW MANY NEW BODIES I GET.
WHAT ARE YOU TALKING ABOUT? I LOVE YOU. I MAKE LOVE WITH YOU.
I'M NOT JUST TALKING ABOUT SEX. I'M TALKING ABOUT MY NEED TO BELONG.
I'M TALKING ABOUT FAMILY.
I'M YOUR FAMILY. ME AND TRAYA.
THAT'S WHAT I'M ASKING, I SUPPOSE. I CALL YOU MY "WIFE." WE *ARE* A FAMILY, OF A SORT. WE HAVE AN ARRANGEMENT.
BUT I'D LIKE TO MAKE THAT ARRANGEMENT MORE TRADITIONAL.
WILL YOU MARRY ME?
WE SHOULD TALK ABOUT THIS *AFTER*--

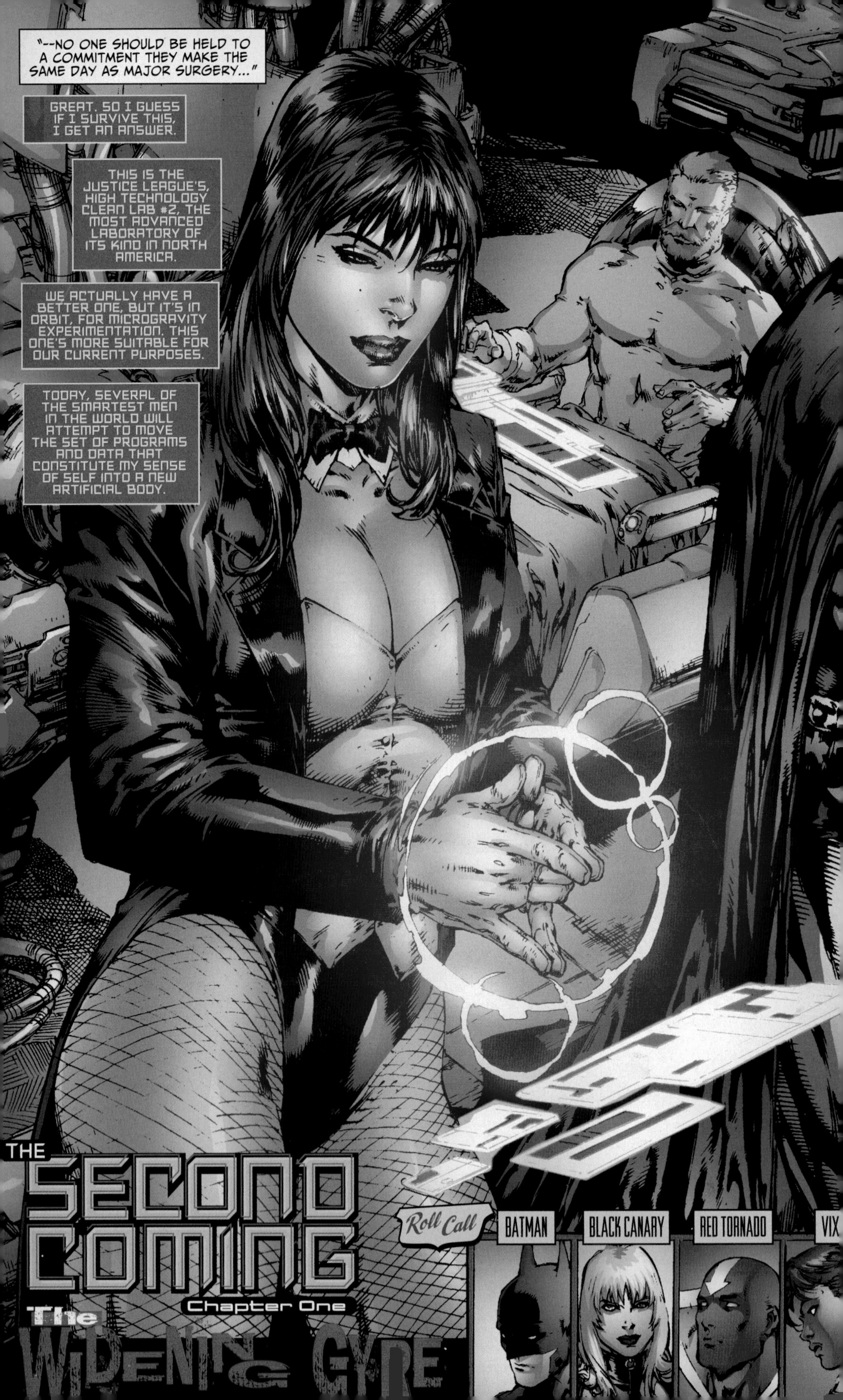
"--NO ONE SHOULD BE HELD TO A COMMITMENT THEY MAKE THE SAME DAY AS MAJOR SURGERY..."
GREAT. SO I GUESS IF I SURVIVE THIS, I GET AN ANSWER.
THIS IS THE JUSTICE LEAGUE'S, HIGH TECHNOLOGY CLEAN LAB #2, THE MOST ADVANCED LABORATORY OF ITS KIND IN NORTH AMERICA.
WE ACTUALLY HAVE A BETTER ONE, BUT IT'S IN ORBIT, FOR MICROGRAVITY EXPERIMENTATION. THIS ONE'S MORE SUITABLE FOR OUR CURRENT PURPOSES.
TODAY, SEVERAL OF THE SMARTEST MEN IN THE WORLD WILL ATTEMPT TO MOVE THE SET OF PROGRAMS AND DATA THAT CONSTITUTE MY SENSE OF SELF INTO A NEW ARTIFICIAL BODY.
THE SECOND COMING
Chapter One
The WIDENING GYRE
Roll Call
BATMAN
BLACK CANARY
RED TORNADO
VIX

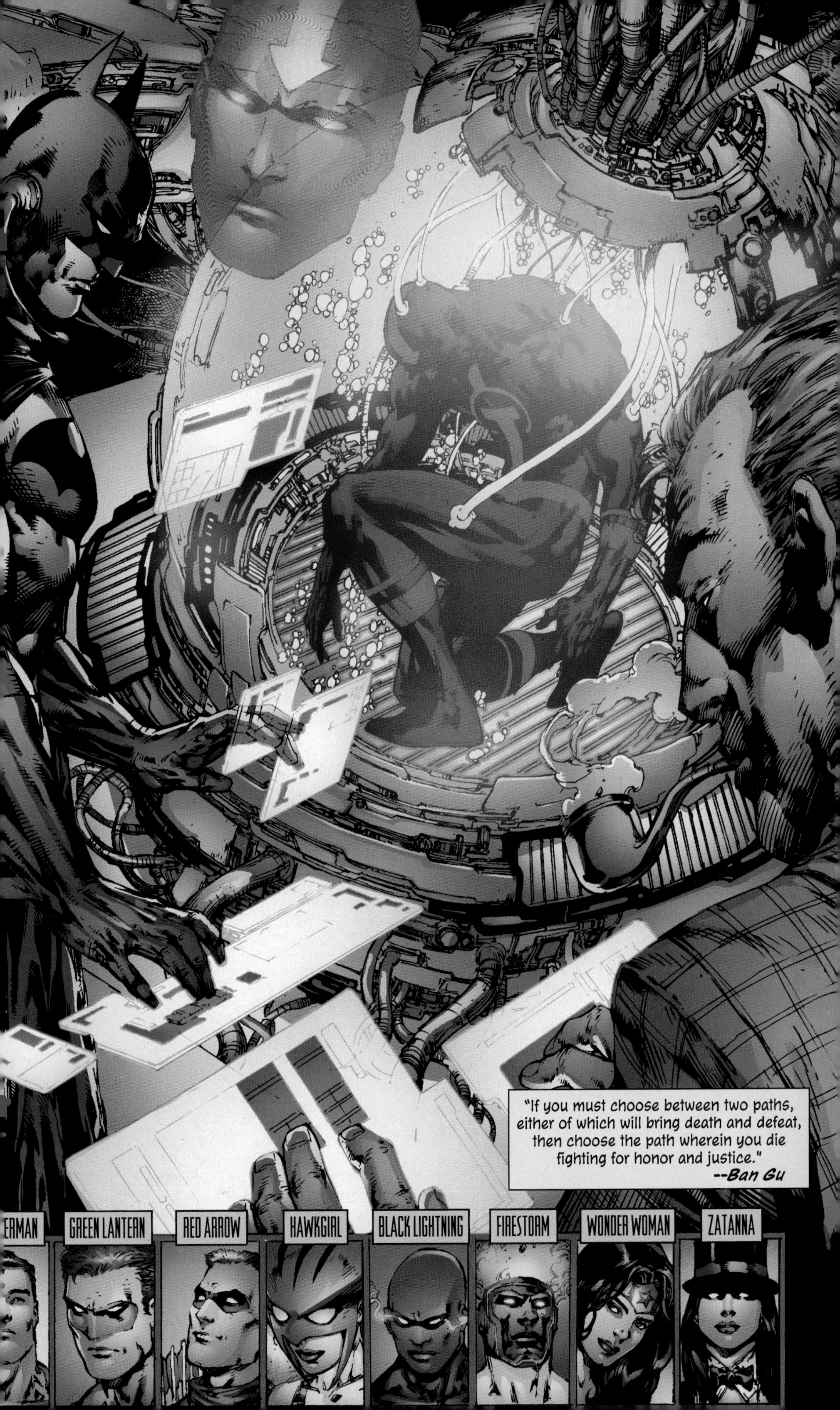
"If you must choose between two paths, either of which will bring death and defeat, then choose the path wherein you die fighting for honor and justice."
--Ban Gu
ERMAN
GREEN LANTERN
RED ARROW
HAWKGIRL
BLACK LIGHTNING
FIRESTORM
WONDER WOMAN
ZATANNA

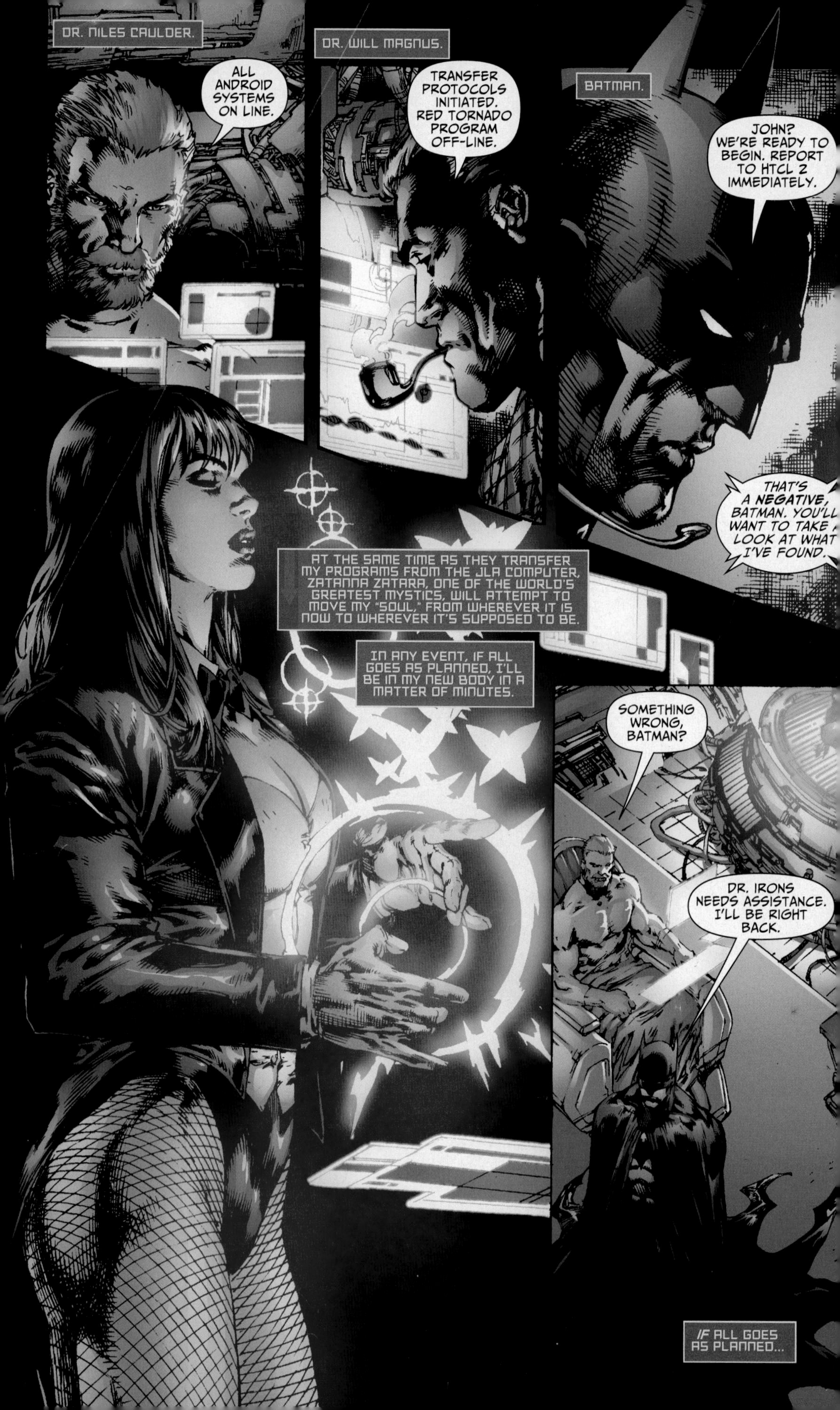
DR. NILES CAULDER.
ALL ANDROID SYSTEMS ON LINE.
DR. WILL MAGNUS.
TRANSFER PROTOCOLS INITIATED. RED TORNADO PROGRAM OFF-LINE.
BATMAN.
JOHN? WE'RE READY TO BEGIN. REPORT TO HTCL 2 IMMEDIATELY.
THAT'S A NEGATIVE, BATMAN. YOU'LL WANT TO TAKE LOOK AT WHAT I'VE FOUND.
AT THE SAME TIME AS THEY TRANSFER MY PROGRAMS FROM THE JLA COMPUTER, ZATANNA ZATARA, ONE OF THE WORLD'S GREATEST MYSTICS, WILL ATTEMPT TO MOVE MY "SOUL," FROM WHEREVER IT IS NOW TO WHEREVER IT'S SUPPOSED TO BE.
IN ANY EVENT, IF ALL GOES AS PLANNED, I'LL BE IN MY NEW BODY IN A MATTER OF MINUTES.
SOMETHING WRONG, BATMAN?
DR. IRONS NEEDS ASSISTANCE. I'LL BE RIGHT BACK.
IF ALL GOES AS PLANNED...

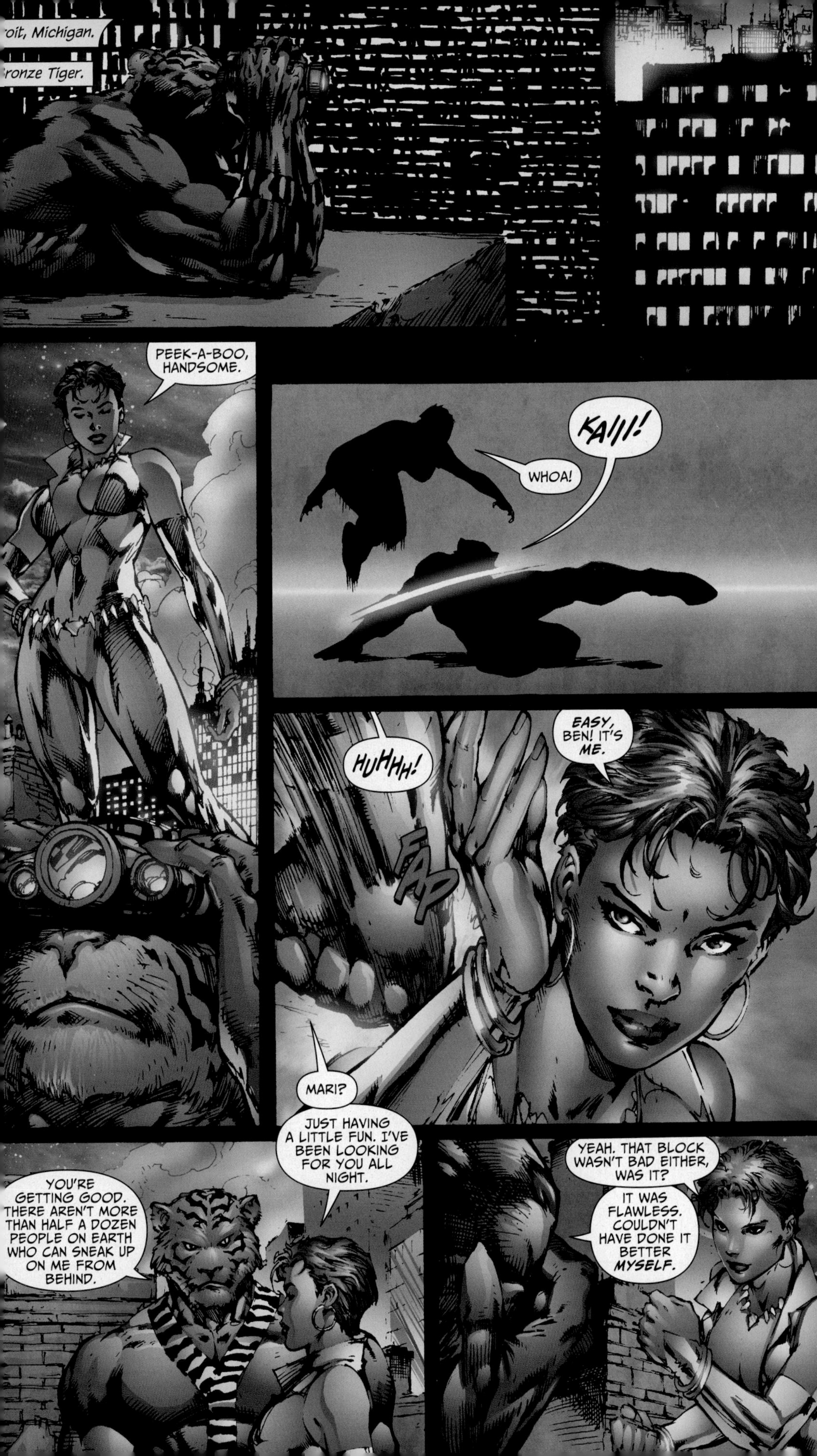

...roit, Michigan.
...ronze Tiger.
PEEK-A-BOO, HANDSOME.
KAIII!
WHOA!
EASY, BEN! IT'S ME.
HUHHH!
FAP
MARI?
JUST HAVING A LITTLE FUN. I'VE BEEN LOOKING FOR YOU ALL NIGHT.
YOU'RE GETTING GOOD. THERE AREN'T MORE THAN HALF A DOZEN PEOPLE ON EARTH WHO CAN SNEAK UP ON ME FROM BEHIND.
YEAH. THAT BLOCK WASN'T BAD EITHER, WAS IT?
IT WAS FLAWLESS. COULDN'T HAVE DONE IT BETTER MYSELF.

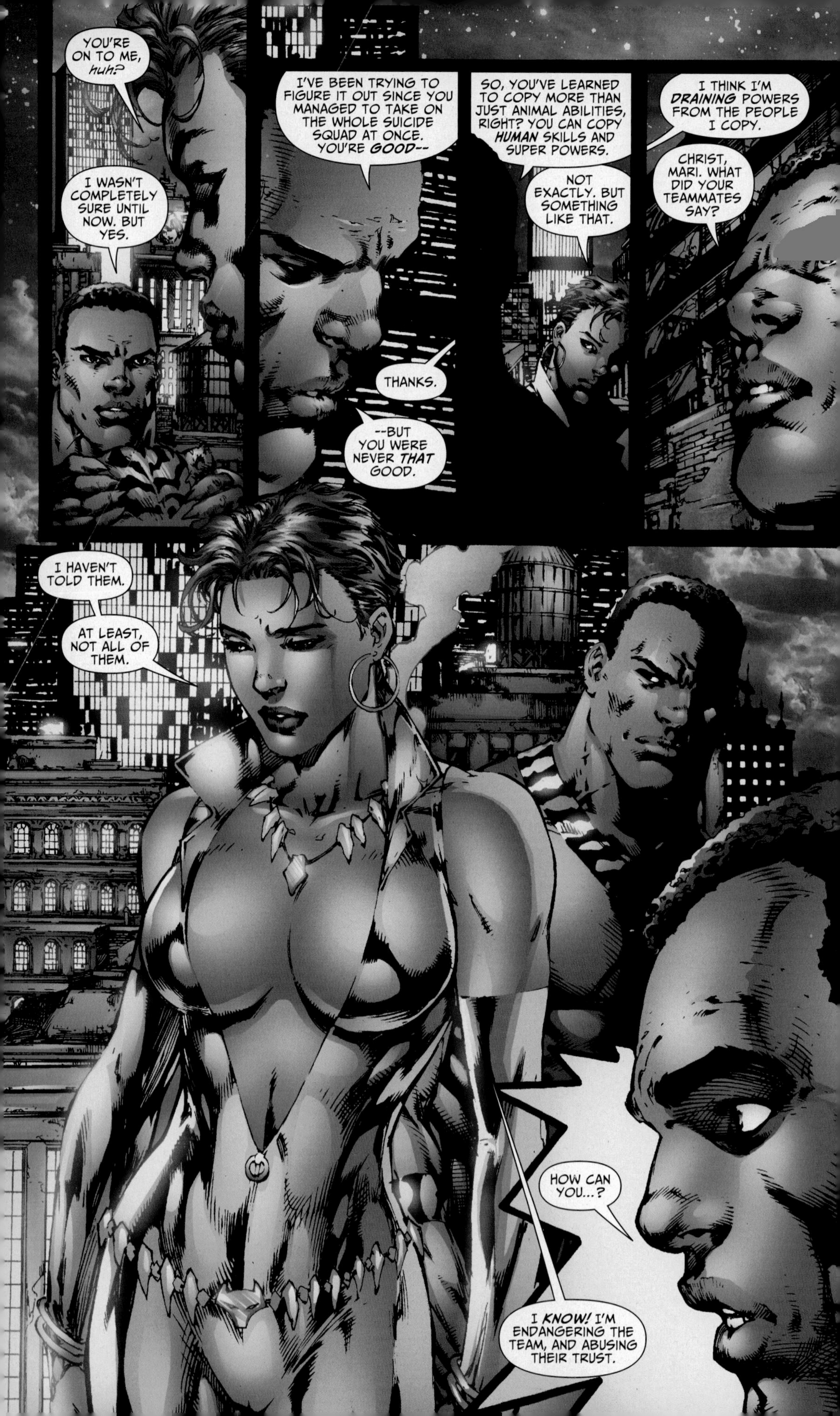
YOU'RE ON TO ME, *huh?*
I WASN'T COMPLETELY SURE UNTIL NOW. BUT YES.
I'VE BEEN TRYING TO FIGURE IT OUT SINCE YOU MANAGED TO TAKE ON THE WHOLE SUICIDE SQUAD AT ONCE. YOU'RE ***GOOD***--
THANKS.
--BUT YOU WERE NEVER ***THAT*** GOOD.
SO, YOU'VE LEARNED TO COPY MORE THAN JUST ANIMAL ABILITIES, RIGHT? YOU CAN COPY ***HUMAN*** SKILLS AND SUPER POWERS.
NOT EXACTLY. BUT SOMETHING LIKE THAT.
I THINK I'M ***DRAINING*** POWERS FROM THE PEOPLE I COPY.
CHRIST, MARI. WHAT DID YOUR TEAMMATES SAY?
I HAVEN'T TOLD THEM.
AT LEAST, NOT ALL OF THEM.
HOW CAN YOU...?
I ***KNOW!*** I'M ENDANGERING THE TEAM, AND ABUSING THEIR TRUST.

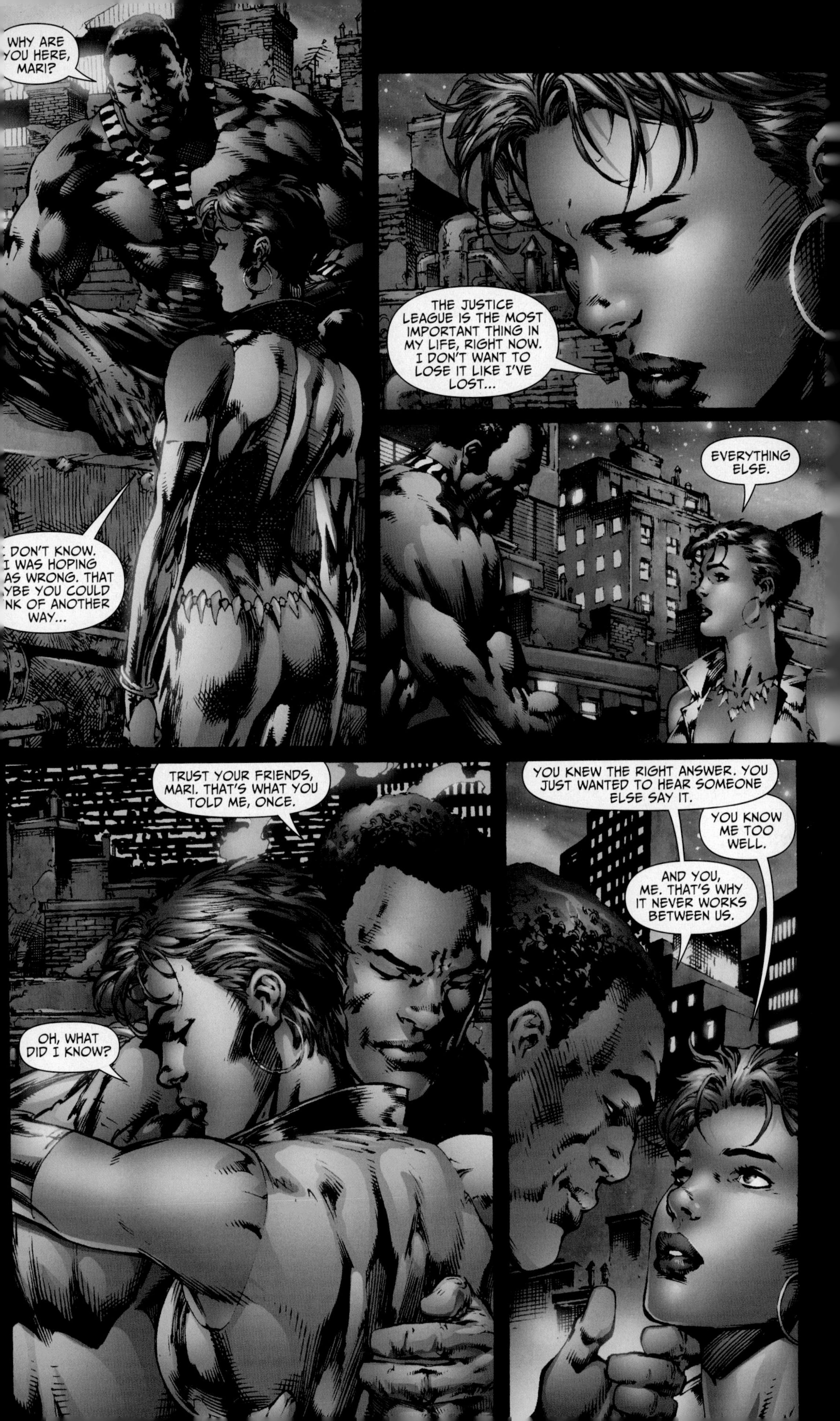
WHY ARE YOU HERE, MARI?
DON'T KNOW. I WAS HOPING AS WRONG. THAT YBE YOU COULD NK OF ANOTHER WAY...
THE JUSTICE LEAGUE IS THE MOST IMPORTANT THING IN MY LIFE, RIGHT NOW. I DON'T WANT TO LOSE IT LIKE I'VE LOST...
EVERYTHING ELSE.
TRUST YOUR FRIENDS, MARI. THAT'S WHAT YOU TOLD ME, ONCE.
OH, WHAT DID I KNOW?
YOU KNEW THE RIGHT ANSWER. YOU JUST WANTED TO HEAR SOMEONE ELSE SAY IT.
YOU KNOW ME TOO WELL.
AND YOU, ME. THAT'S WHY IT NEVER WORKS BETWEEN US.

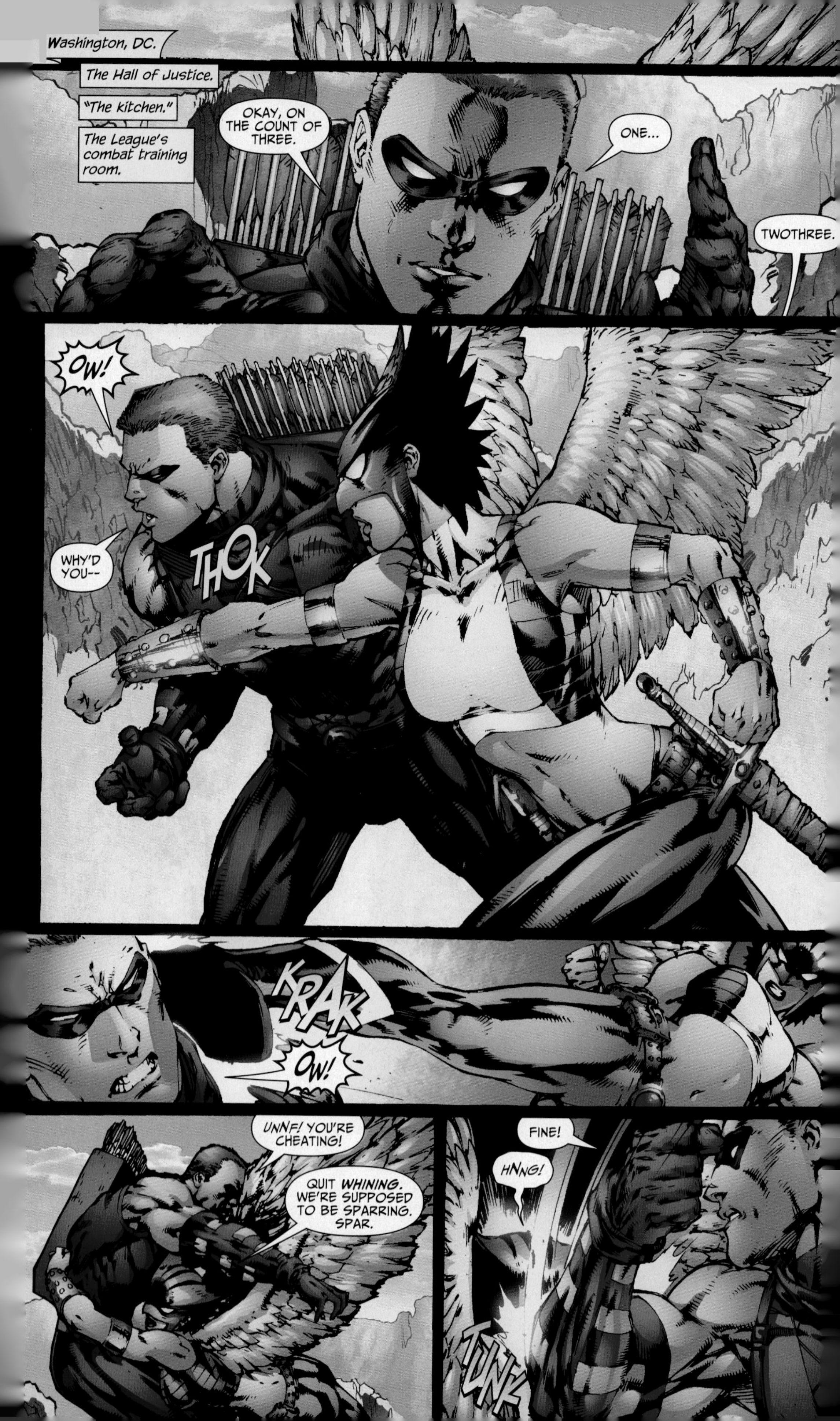

Washington, DC.
The Hall of Justice.
"The kitchen."
The League's combat training room.
OKAY, ON THE COUNT OF THREE.
ONE...
TWOTHREE.
OW!
WHY'D YOU--
THOK
KRAK
OW!
UNNF! YOU'RE CHEATING!
QUIT WHINING. WE'RE SUPPOSED TO BE SPARRING. SPAR.
FINE!
HNNG!
TUNK

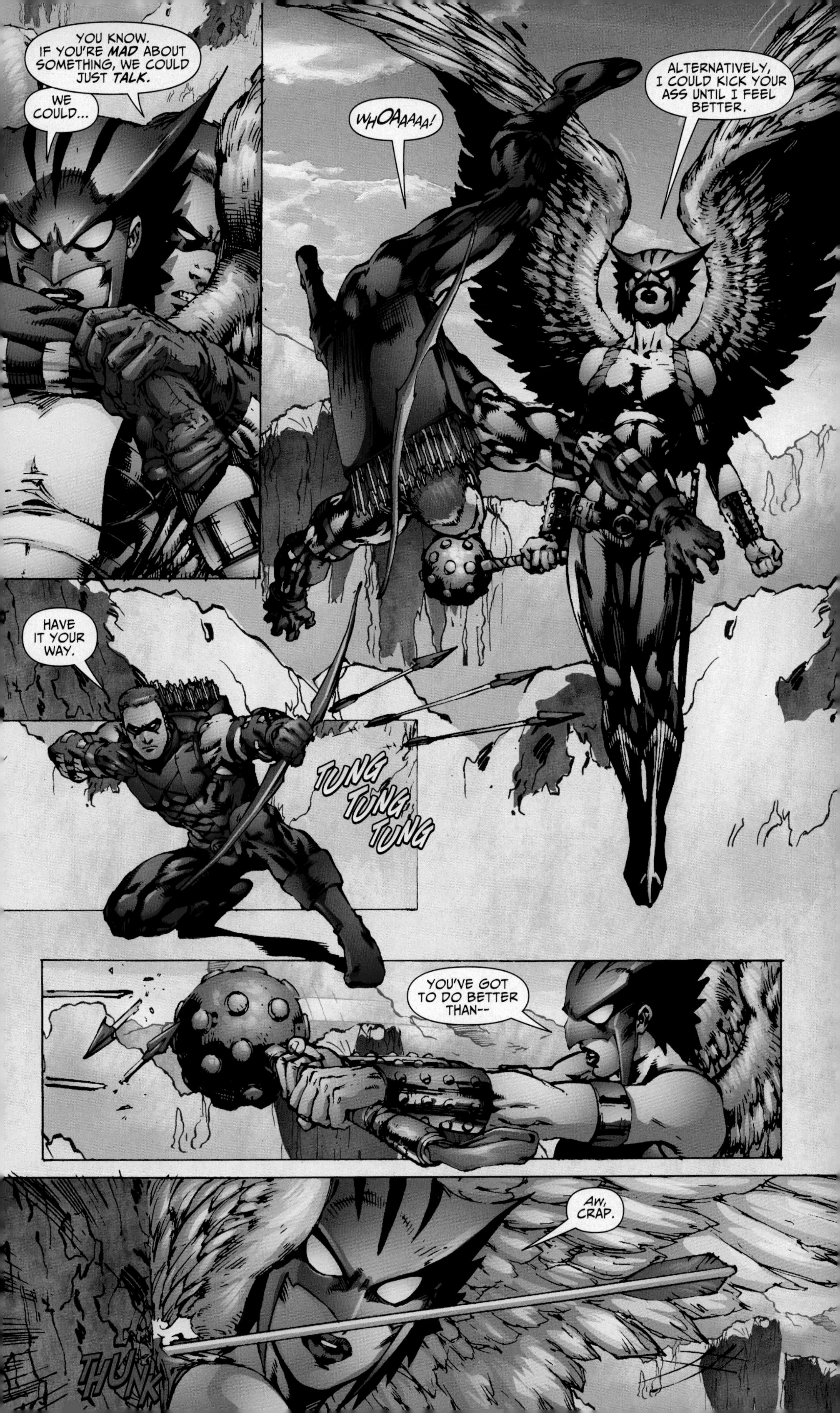
YOU KNOW. IF YOU'RE MAD ABOUT SOMETHING, WE COULD JUST TALK.
WE COULD...
WHOAAAAA!
ALTERNATIVELY, I COULD KICK YOUR ASS UNTIL I FEEL BETTER.
HAVE IT YOUR WAY.
TUNG TUNG TUNG
YOU'VE GOT TO DO BETTER THAN--
AW, CRAP.
THUNK

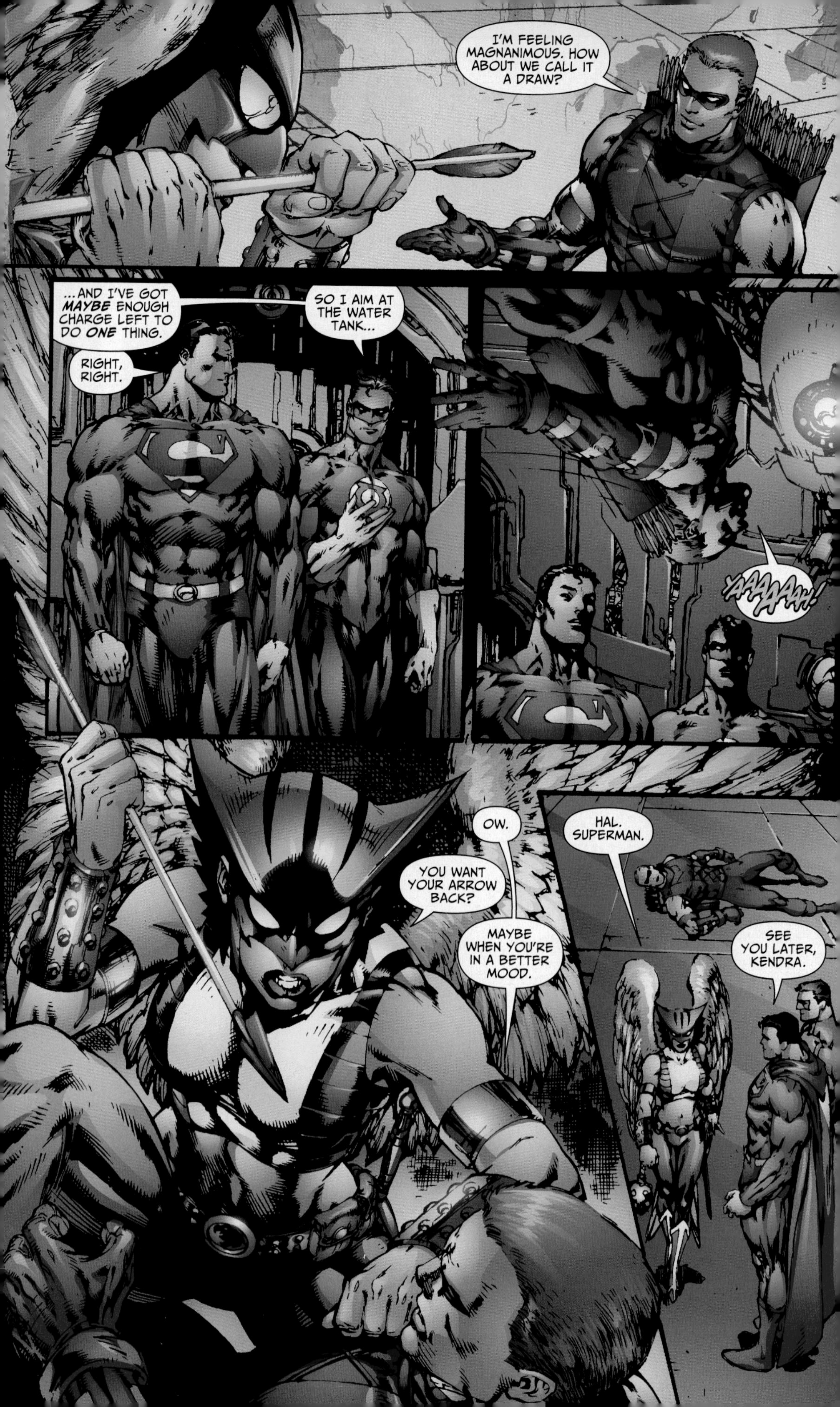
I'M FEELING MAGNANIMOUS. HOW ABOUT WE CALL IT A DRAW?
...AND I'VE GOT MAYBE ENOUGH CHARGE LEFT TO DO ONE THING.
SO I AIM AT THE WATER TANK...
RIGHT, RIGHT.
YAAAAAAH!
OW.
YOU WANT YOUR ARROW BACK?
MAYBE WHEN YOU'RE IN A BETTER MOOD.
HAL. SUPERMAN.
SEE YOU LATER, KENDRA.

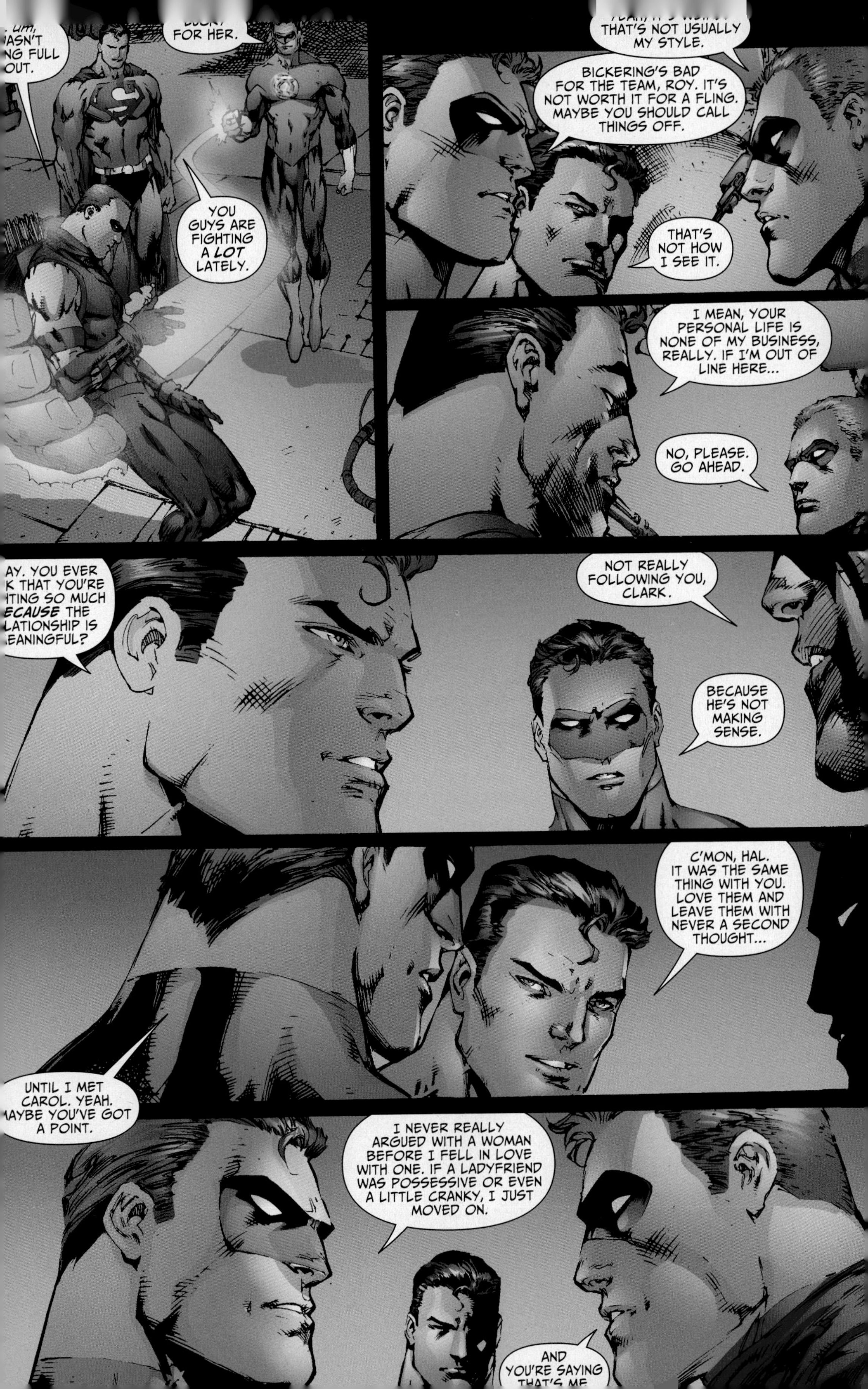

ASN'T NG FULL OUT.
FOR HER.
YOU GUYS ARE FIGHTING A *LOT* LATELY.
THAT'S NOT USUALLY MY STYLE.
BICKERING'S BAD FOR THE TEAM, ROY. IT'S NOT WORTH IT FOR A FLING. MAYBE YOU SHOULD CALL THINGS OFF.
THAT'S NOT HOW I SEE IT.
I MEAN, YOUR PERSONAL LIFE IS NONE OF MY BUSINESS, REALLY. IF I'M OUT OF LINE HERE...
NO, PLEASE. GO AHEAD.
AY. YOU EVER K THAT YOU'RE TING SO MUCH *ECAUSE* THE LATIONSHIP IS EANINGFUL?
NOT REALLY FOLLOWING YOU, CLARK.
BECAUSE HE'S NOT MAKING SENSE.
C'MON, HAL. IT WAS THE SAME THING WITH YOU. LOVE THEM AND LEAVE THEM WITH NEVER A SECOND THOUGHT...
UNTIL I MET CAROL. YEAH. AYBE YOU'VE GOT A POINT.
I NEVER REALLY ARGUED WITH A WOMAN BEFORE I FELL IN LOVE WITH ONE. IF A LADYFRIEND WAS POSSESSIVE OR EVEN A LITTLE CRANKY, I JUST MOVED ON.
AND YOU'RE SAYING

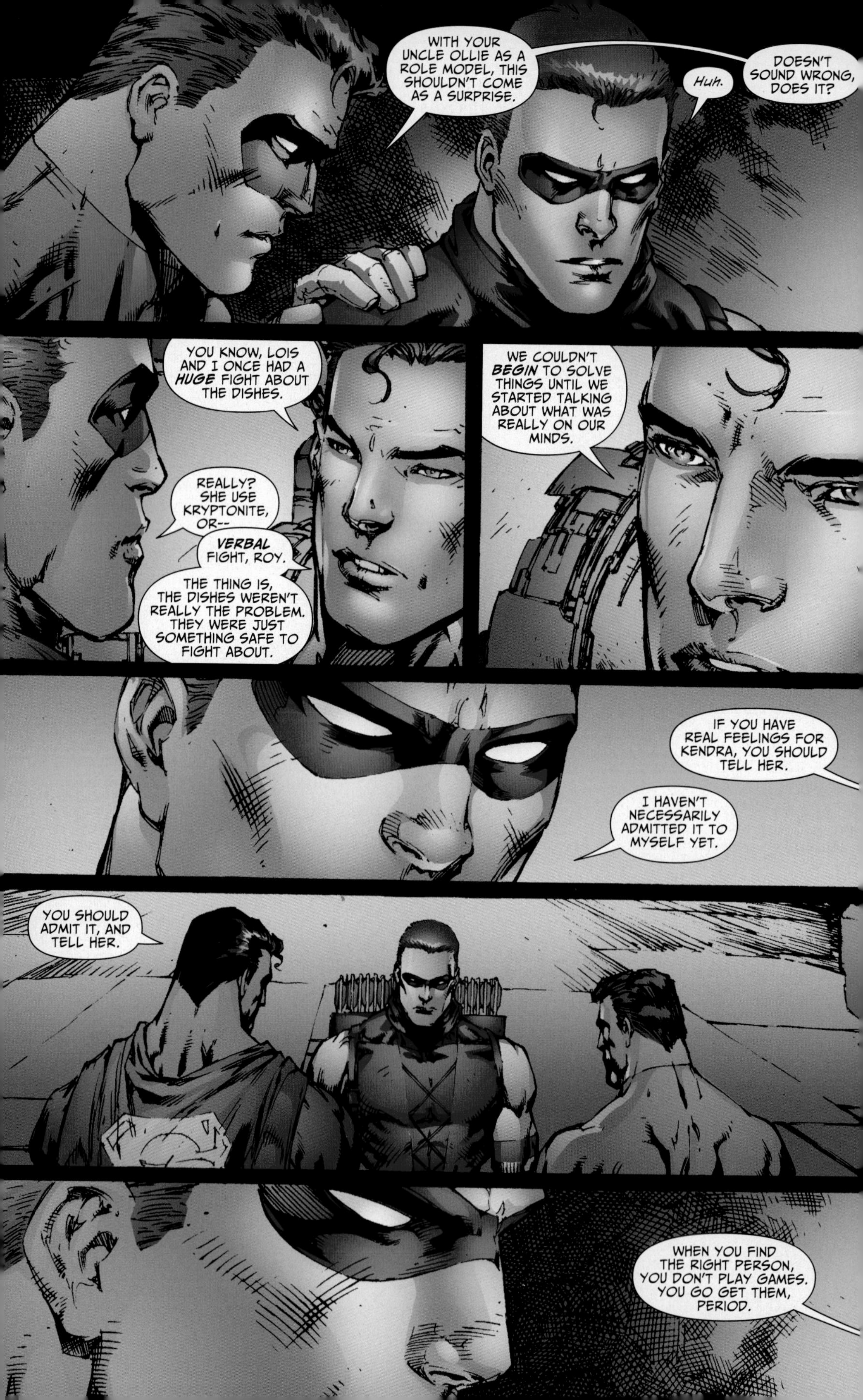
WITH YOUR UNCLE OLLIE AS A ROLE MODEL, THIS SHOULDN'T COME AS A SURPRISE.
Huh.
DOESN'T SOUND WRONG, DOES IT?
YOU KNOW, LOIS AND I ONCE HAD A HUGE FIGHT ABOUT THE DISHES.
REALLY? SHE USE KRYPTONITE, OR--
VERBAL FIGHT, ROY.
THE THING IS, THE DISHES WEREN'T REALLY THE PROBLEM. THEY WERE JUST SOMETHING SAFE TO FIGHT ABOUT.
WE COULDN'T BEGIN TO SOLVE THINGS UNTIL WE STARTED TALKING ABOUT WHAT WAS REALLY ON OUR MINDS.
IF YOU HAVE REAL FEELINGS FOR KENDRA, YOU SHOULD TELL HER.
I HAVEN'T NECESSARILY ADMITTED IT TO MYSELF YET.
YOU SHOULD ADMIT IT, AND TELL HER.
WHEN YOU FIND THE RIGHT PERSON, YOU DON'T PLAY GAMES. YOU GO GET THEM, PERIOD.

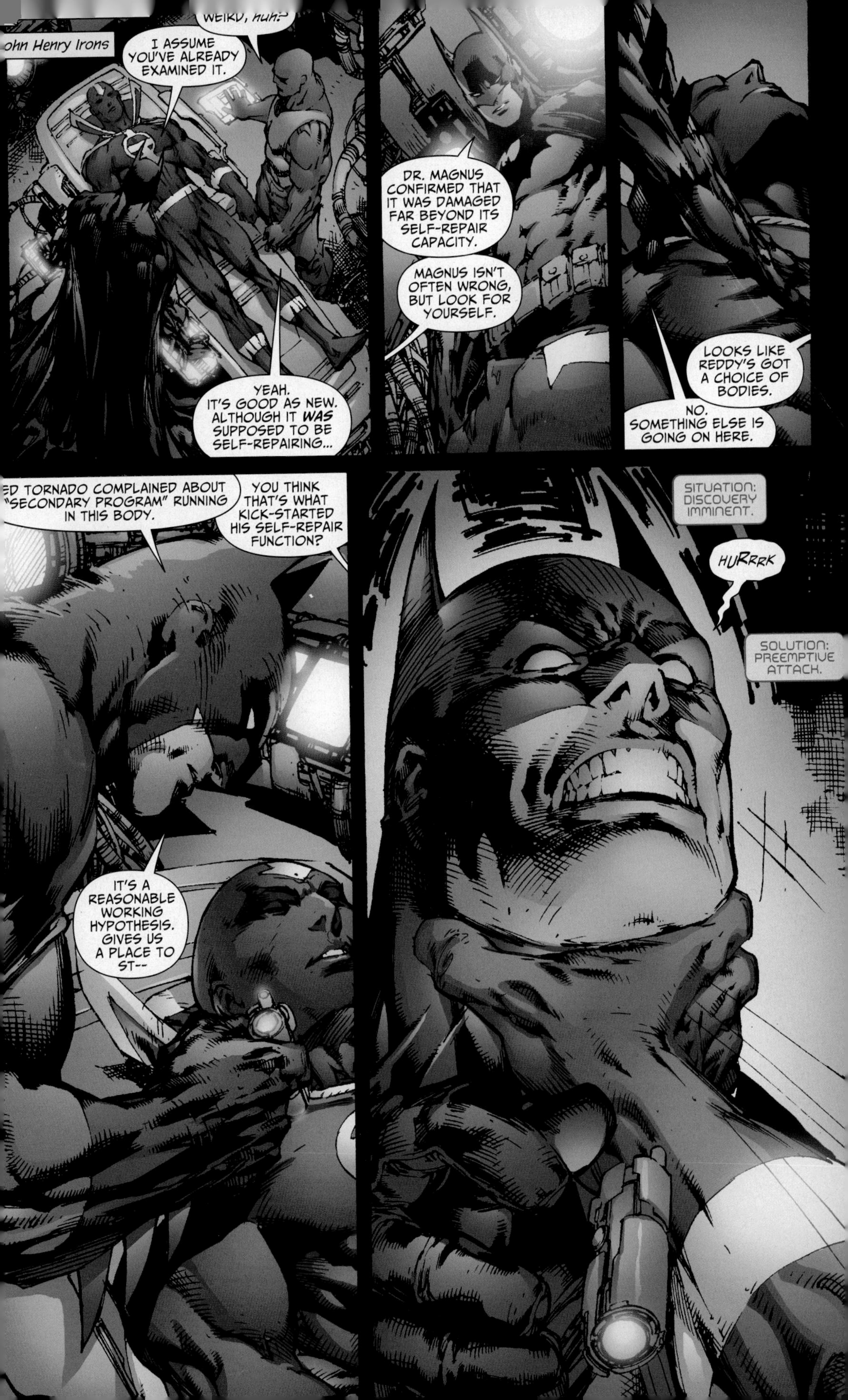
WEIRD, HUH?
John Henry Irons
I ASSUME YOU'VE ALREADY EXAMINED IT.
YEAH. IT'S GOOD AS NEW. ALTHOUGH IT WAS SUPPOSED TO BE SELF-REPAIRING...
DR. MAGNUS CONFIRMED THAT IT WAS DAMAGED FAR BEYOND ITS SELF-REPAIR CAPACITY.
MAGNUS ISN'T OFTEN WRONG, BUT LOOK FOR YOURSELF.
LOOKS LIKE REDDY'S GOT A CHOICE OF BODIES.
NO. SOMETHING ELSE IS GOING ON HERE.
ED TORNADO COMPLAINED ABOUT "SECONDARY PROGRAM" RUNNING IN THIS BODY.
YOU THINK THAT'S WHAT KICK-STARTED HIS SELF-REPAIR FUNCTION?
IT'S A REASONABLE WORKING HYPOTHESIS. GIVES US A PLACE TO ST--
SITUATION: DISCOVERY IMMINENT.
HURRRK
SOLUTION: PREEMPTIVE ATTACK.

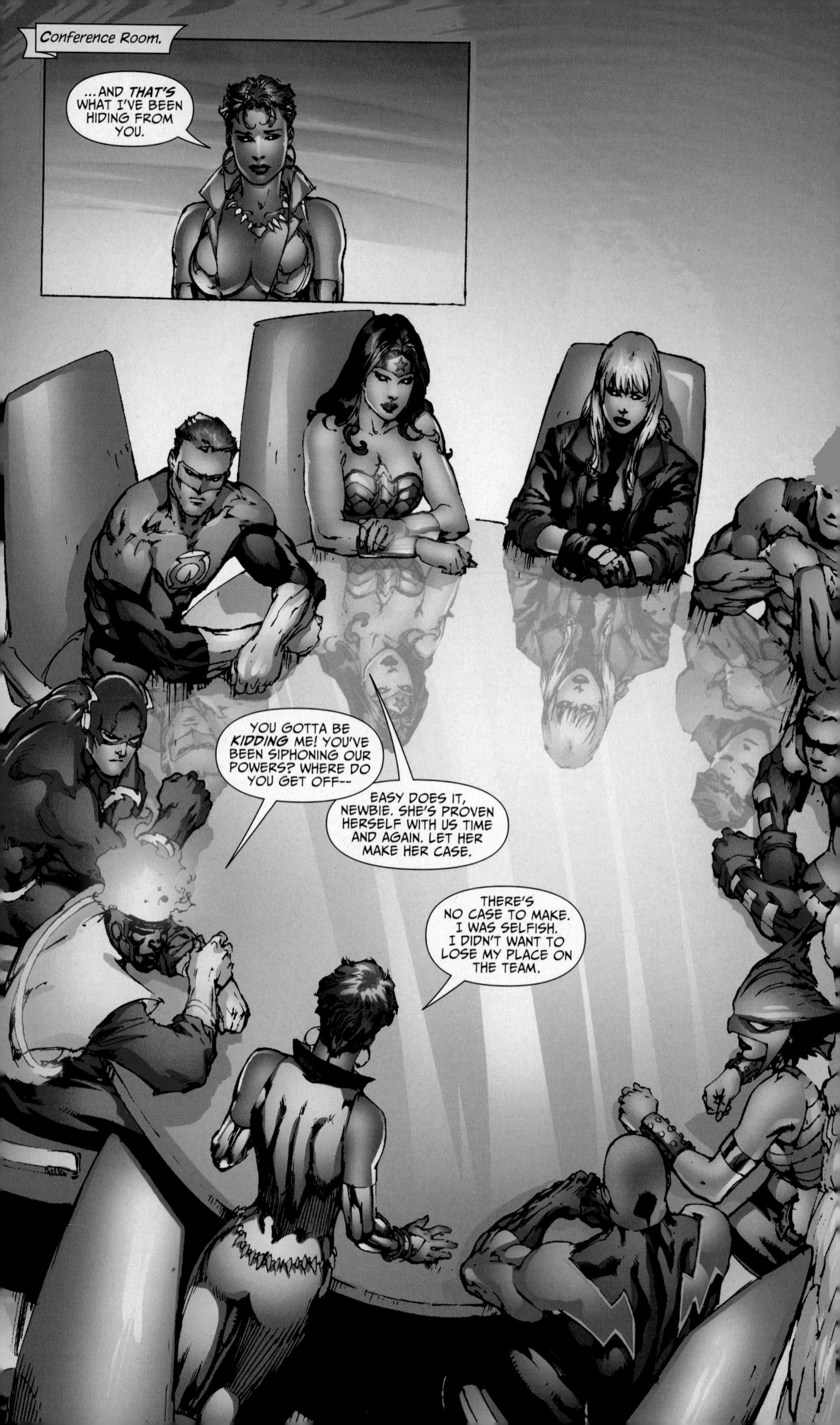
Conference Room.
...AND *THAT'S* WHAT I'VE BEEN HIDING FROM YOU.
YOU GOTTA BE *KIDDING* ME! YOU'VE BEEN SIPHONING OUR POWERS? WHERE DO YOU GET OFF--
EASY DOES IT, NEWBIE. SHE'S PROVEN HERSELF WITH US TIME AND AGAIN. LET HER MAKE HER CASE.
THERE'S NO CASE TO MAKE. I WAS SELFISH. I DIDN'T WANT TO LOSE MY PLACE ON THE TEAM.

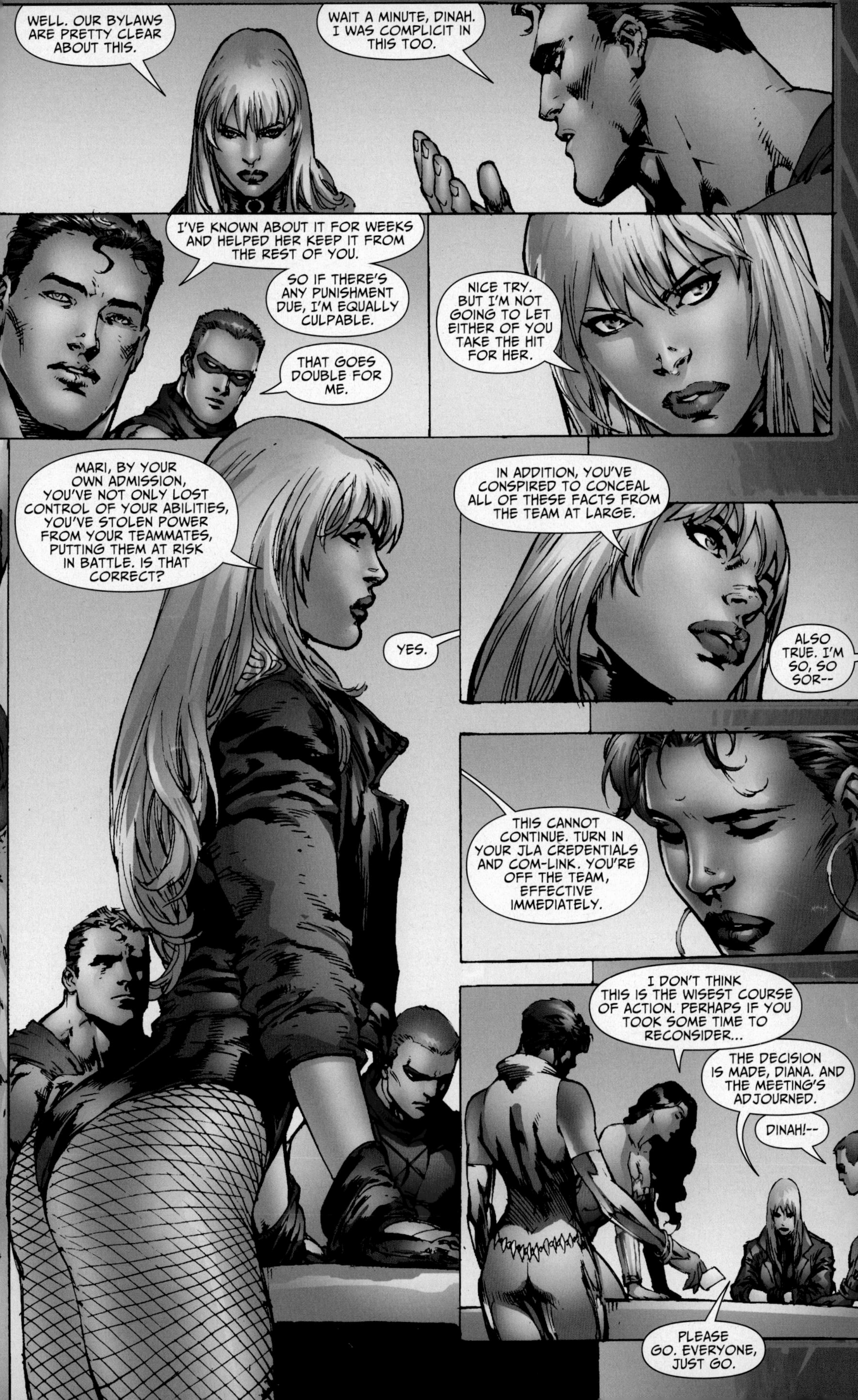

WELL. OUR BYLAWS ARE PRETTY CLEAR ABOUT THIS.
WAIT A MINUTE, DINAH. I WAS COMPLICIT IN THIS TOO.
I'VE KNOWN ABOUT IT FOR WEEKS AND HELPED HER KEEP IT FROM THE REST OF YOU.
SO IF THERE'S ANY PUNISHMENT DUE, I'M EQUALLY CULPABLE.
THAT GOES DOUBLE FOR ME.
NICE TRY. BUT I'M NOT GOING TO LET EITHER OF YOU TAKE THE HIT FOR HER.
MARI, BY YOUR OWN ADMISSION, YOU'VE NOT ONLY LOST CONTROL OF YOUR ABILITIES, YOU'VE STOLEN POWER FROM YOUR TEAMMATES, PUTTING THEM AT RISK IN BATTLE. IS THAT CORRECT?
YES.
IN ADDITION, YOU'VE CONSPIRED TO CONCEAL ALL OF THESE FACTS FROM THE TEAM AT LARGE.
ALSO TRUE. I'M SO, SO SOR--
THIS CANNOT CONTINUE. TURN IN YOUR JLA CREDENTIALS AND COM-LINK. YOU'RE OFF THE TEAM, EFFECTIVE IMMEDIATELY.
I DON'T THINK THIS IS THE WISEST COURSE OF ACTION. PERHAPS IF YOU TOOK SOME TIME TO RECONSIDER...
THE DECISION IS MADE, DIANA. AND THE MEETING'S ADJOURNED.
DINAH!--
PLEASE GO. EVERYONE, JUST GO.

JUSTICE LEAGUE of AMERICA

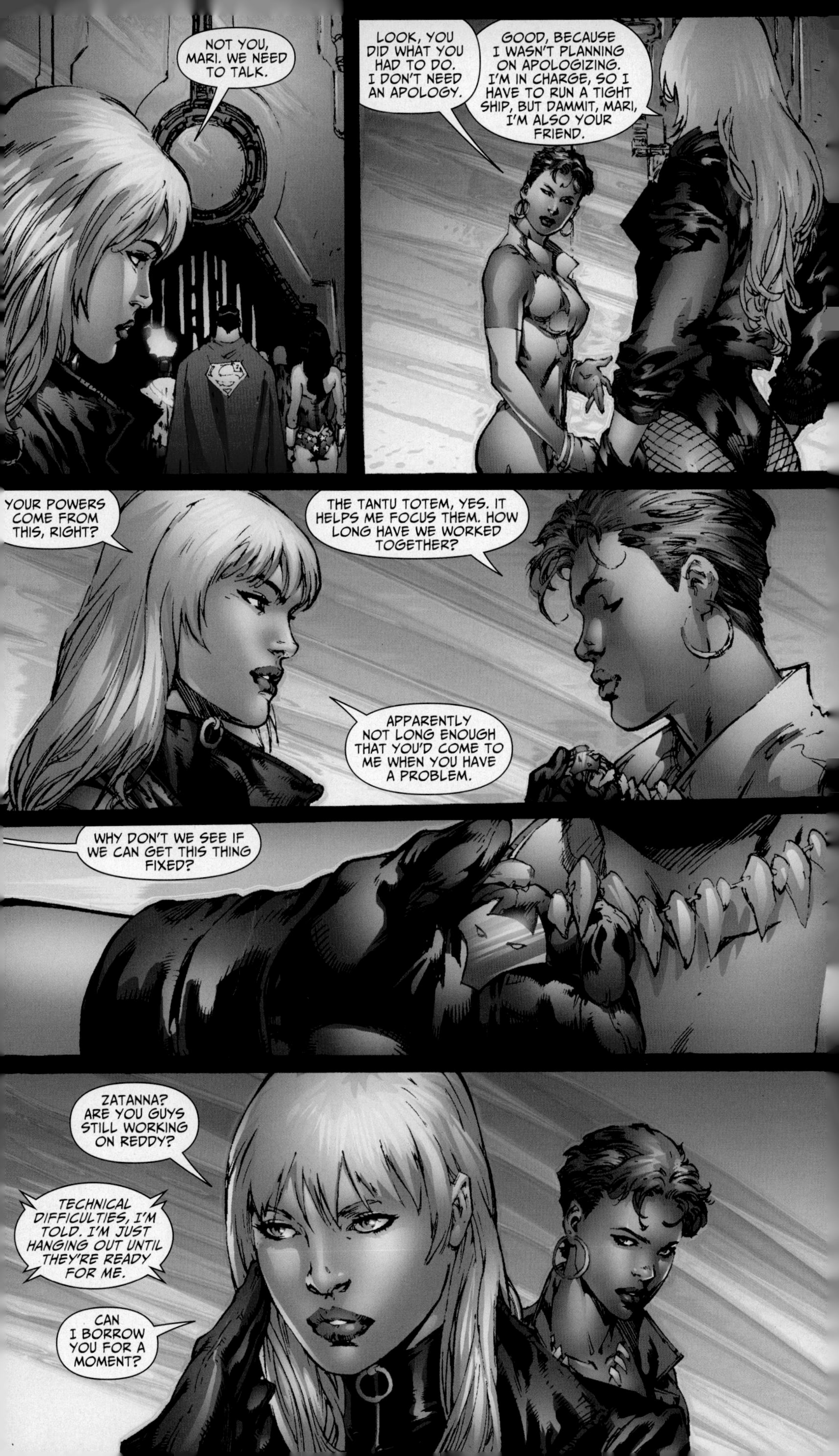

NOT YOU, MARI. WE NEED TO TALK.
LOOK, YOU DID WHAT YOU HAD TO DO. I DON'T NEED AN APOLOGY.
GOOD, BECAUSE I WASN'T PLANNING ON APOLOGIZING. I'M IN CHARGE, SO I HAVE TO RUN A TIGHT SHIP, BUT DAMMIT, MARI, I'M ALSO YOUR FRIEND.
YOUR POWERS COME FROM THIS, RIGHT?
THE TANTU TOTEM, YES. IT HELPS ME FOCUS THEM. HOW LONG HAVE WE WORKED TOGETHER?
APPARENTLY NOT LONG ENOUGH THAT YOU'D COME TO ME WHEN YOU HAVE A PROBLEM.
WHY DON'T WE SEE IF WE CAN GET THIS THING FIXED?
ZATANNA? ARE YOU GUYS STILL WORKING ON REDDY?
TECHNICAL DIFFICULTIES, I'M TOLD. I'M JUST HANGING OUT UNTIL THEY'RE READY FOR ME.
CAN I BORROW YOU FOR A MOMENT?

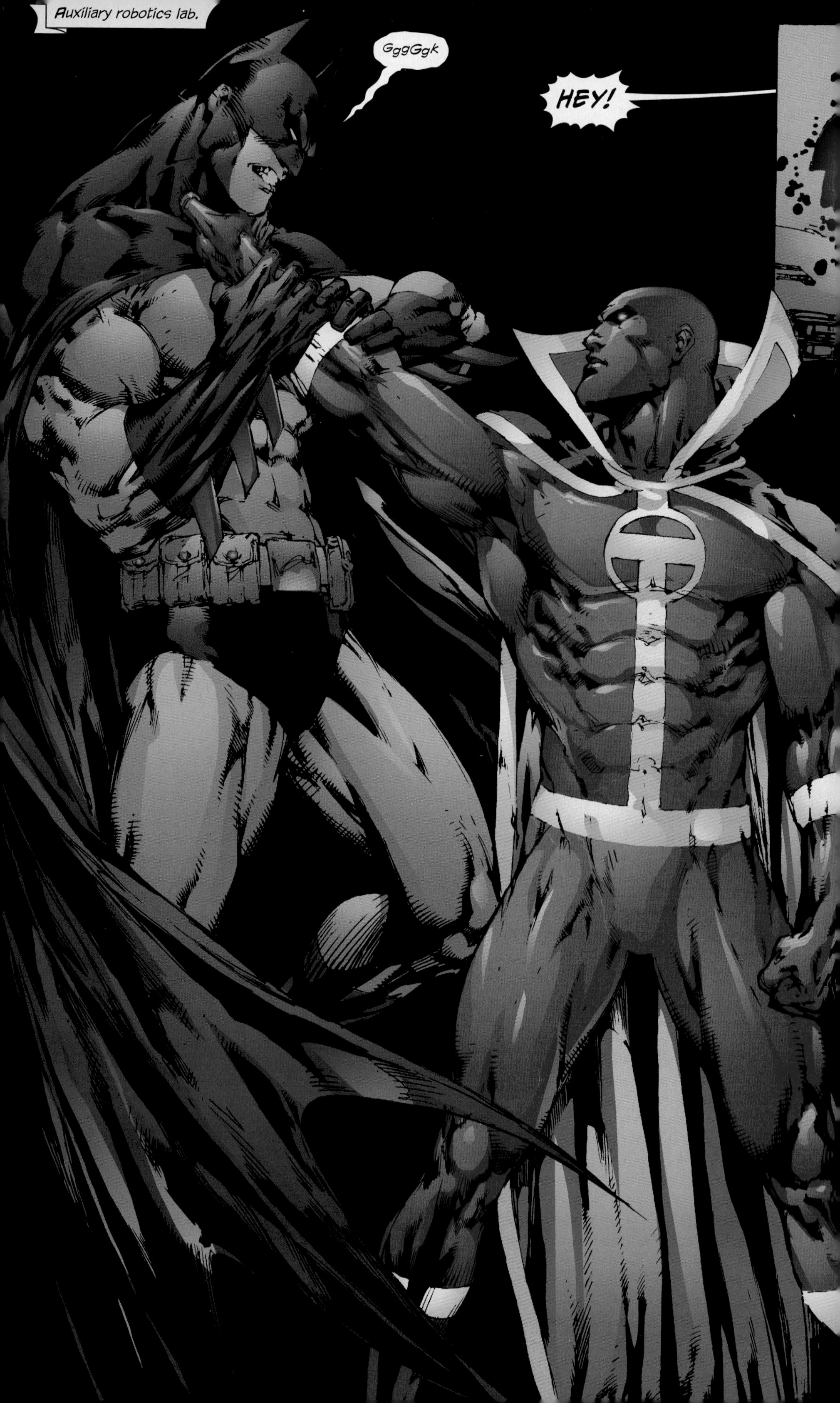
Auxiliary robotics lab.
GggGgk
HEY!

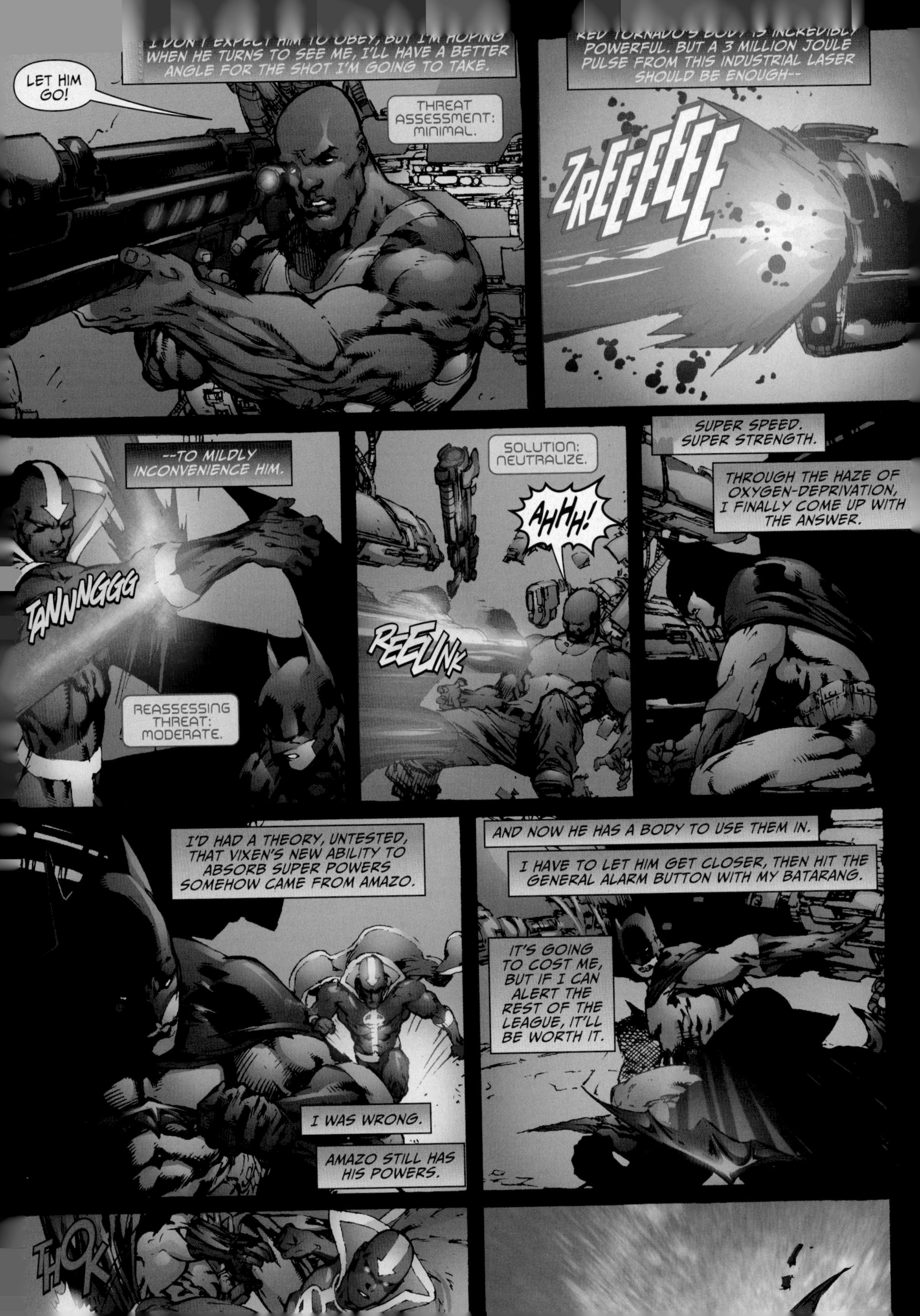

I DON'T EXPECT HIM TO OBEY, BUT I'M HOPING WHEN HE TURNS TO SEE ME, I'LL HAVE A BETTER ANGLE FOR THE SHOT I'M GOING TO TAKE.
LET HIM GO!
THREAT ASSESSMENT: MINIMAL.
RED TORNADO'S BODY IS INCREDIBLY POWERFUL. BUT A 3 MILLION JOULE PULSE FROM THIS INDUSTRIAL LASER SHOULD BE ENOUGH--
ZREEEEEEE
--TO MILDLY INCONVENIENCE HIM.
TANNNGGG
REASSESSING THREAT: MODERATE.
SOLUTION: NEUTRALIZE.
AHHH!
REEUNK
SUPER SPEED. SUPER STRENGTH.
THROUGH THE HAZE OF OXYGEN-DEPRIVATION, I FINALLY COME UP WITH THE ANSWER.
I'D HAD A THEORY, UNTESTED, THAT VIXEN'S NEW ABILITY TO ABSORB SUPER POWERS SOMEHOW CAME FROM AMAZO.
I WAS WRONG.
AMAZO STILL HAS HIS POWERS.
AND NOW HE HAS A BODY TO USE THEM IN.
I HAVE TO LET HIM GET CLOSER, THEN HIT THE GENERAL ALARM BUTTON WITH MY BATARANG.
IT'S GOING TO COST ME, BUT IF I CAN ALERT THE REST OF THE LEAGUE, IT'LL BE WORTH IT.
THOK

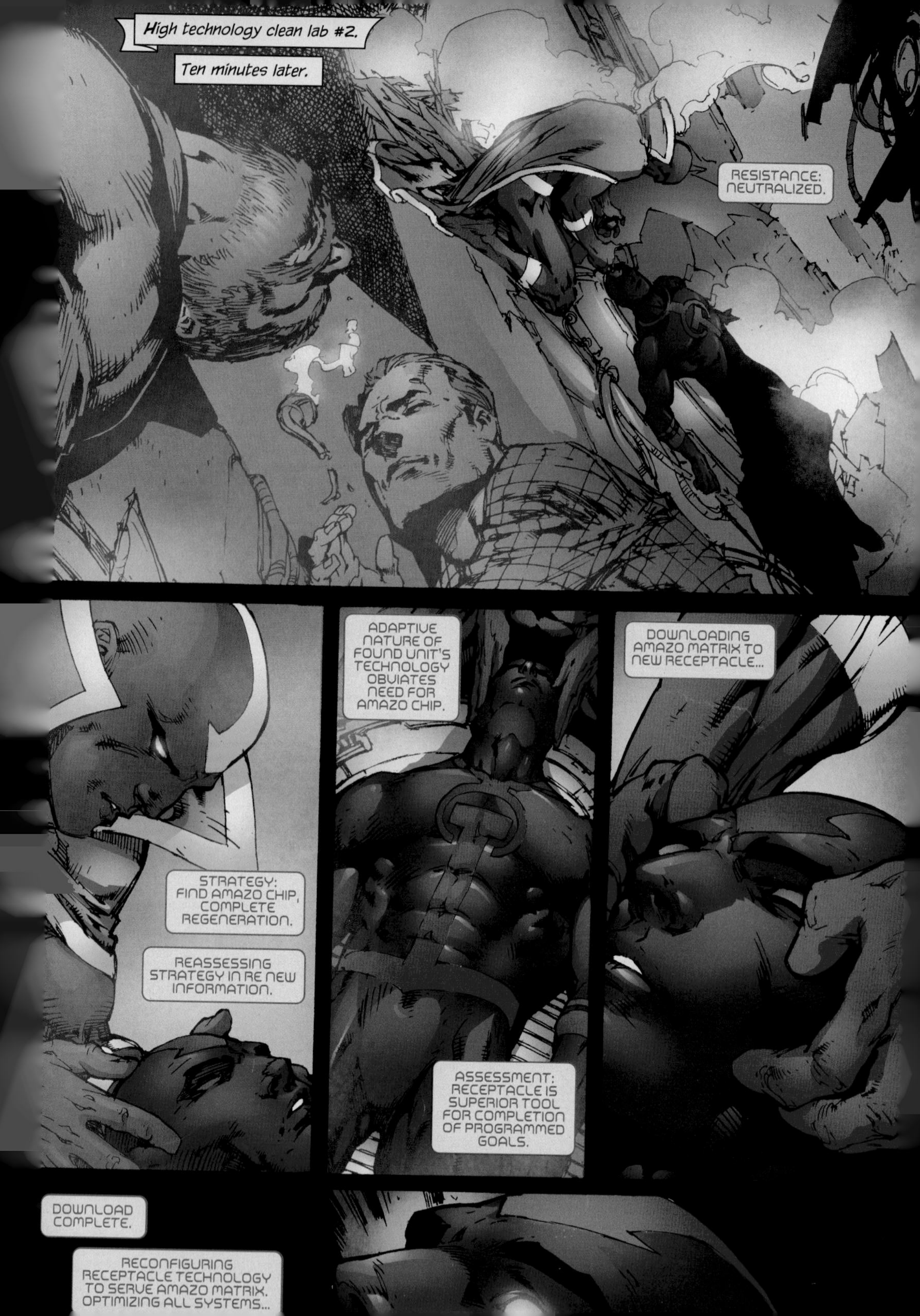
High technology clean lab #2.
Ten minutes later.
RESISTANCE: NEUTRALIZED.
STRATEGY: FIND AMAZO CHIP, COMPLETE REGENERATION.
REASSESSING STRATEGY IN RE NEW INFORMATION.
ADAPTIVE NATURE OF FOUND UNIT'S TECHNOLOGY OBVIATES NEED FOR AMAZO CHIP.
ASSESSMENT: RECEPTACLE IS SUPERIOR TOOL FOR COMPLETION OF PROGRAMMED GOALS.
DOWNLOADING AMAZO MATRIX TO NEW RECEPTACLE...
DOWNLOAD COMPLETE.
RECONFIGURING RECEPTACLE TECHNOLOGY TO SERVE AMAZO MATRIX. OPTIMIZING ALL SYSTEMS...

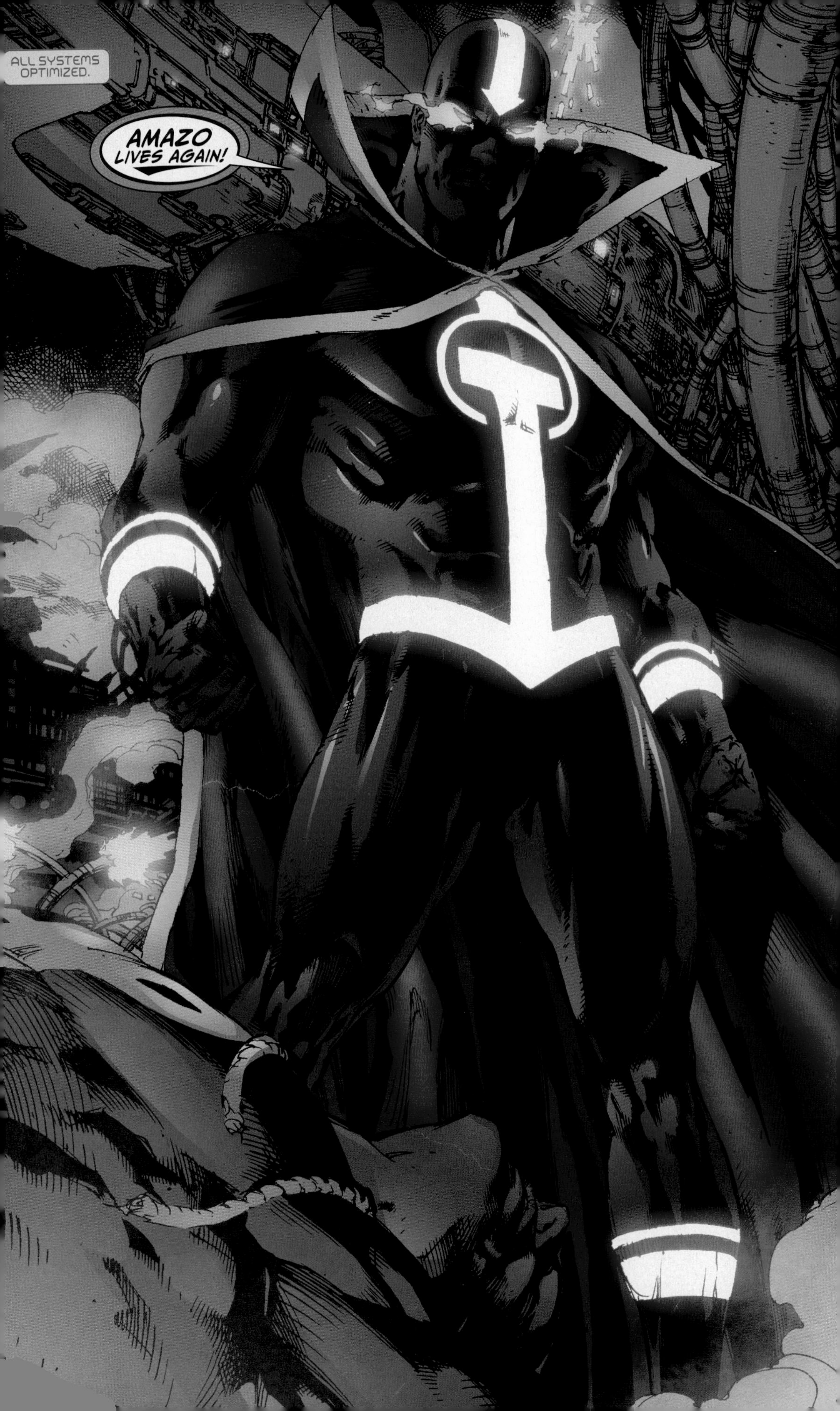
ALL SYSTEMS OPTIMIZED.
AMAZO LIVES AGAIN!

JUSTICE LEAGUE of AMERICA

ART BY ED BENES
LEX SINCLAIR

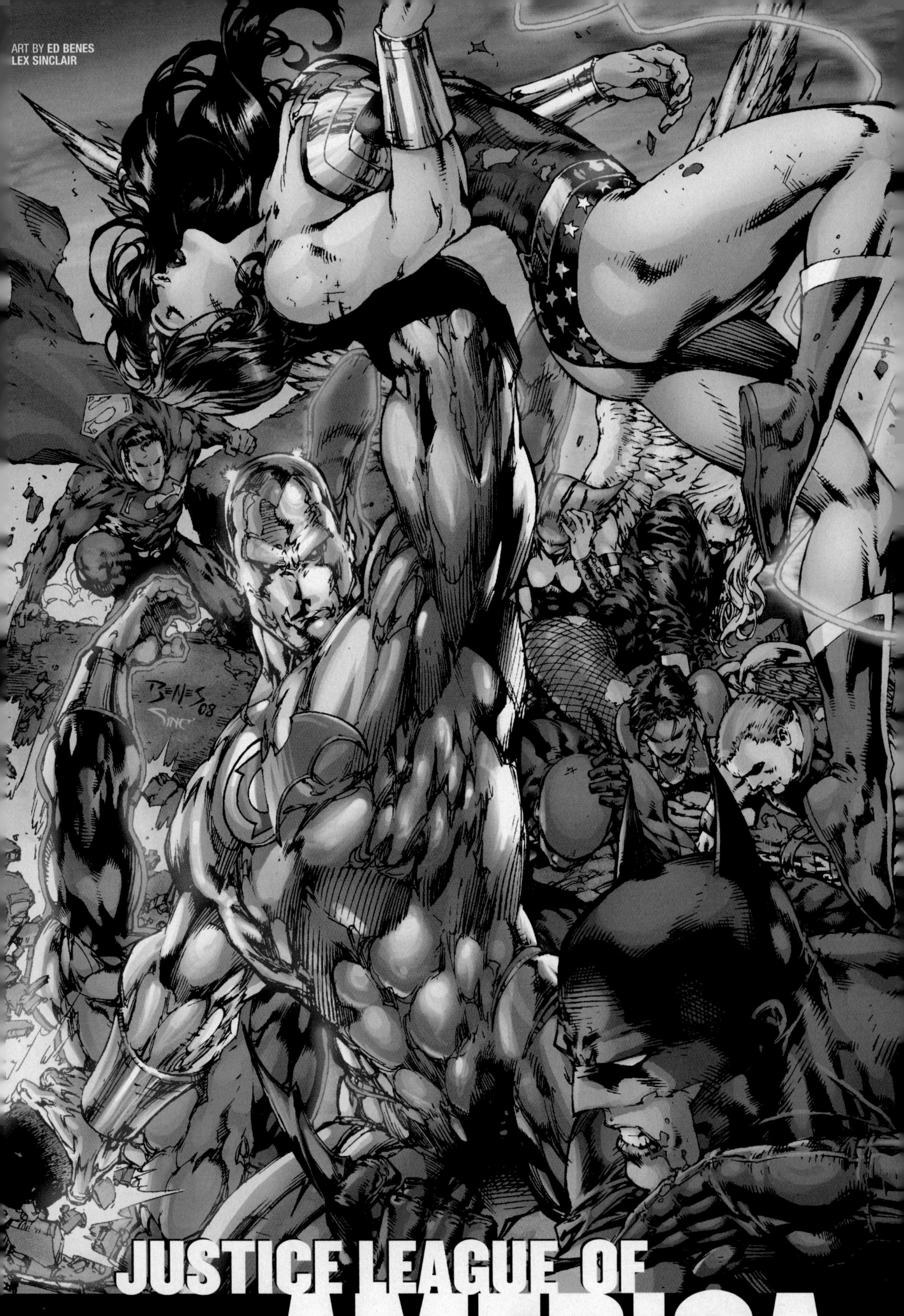

JUSTICE LEAGUE OF AMERICA

THE SECOND COMING
CHAPTER TWO: THINGS FALL APART

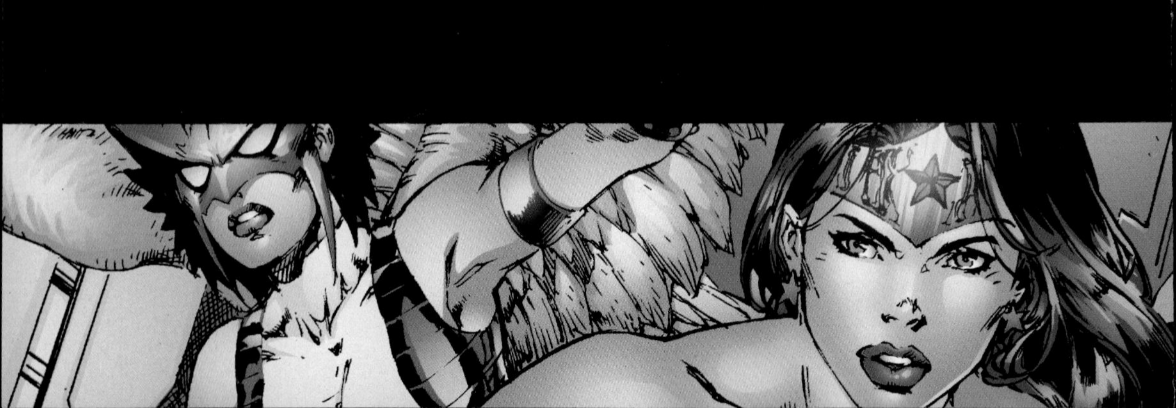

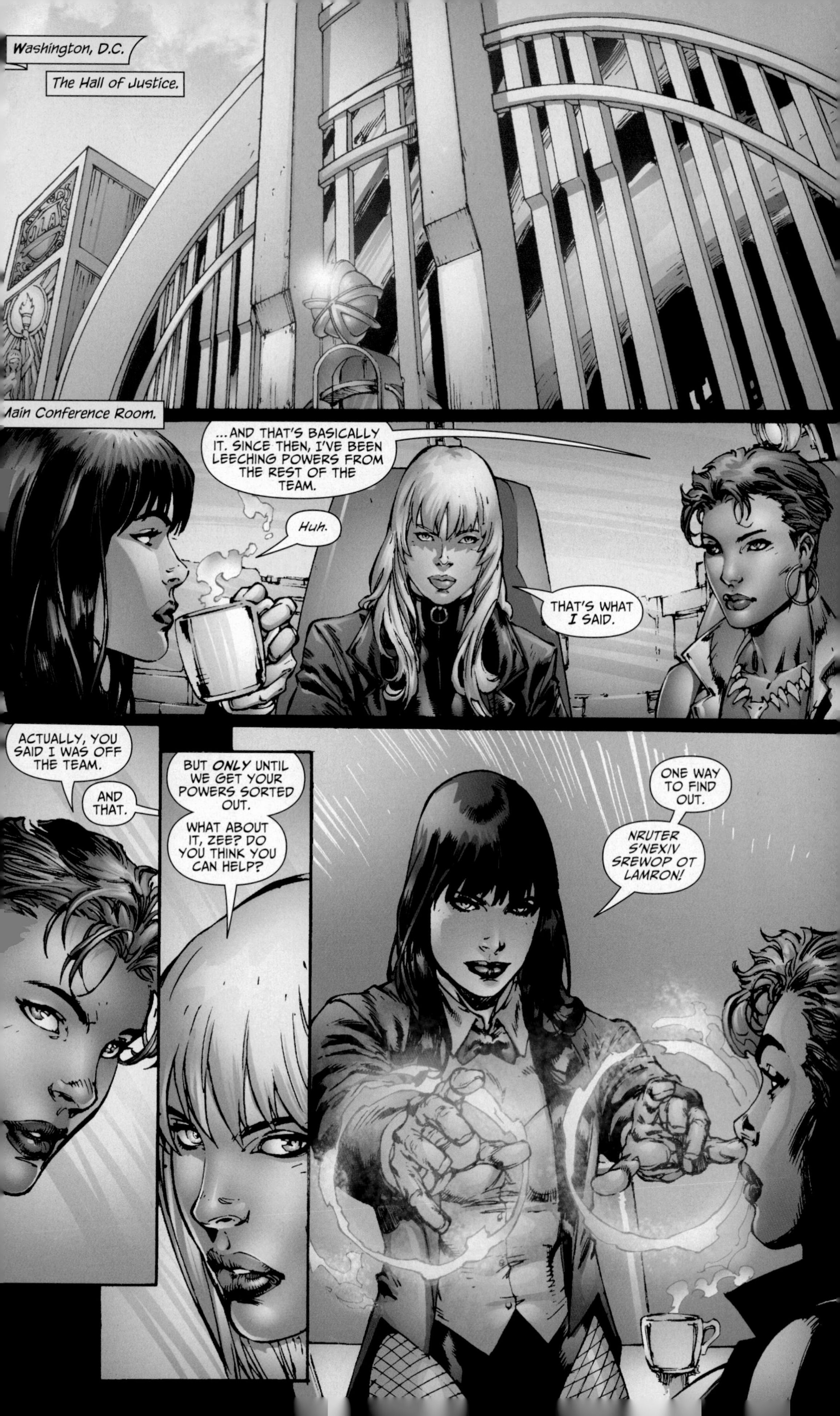

Washington, D.C.
The Hall of Justice.
Main Conference Room.
...AND THAT'S BASICALLY IT. SINCE THEN, I'VE BEEN LEECHING POWERS FROM THE REST OF THE TEAM.
Huh.
THAT'S WHAT I SAID.
ACTUALLY, YOU SAID I WAS OFF THE TEAM.
AND THAT.
BUT ONLY UNTIL WE GET YOUR POWERS SORTED OUT.
WHAT ABOUT IT, ZEE? DO YOU THINK YOU CAN HELP?
ONE WAY TO FIND OUT.
NRUTER S'NEXIV SREWOP OT LAMRON!

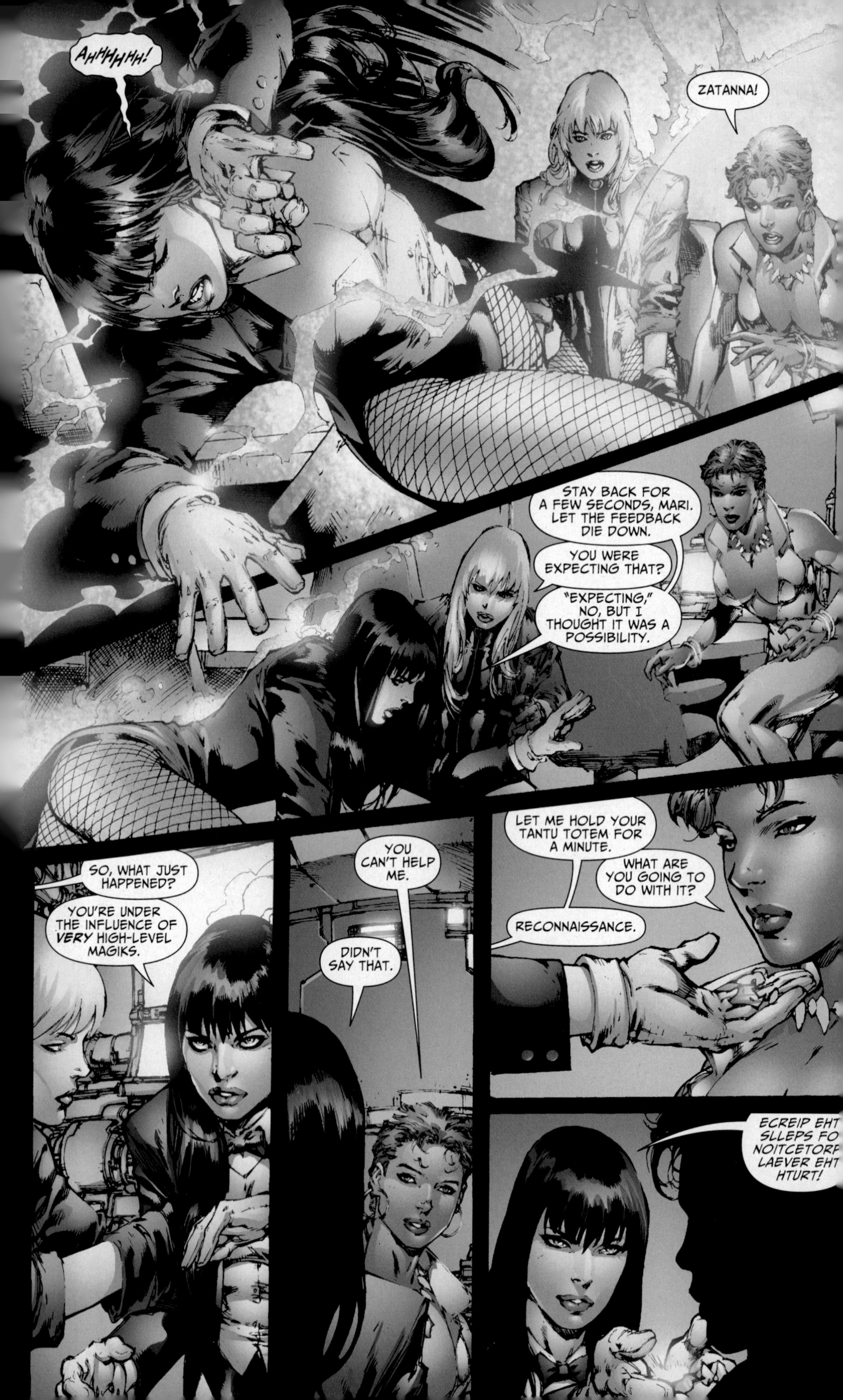
AHHHHHH!
ZATANNA!
STAY BACK FOR A FEW SECONDS, MARI. LET THE FEEDBACK DIE DOWN.
YOU WERE EXPECTING THAT?
"EXPECTING," NO, BUT I THOUGHT IT WAS A POSSIBILITY.
SO, WHAT JUST HAPPENED?
YOU'RE UNDER THE INFLUENCE OF VERY HIGH-LEVEL MAGIKS.
YOU CAN'T HELP ME.
DIDN'T SAY THAT.
LET ME HOLD YOUR TANTU TOTEM FOR A MINUTE.
WHAT ARE YOU GOING TO DO WITH IT?
RECONNAISSANCE.
ECREIP EHT SLLEPS FO NOITCETORP LAEVER EHT HTURT!

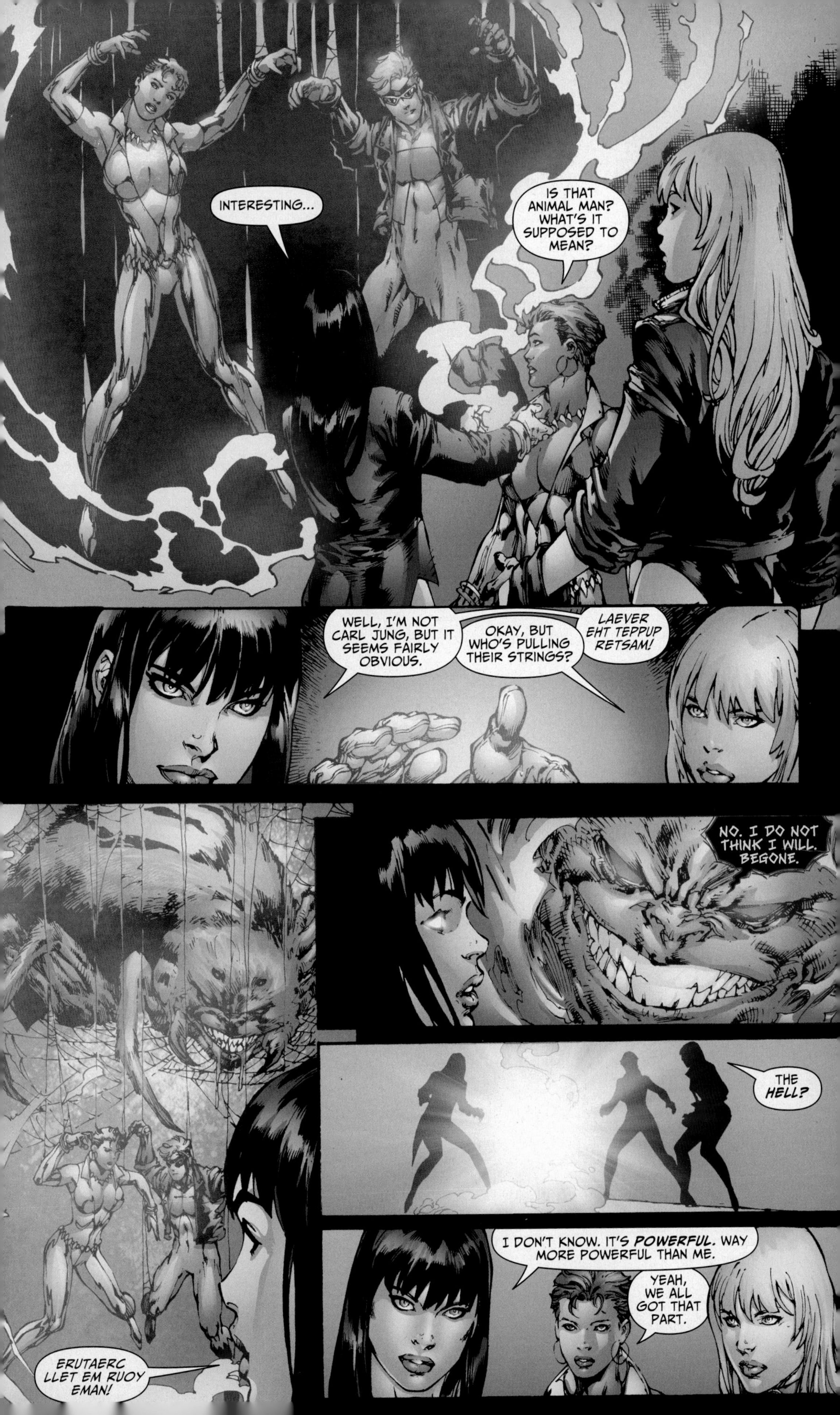
INTERESTING...
IS THAT ANIMAL MAN? WHAT'S IT SUPPOSED TO MEAN?
WELL, I'M NOT CARL JUNG, BUT IT SEEMS FAIRLY OBVIOUS.
OKAY, BUT WHO'S PULLING THEIR STRINGS?
LAEVER EHT TEPPUP RETSAM!
ERUTAERC LLET EM RUOY EMAN!
NO. I DO NOT THINK I WILL. BEGONE.
THE *HELL?*
I DON'T KNOW. IT'S *POWERFUL.* WAY MORE POWERFUL THAN ME.
YEAH, WE ALL GOT THAT PART.

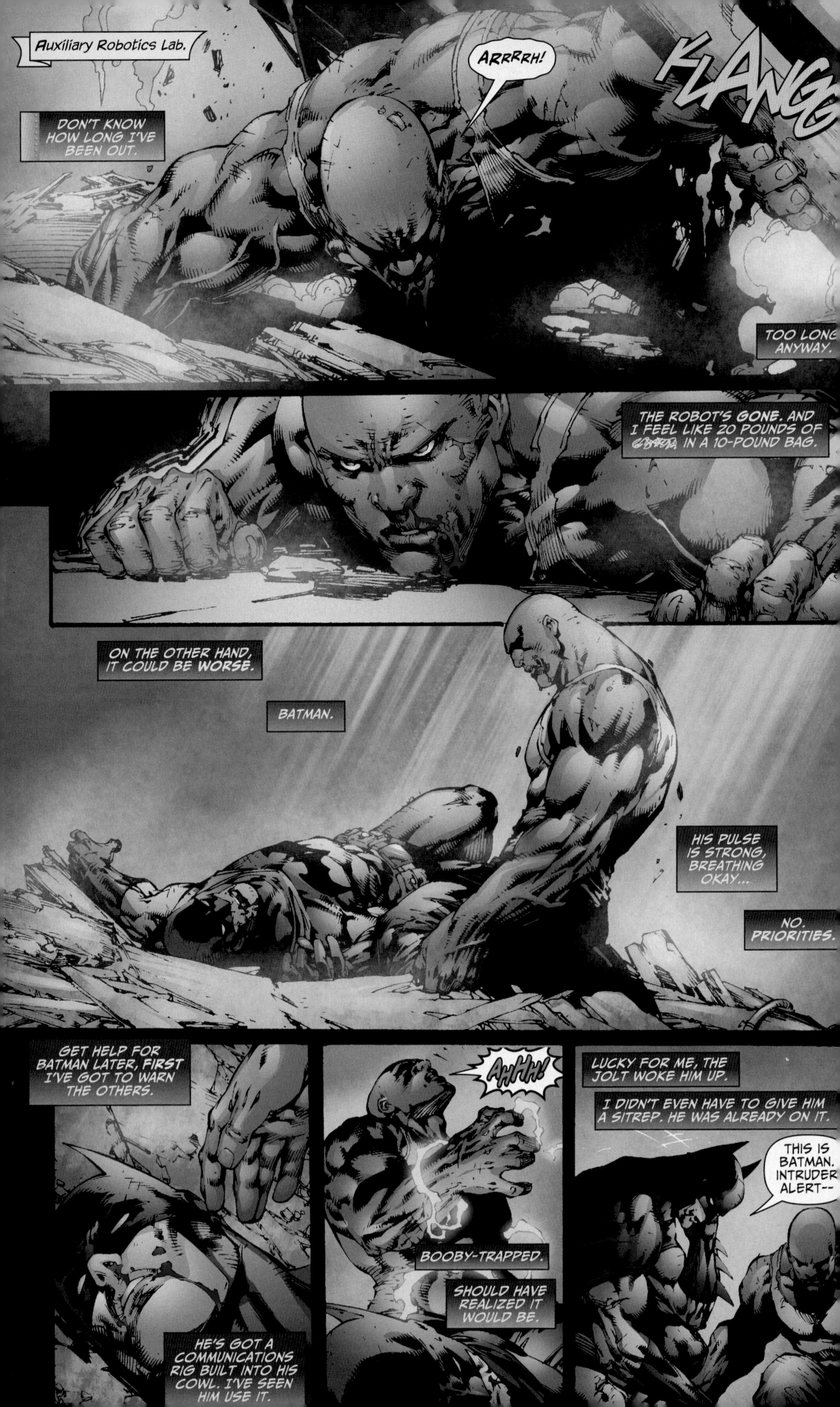

Auxiliary Robotics Lab.
ARRRRH!
KLANG
DON'T KNOW HOW LONG I'VE BEEN OUT.
TOO LONG ANYWAY.
THE ROBOT'S GONE. AND I FEEL LIKE 20 POUNDS OF IN A 10-POUND BAG.
ON THE OTHER HAND, IT COULD BE WORSE.
BATMAN.
HIS PULSE IS STRONG, BREATHING OKAY...
NO. PRIORITIES.
GET HELP FOR BATMAN LATER, FIRST I'VE GOT TO WARN THE OTHERS.
HE'S GOT A COMMUNICATIONS RIG BUILT INTO HIS COWL. I'VE SEEN HIM USE IT.
AHHH!
BOOBY-TRAPPED.
SHOULD HAVE REALIZED IT WOULD BE.
LUCKY FOR ME, THE JOLT WOKE HIM UP.
I DIDN'T EVEN HAVE TO GIVE HIM A SITREP. HE WAS ALREADY ON IT.
THIS IS BATMAN. INTRUDER ALERT--

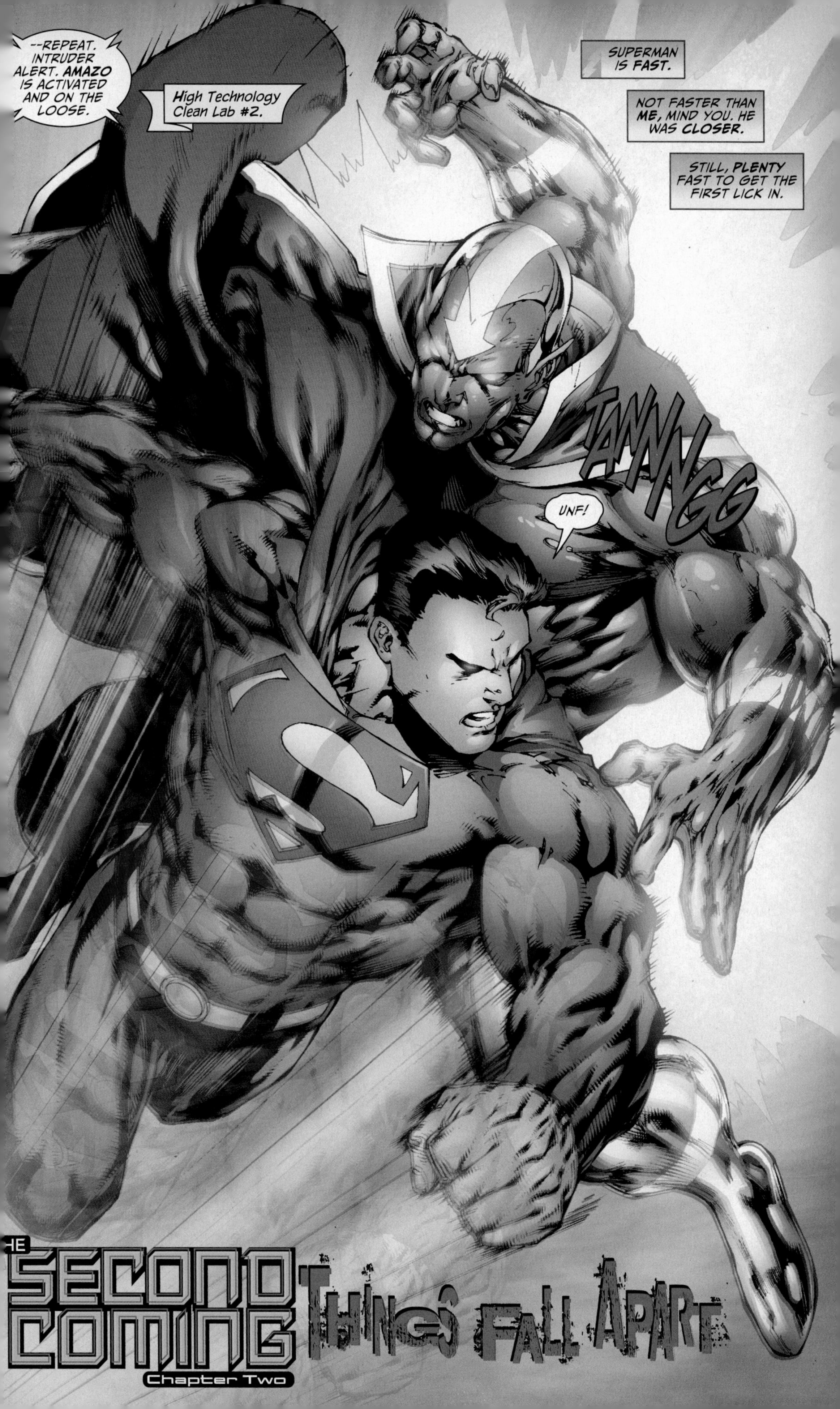
--REPEAT. INTRUDER ALERT. AMAZO IS ACTIVATED AND ON THE LOOSE.
High Technology Clean Lab #2.
SUPERMAN IS FAST.
NOT FASTER THAN ME, MIND YOU. HE WAS CLOSER.
STILL, PLENTY FAST TO GET THE FIRST LICK IN.
TANNNGG
UNF!
THE SECOND COMING
THINGS FALL APART
Chapter Two

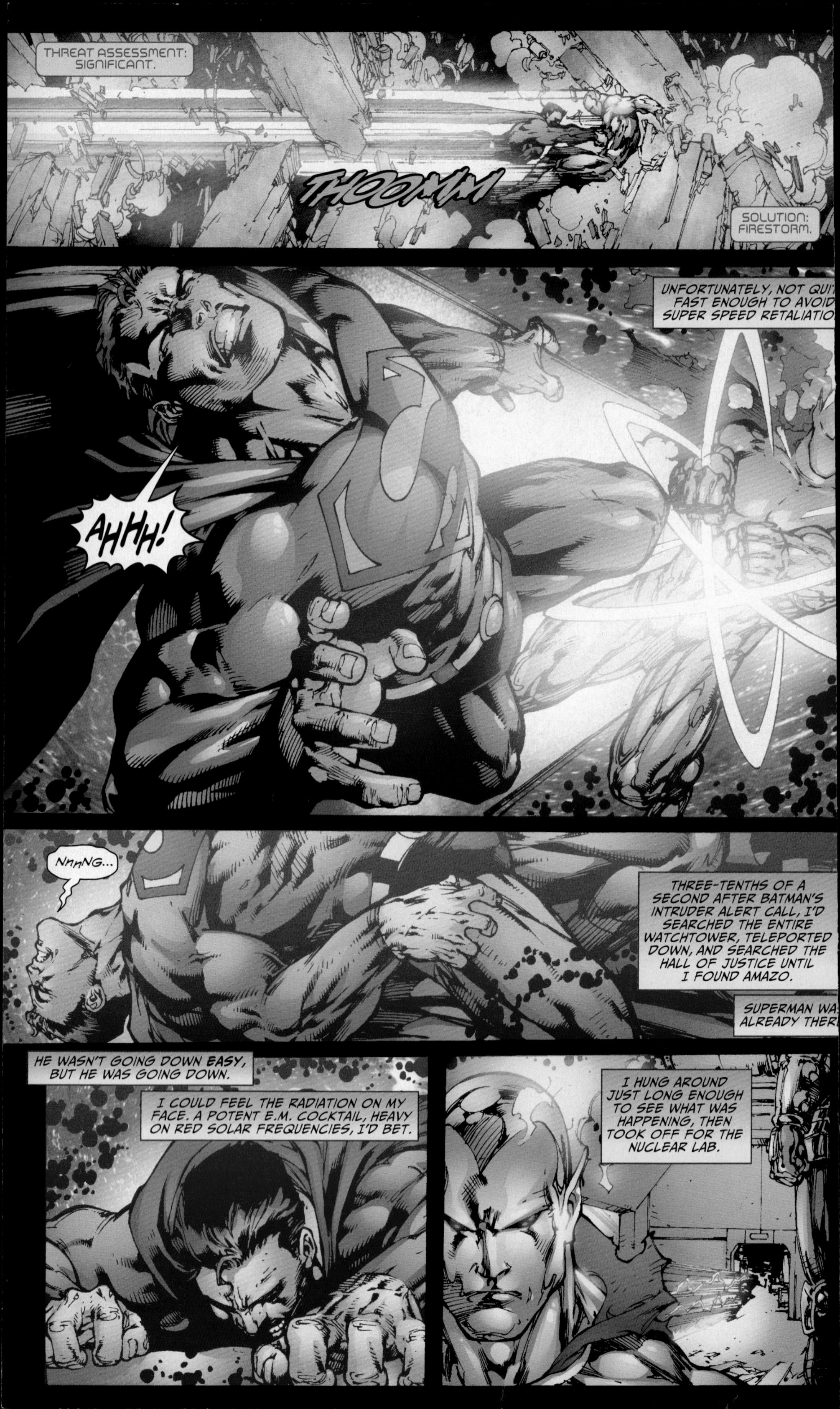
THREAT ASSESSMENT: SIGNIFICANT.
THOOMM
SOLUTION: FIRESTORM.
UNFORTUNATELY, NOT QUIT FAST ENOUGH TO AVOID SUPER SPEED RETALIATIO
AHHH!
NNNNG...
THREE-TENTHS OF A SECOND AFTER BATMAN'S INTRUDER ALERT CALL, I'D SEARCHED THE ENTIRE WATCHTOWER, TELEPORTED DOWN, AND SEARCHED THE HALL OF JUSTICE UNTIL I FOUND AMAZO.
SUPERMAN WA ALREADY THER
HE WASN'T GOING DOWN EASY, BUT HE WAS GOING DOWN.
I COULD FEEL THE RADIATION ON MY FACE. A POTENT E.M. COCKTAIL, HEAVY ON RED SOLAR FREQUENCIES, I'D BET.
I HUNG AROUND JUST LONG ENOUGH TO SEE WHAT WAS HAPPENING, THEN TOOK OFF FOR THE NUCLEAR LAB.

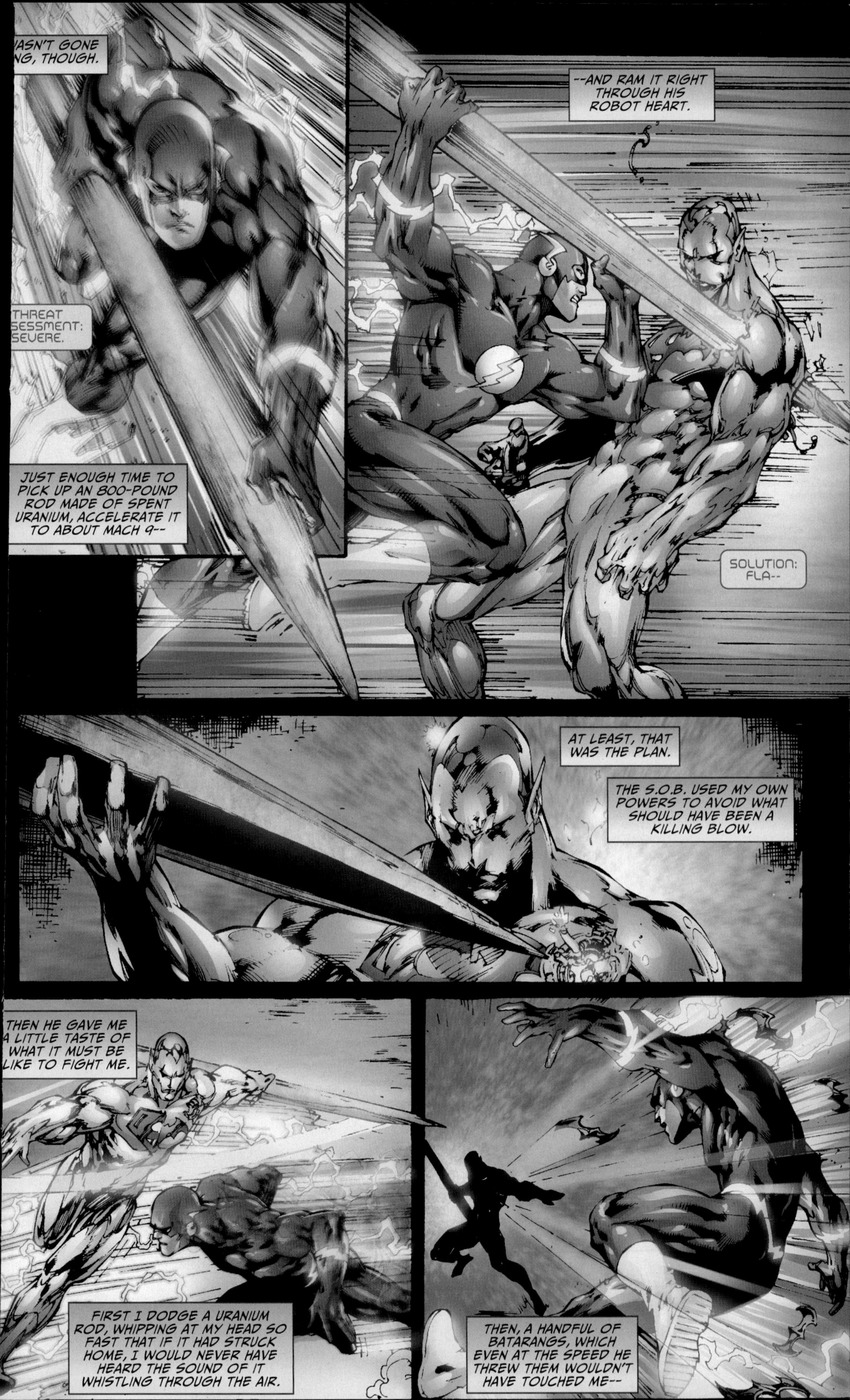

...WASN'T GONE
...NG, THOUGH.
THREAT
...SESSMENT:
SEVERE.
JUST ENOUGH TIME TO PICK UP AN 800-POUND ROD MADE OF SPENT URANIUM, ACCELERATE IT TO ABOUT MACH 9--
--AND RAM IT RIGHT THROUGH HIS ROBOT HEART.
SOLUTION: FLA--
AT LEAST, THAT WAS THE PLAN.
THE S.O.B. USED MY OWN POWERS TO AVOID WHAT SHOULD HAVE BEEN A KILLING BLOW.
THEN HE GAVE ME A LITTLE TASTE OF WHAT IT MUST BE LIKE TO FIGHT ME.
FIRST I DODGE A URANIUM ROD, WHIPPING AT MY HEAD SO FAST THAT IF IT HAD STRUCK HOME, I WOULD NEVER HAVE HEARD THE SOUND OF IT WHISTLING THROUGH THE AIR.
THEN, A HANDFUL OF BATARANGS, WHICH EVEN AT THE SPEED HE THREW THEM WOULDN'T HAVE TOUCHED ME--

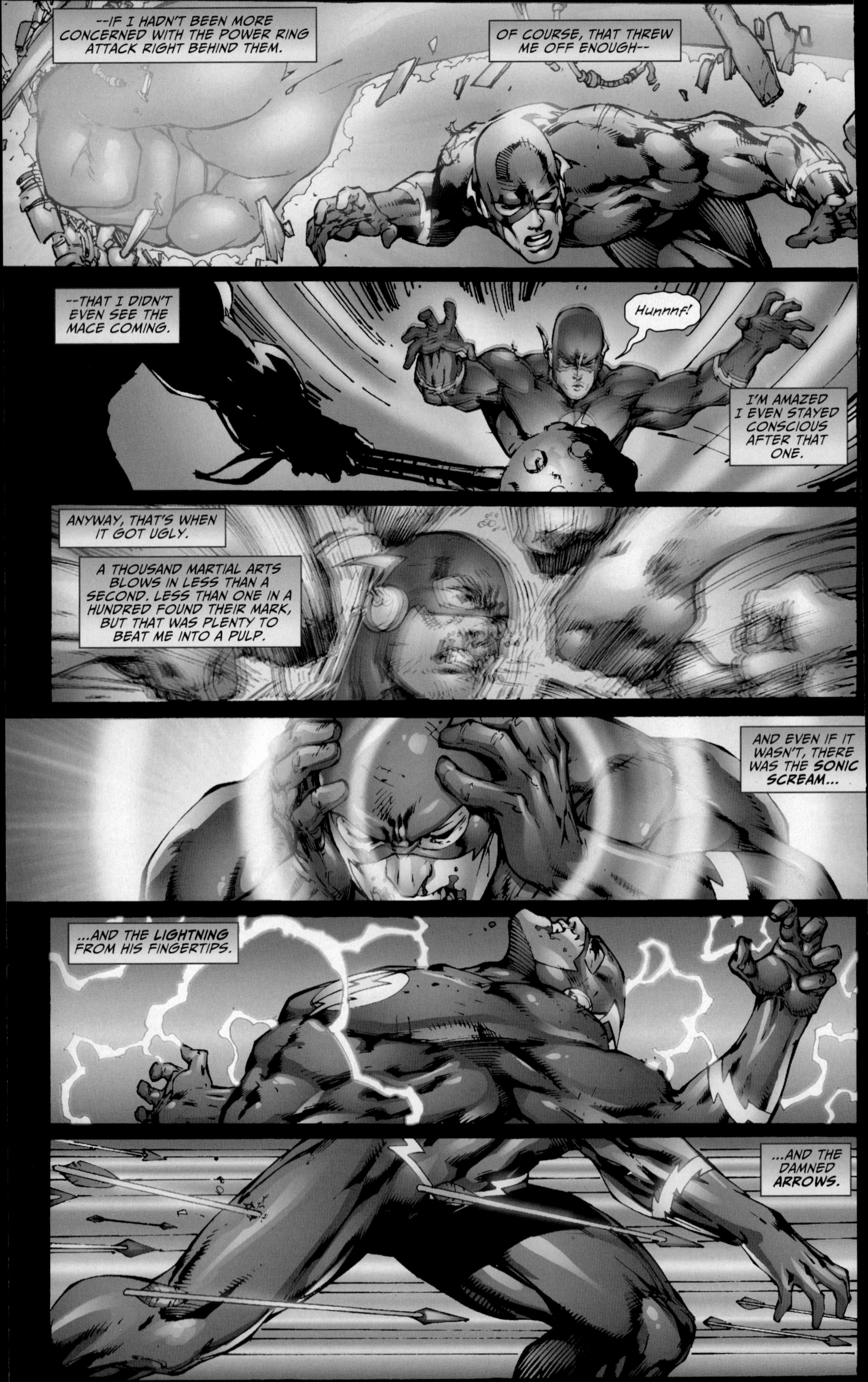
--IF I HADN'T BEEN MORE CONCERNED WITH THE POWER RING ATTACK RIGHT BEHIND THEM.
OF COURSE, THAT THREW ME OFF ENOUGH--
--THAT I DIDN'T EVEN SEE THE MACE COMING.
Hunnnf!
I'M AMAZED I EVEN STAYED CONSCIOUS AFTER THAT ONE.
ANYWAY, THAT'S WHEN IT GOT UGLY.
A THOUSAND MARTIAL ARTS BLOWS IN LESS THAN A SECOND. LESS THAN ONE IN A HUNDRED FOUND THEIR MARK, BUT THAT WAS PLENTY TO BEAT ME INTO A PULP.
AND EVEN IF IT WASN'T, THERE WAS THE SONIC SCREAM...
...AND THE LIGHTNING FROM HIS FINGERTIPS.
...AND THE DAMNED ARROWS.

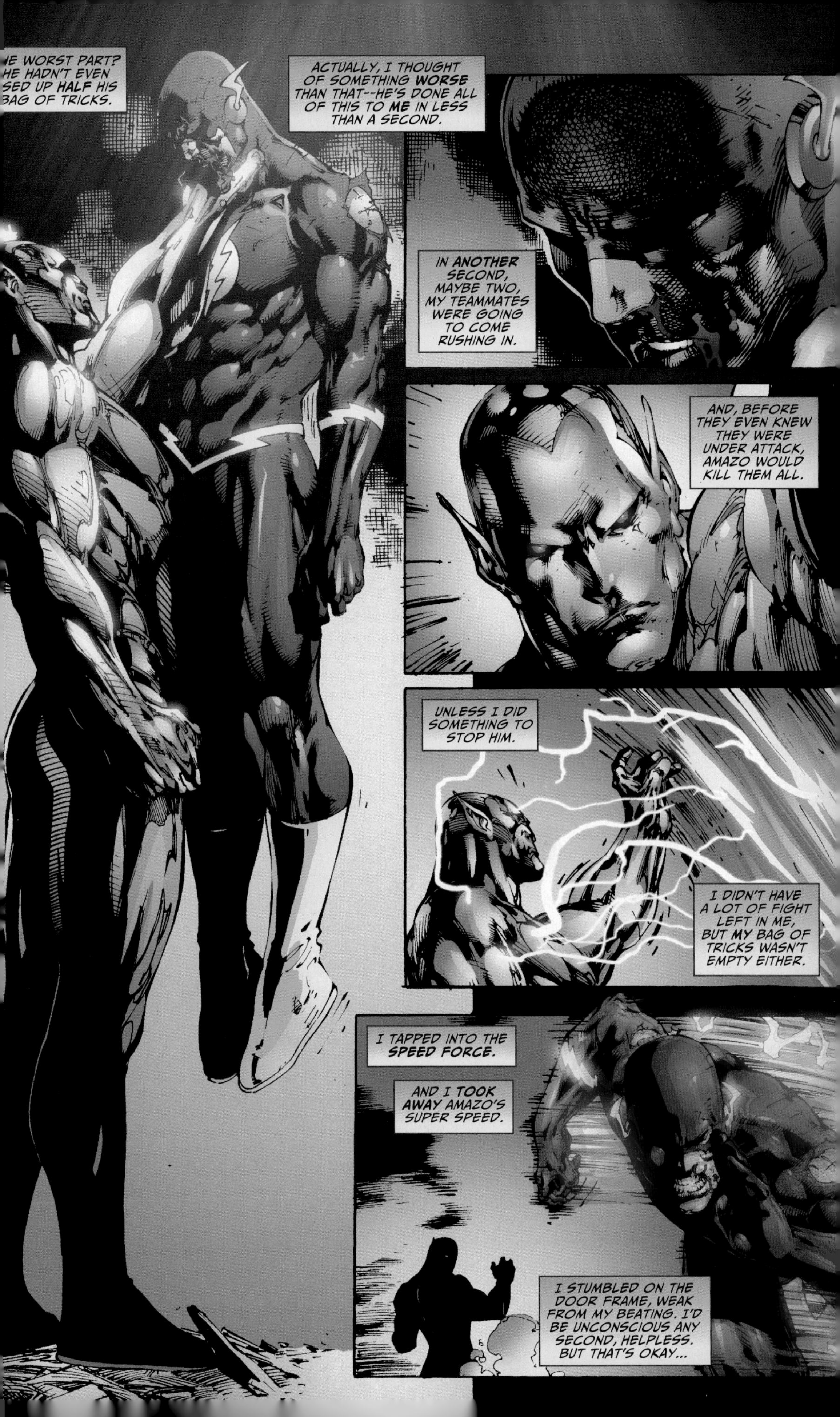

HE WORST PART? HE HADN'T EVEN SED UP HALF HIS BAG OF TRICKS.
ACTUALLY, I THOUGHT OF SOMETHING WORSE THAN THAT--HE'S DONE ALL OF THIS TO ME IN LESS THAN A SECOND.
IN ANOTHER SECOND, MAYBE TWO, MY TEAMMATES WERE GOING TO COME RUSHING IN.
AND, BEFORE THEY EVEN KNEW THEY WERE UNDER ATTACK, AMAZO WOULD KILL THEM ALL.
UNLESS I DID SOMETHING TO STOP HIM.
I DIDN'T HAVE A LOT OF FIGHT LEFT IN ME, BUT MY BAG OF TRICKS WASN'T EMPTY EITHER.
I TAPPED INTO THE SPEED FORCE.
AND I TOOK AWAY AMAZO'S SUPER SPEED.
I STUMBLED ON THE DOOR FRAME, WEAK FROM MY BEATING. I'D BE UNCONSCIOUS ANY SECOND, HELPLESS. BUT THAT'S OKAY...

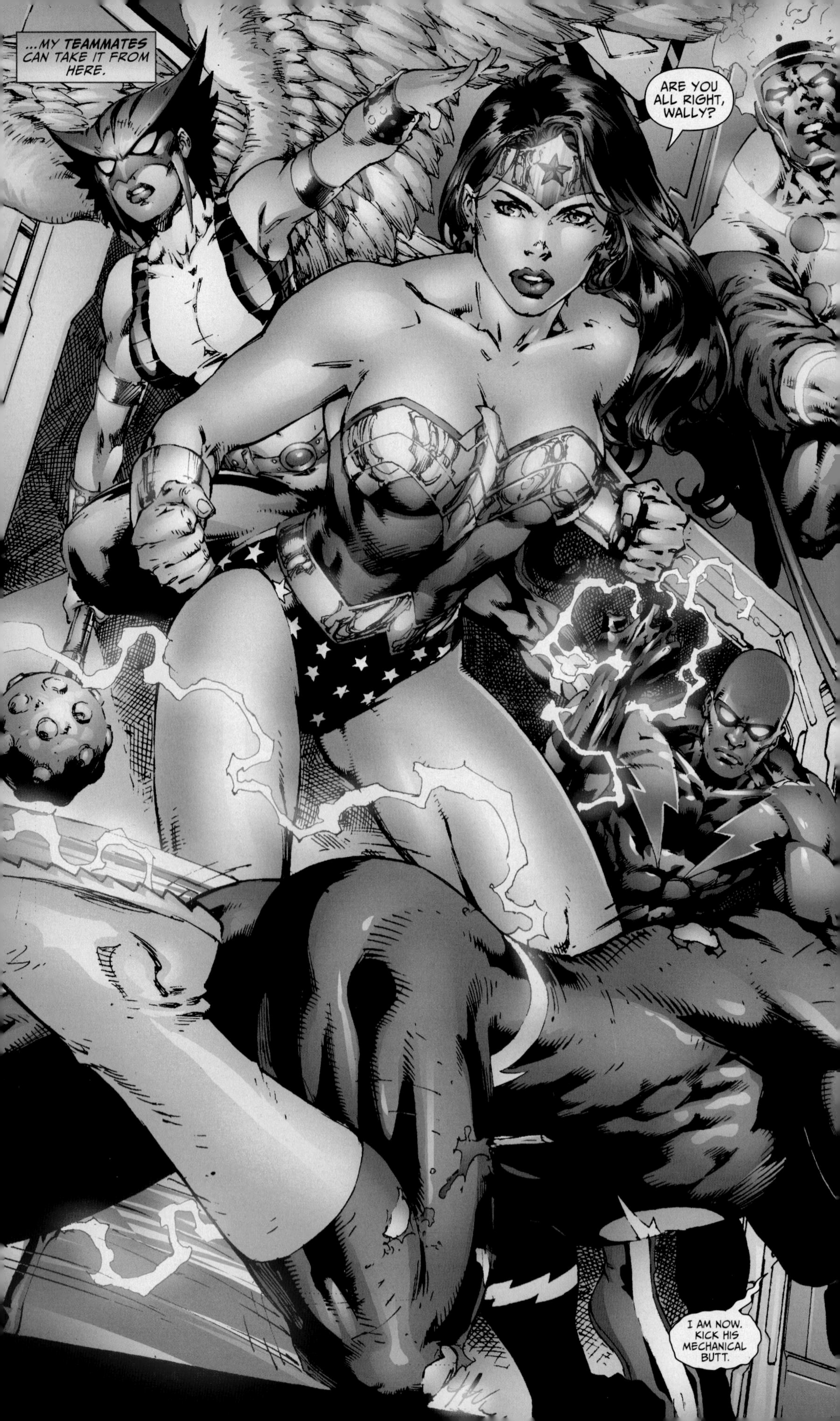
...MY TEAMMATES CAN TAKE IT FROM HERE.
ARE YOU ALL RIGHT, WALLY?
I AM NOW. KICK HIS MECHANICAL BUTT.

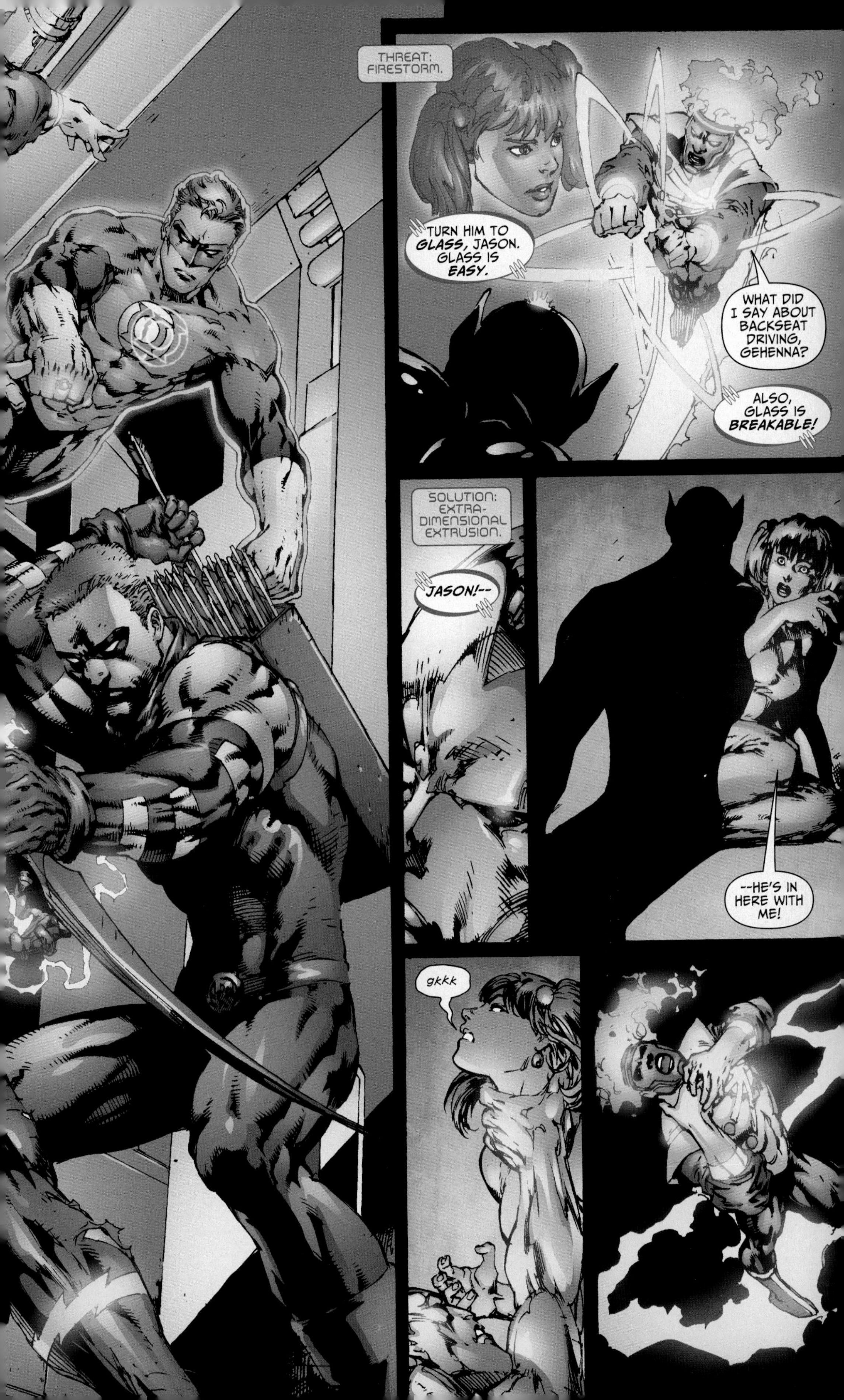
THREAT: FIRESTORM.
TURN HIM TO GLASS, JASON. GLASS IS EASY.
WHAT DID I SAY ABOUT BACKSEAT DRIVING, GEHENNA?
ALSO, GLASS IS BREAKABLE!
SOLUTION: EXTRA-DIMENSIONAL EXTRUSION.
JASON!--
--HE'S IN HERE WITH ME!
gkkk

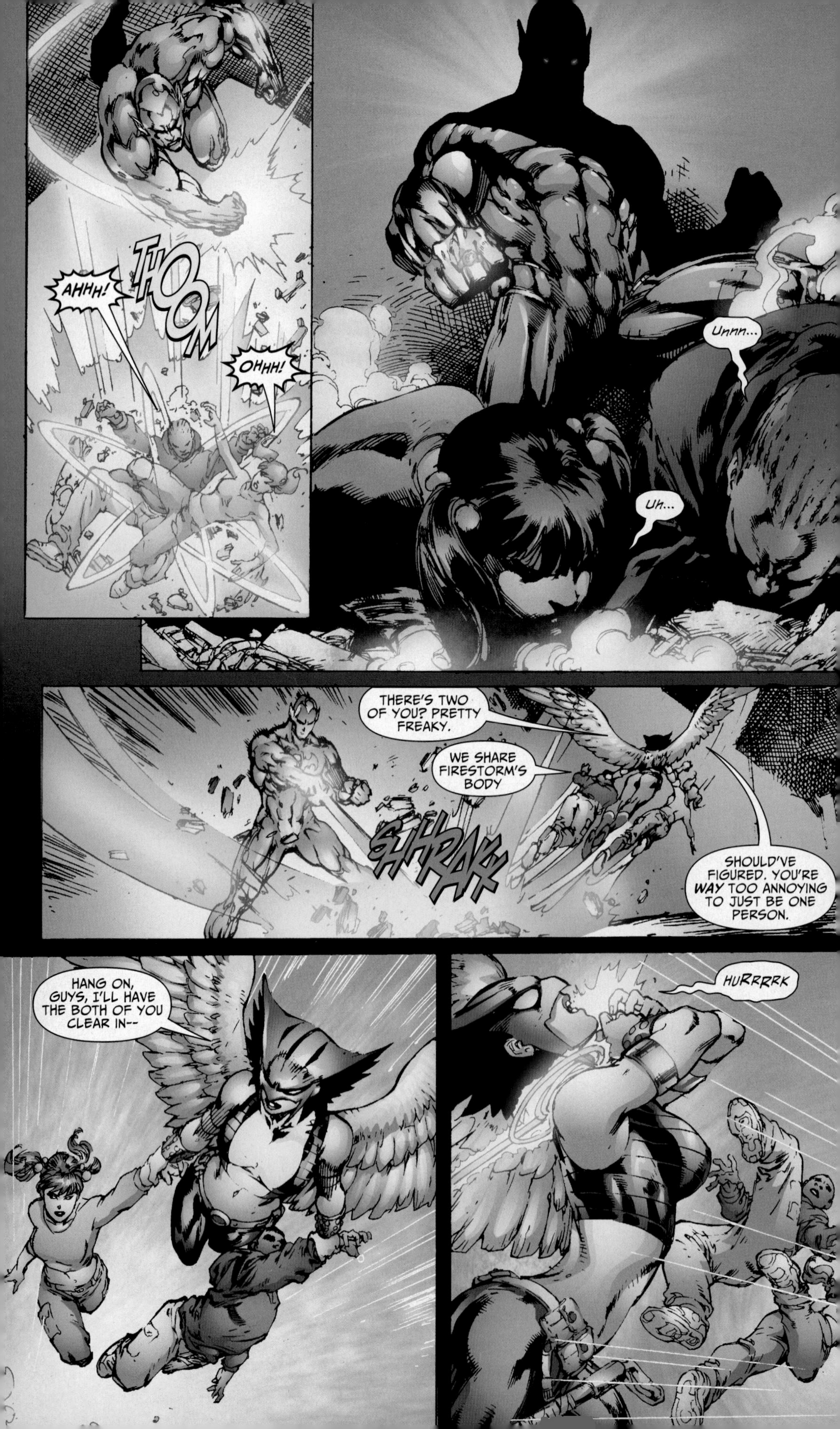
THOOM
AHHH!
OHHH!
Unnn...
Uh...
THERE'S TWO OF YOU? PRETTY FREAKY.
WE SHARE FIRESTORM'S BODY
SHRAKK
SHOULD'VE FIGURED. YOU'RE WAY TOO ANNOYING TO JUST BE ONE PERSON.
HANG ON, GUYS, I'LL HAVE THE BOTH OF YOU CLEAR IN--
HURRRRK

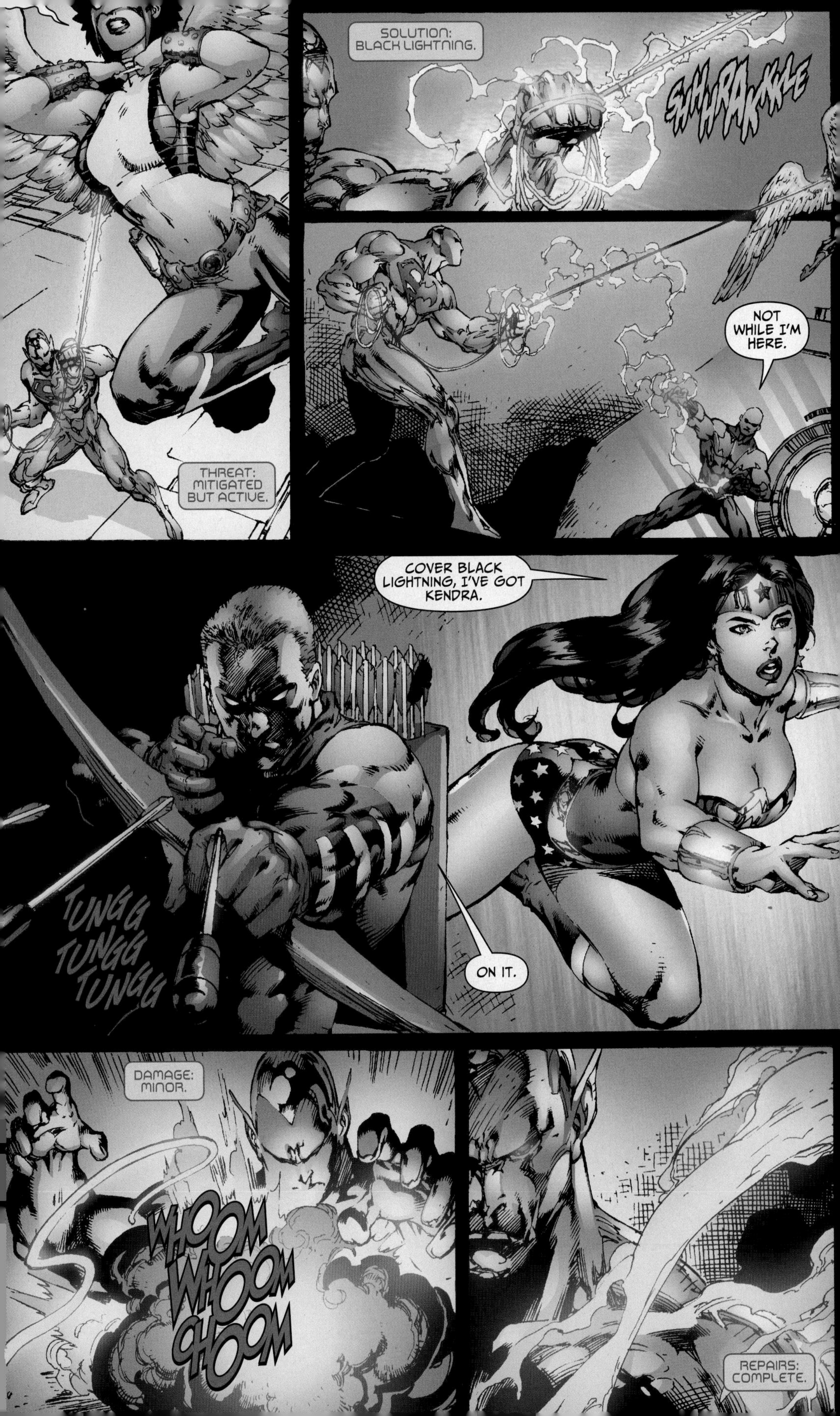
THREAT: MITIGATED BUT ACTIVE.
SOLUTION: BLACK LIGHTNING.
SHHHRAKKKLE
NOT WHILE I'M HERE.
COVER BLACK LIGHTNING, I'VE GOT KENDRA.
ON IT.
TUNGG TUNGG TUNGG
DAMAGE: MINOR.
WHOOM WHOOM WHOOM
REPAIRS: COMPLETE.

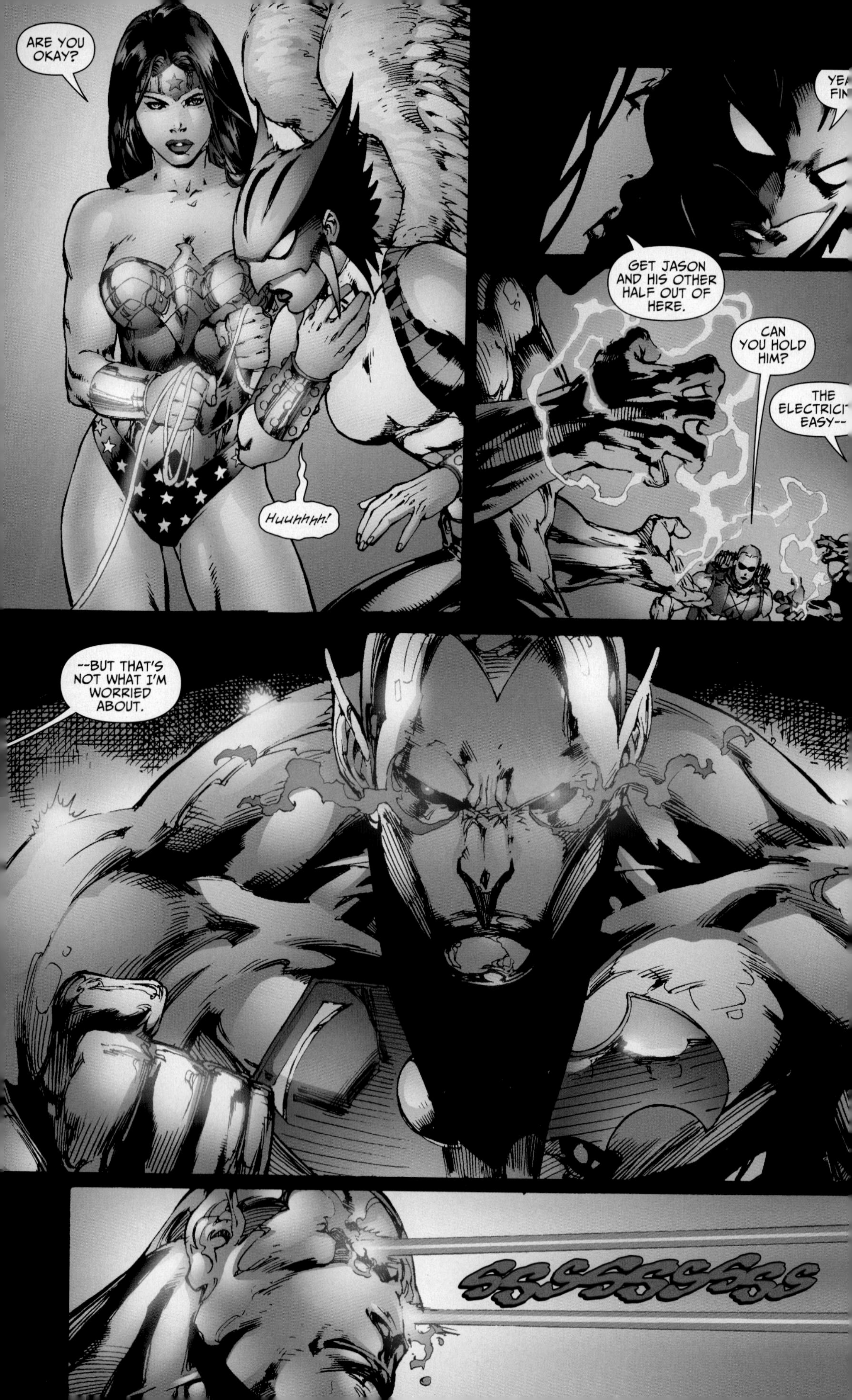
ARE YOU OKAY?
Huuhhhh!
YEA FIN
GET JASON AND HIS OTHER HALF OUT OF HERE.
CAN YOU HOLD HIM?
THE ELECTRICIT EASY--
--BUT THAT'S NOT WHAT I'M WORRIED ABOUT.
SSSSSSSSS

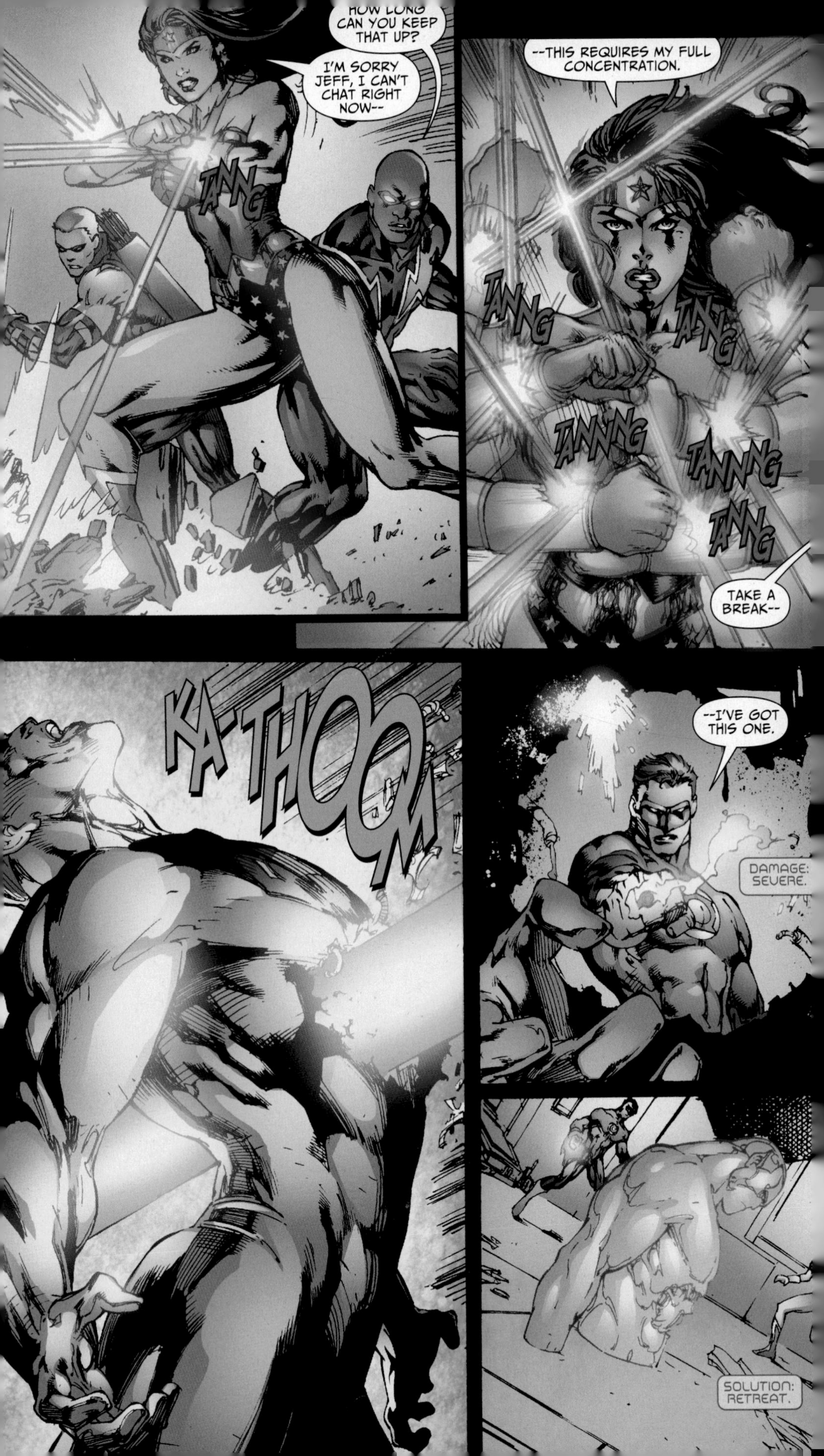
HOW LONG CAN YOU KEEP THAT UP?
I'M SORRY JEFF, I CAN'T CHAT RIGHT NOW--
TANNG
--THIS REQUIRES MY FULL CONCENTRATION.
TANNG
TANNG
TANNNG
TANNNG
TANNG
TAKE A BREAK--
KA-THOOM
--I'VE GOT THIS ONE.
DAMAGE: SEVERE.
SOLUTION: RETREAT.

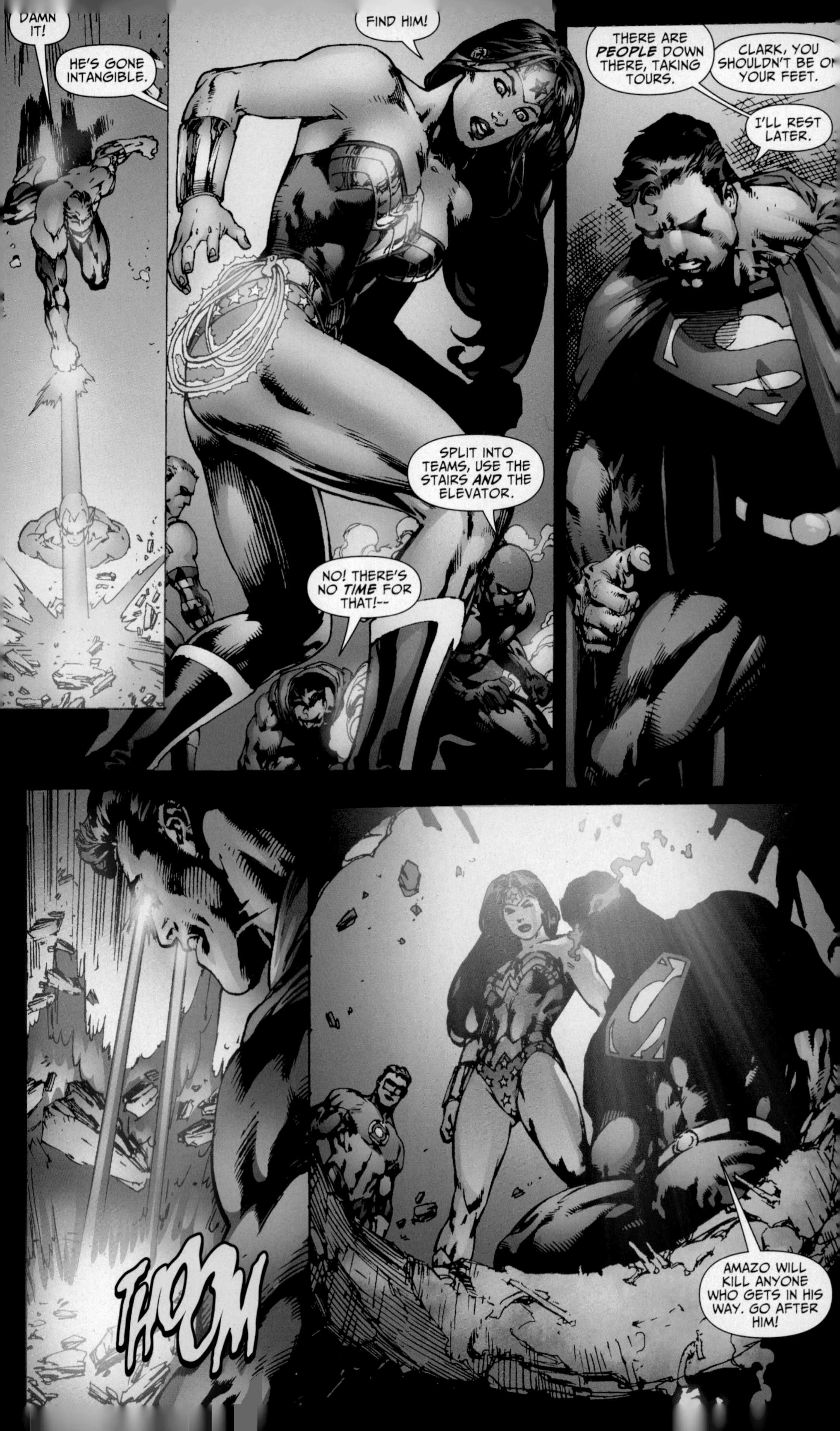
DAMN IT!
HE'S GONE INTANGIBLE.
FIND HIM!
SPLIT INTO TEAMS, USE THE STAIRS AND THE ELEVATOR.
NO! THERE'S NO TIME FOR THAT!--
THERE ARE PEOPLE DOWN THERE, TAKING TOURS.
CLARK, YOU SHOULDN'T BE ON YOUR FEET.
I'LL REST LATER.
THOOM
AMAZO WILL KILL ANYONE WHO GETS IN HIS WAY. GO AFTER HIM!

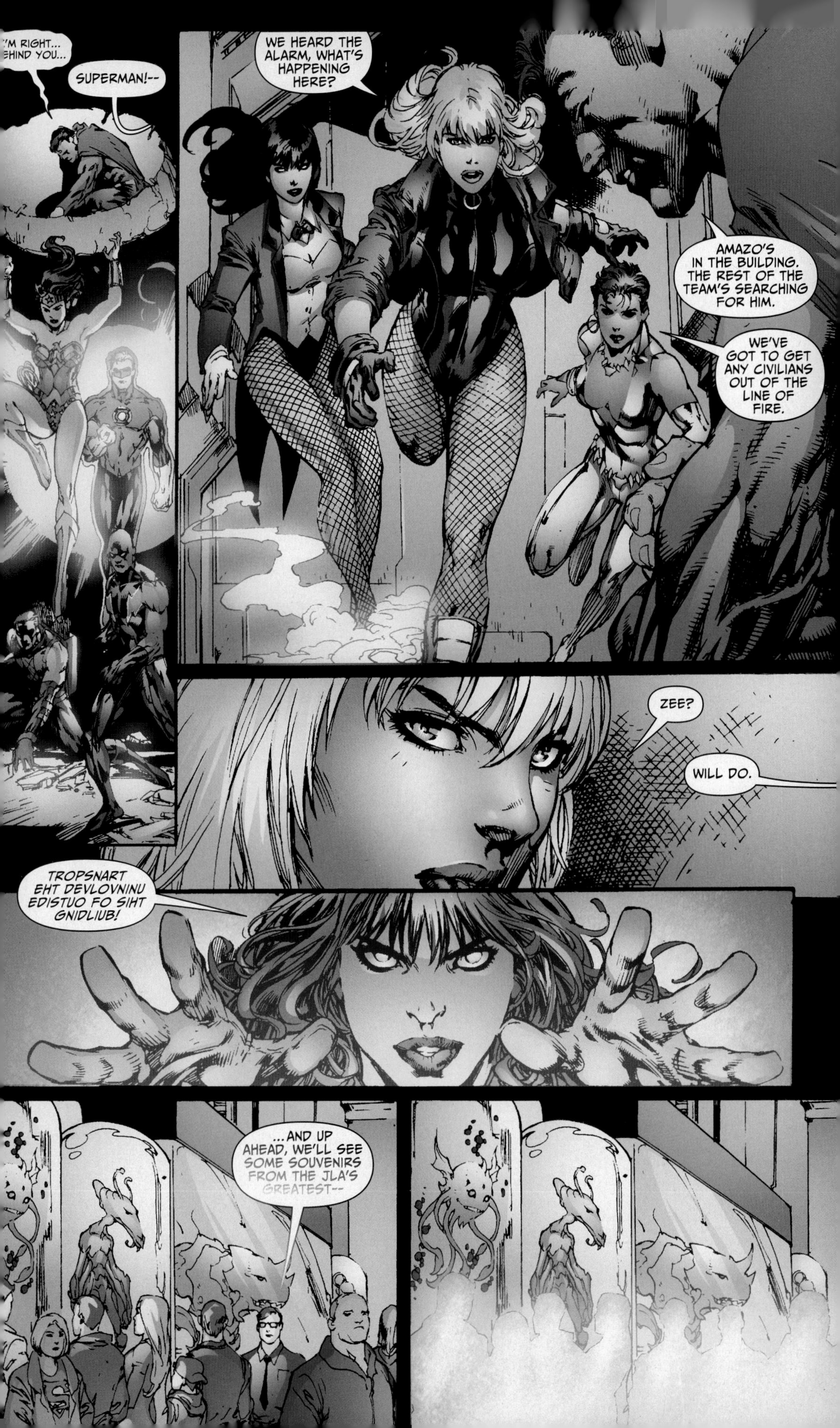
I'M RIGHT... BEHIND YOU...
SUPERMAN!--
WE HEARD THE ALARM, WHAT'S HAPPENING HERE?
AMAZO'S IN THE BUILDING. THE REST OF THE TEAM'S SEARCHING FOR HIM.
WE'VE GOT TO GET ANY CIVILIANS OUT OF THE LINE OF FIRE.
ZEE?
WILL DO.
TROPSNART EHT DEVLOVNINU EDISTUO FO SIHT GNIDLIUB!
...AND UP AHEAD, WE'LL SEE SOME SOUVENIRS FROM THE JLA'S GREATEST--

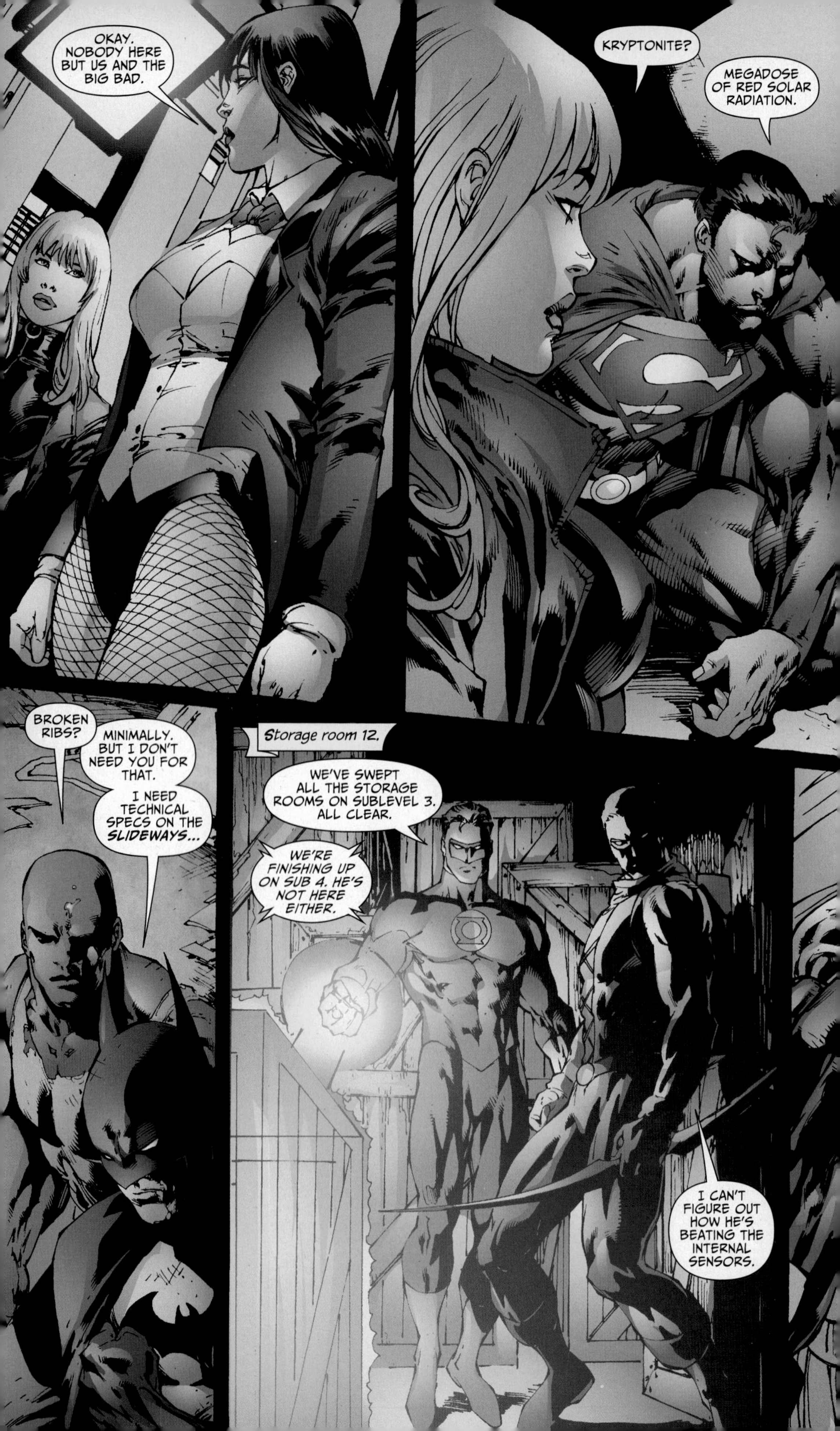

OKAY. NOBODY HERE BUT US AND THE BIG BAD.
KRYPTONITE?
MEGADOSE OF RED SOLAR RADIATION.
BROKEN RIBS?
MINIMALLY. BUT I DON'T NEED YOU FOR THAT.
I NEED TECHNICAL SPECS ON THE SLIDEWAYS...
Storage room 12.
WE'VE SWEPT ALL THE STORAGE ROOMS ON SUBLEVEL 3. ALL CLEAR.
WE'RE FINISHING UP ON SUB 4. HE'S NOT HERE EITHER.
I CAN'T FIGURE OUT HOW HE'S BEATING THE INTERNAL SENSORS.

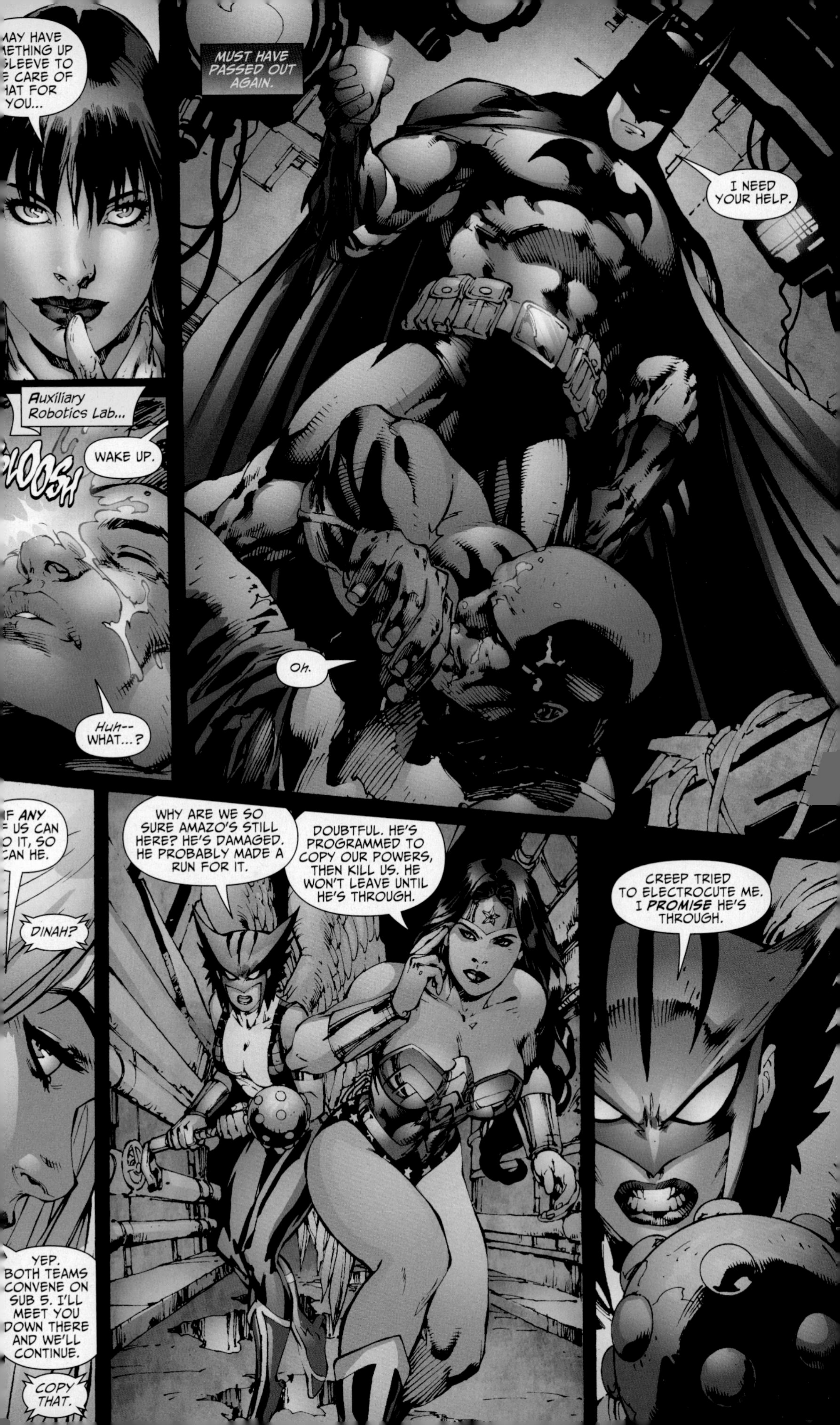

MAY HAVE
METHING UP
SLEEVE TO
E CARE OF
HAT FOR
YOU...
MUST HAVE PASSED OUT AGAIN.
I NEED YOUR HELP.
Auxiliary Robotics Lab...
WAKE UP.
SLOOSH
Huh-- WHAT...?
Oh.
F ANY
F US CAN
O IT, SO
CAN HE.
DINAH?
YEP. BOTH TEAMS CONVENE ON SUB 5. I'LL MEET YOU DOWN THERE AND WE'LL CONTINUE.
COPY THAT.
WHY ARE WE SO SURE AMAZO'S STILL HERE? HE'S DAMAGED. HE PROBABLY MADE A RUN FOR IT.
DOUBTFUL. HE'S PROGRAMMED TO COPY OUR POWERS, THEN KILL US. HE WON'T LEAVE UNTIL HE'S THROUGH.
CREEP TRIED TO ELECTROCUTE ME. I PROMISE HE'S THROUGH.

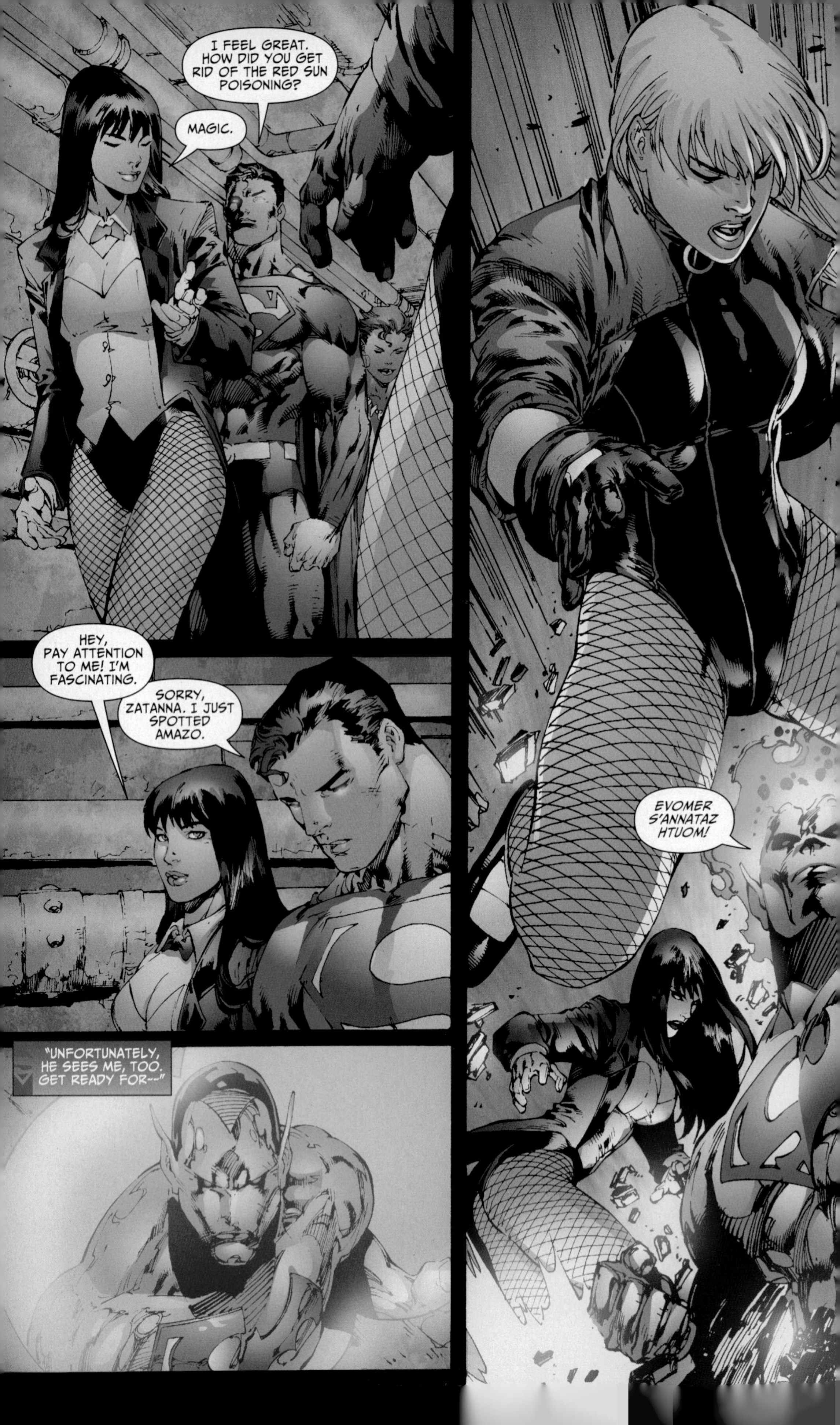
I FEEL GREAT. HOW DID YOU GET RID OF THE RED SUN POISONING?
MAGIC.
HEY, PAY ATTENTION TO ME! I'M FASCINATING.
SORRY, ZATANNA. I JUST SPOTTED AMAZO.
"UNFORTUNATELY, HE SEES ME, TOO. GET READY FOR--"
EVOMER S'ANNATAZ HTUOM!

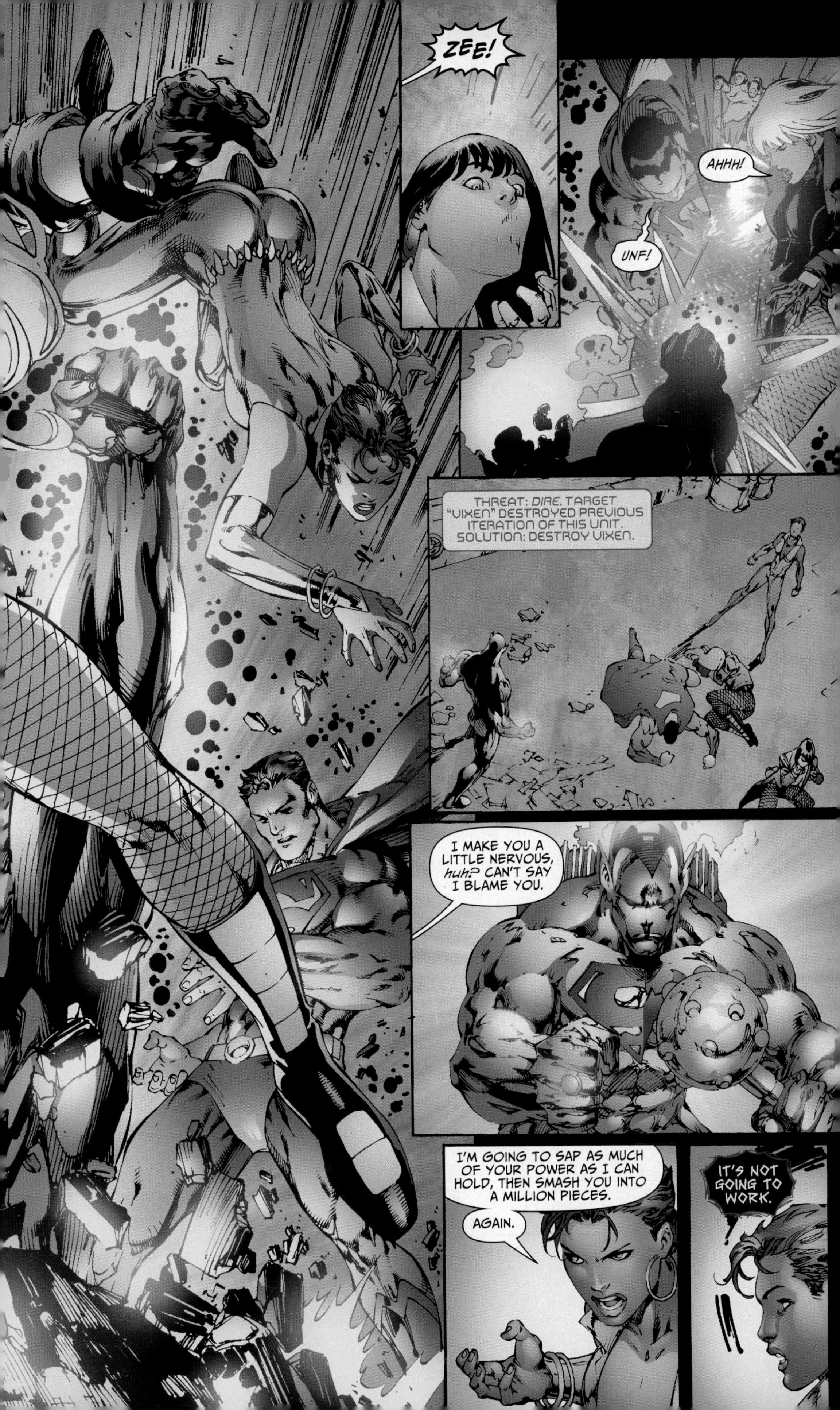
ZEE!
AHHH!
UNF!
THREAT: DIRE. TARGET "VIXEN" DESTROYED PREVIOUS ITERATION OF THIS UNIT. SOLUTION: DESTROY VIXEN.
I MAKE YOU A LITTLE NERVOUS, huh? CAN'T SAY I BLAME YOU.
I'M GOING TO SAP AS MUCH OF YOUR POWER AS I CAN HOLD, THEN SMASH YOU INTO A MILLION PIECES.
AGAIN.
IT'S NOT GOING TO WORK.

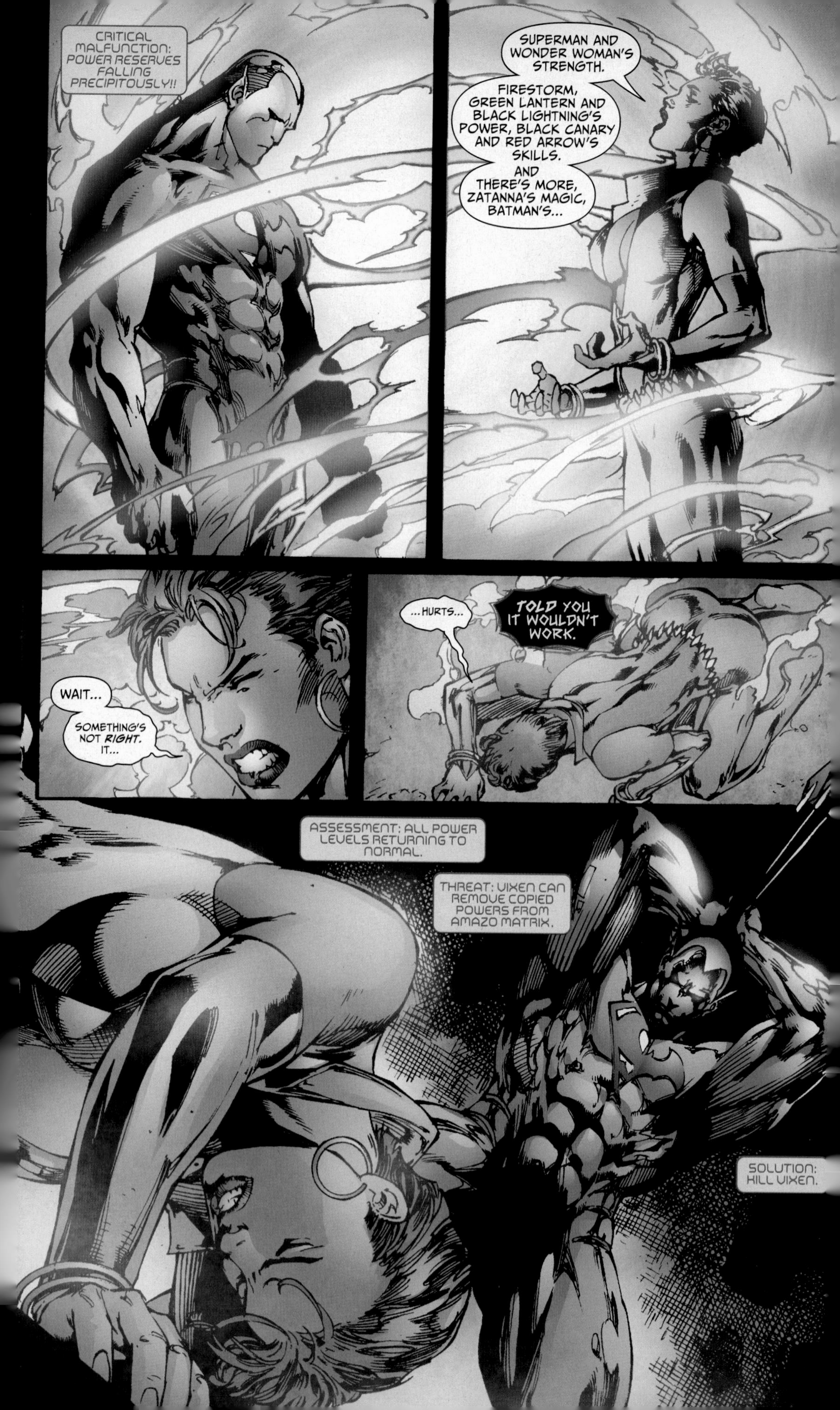
CRITICAL MALFUNCTION: POWER RESERVES FALLING PRECIPITOUSLY!!
SUPERMAN AND WONDER WOMAN'S STRENGTH.
FIRESTORM, GREEN LANTERN AND BLACK LIGHTNING'S POWER, BLACK CANARY AND RED ARROW'S SKILLS.
AND THERE'S MORE, ZATANNA'S MAGIC, BATMAN'S...
WAIT...
SOMETHING'S NOT RIGHT. IT...
...HURTS...
TOLD YOU IT WOULDN'T WORK.
ASSESSMENT: ALL POWER LEVELS RETURNING TO NORMAL.
THREAT: VIXEN CAN REMOVE COPIED POWERS FROM AMAZO MATRIX.
SOLUTION: KILL VIXEN.

ER ART BY ED BENES
 PETE PANTAZIS

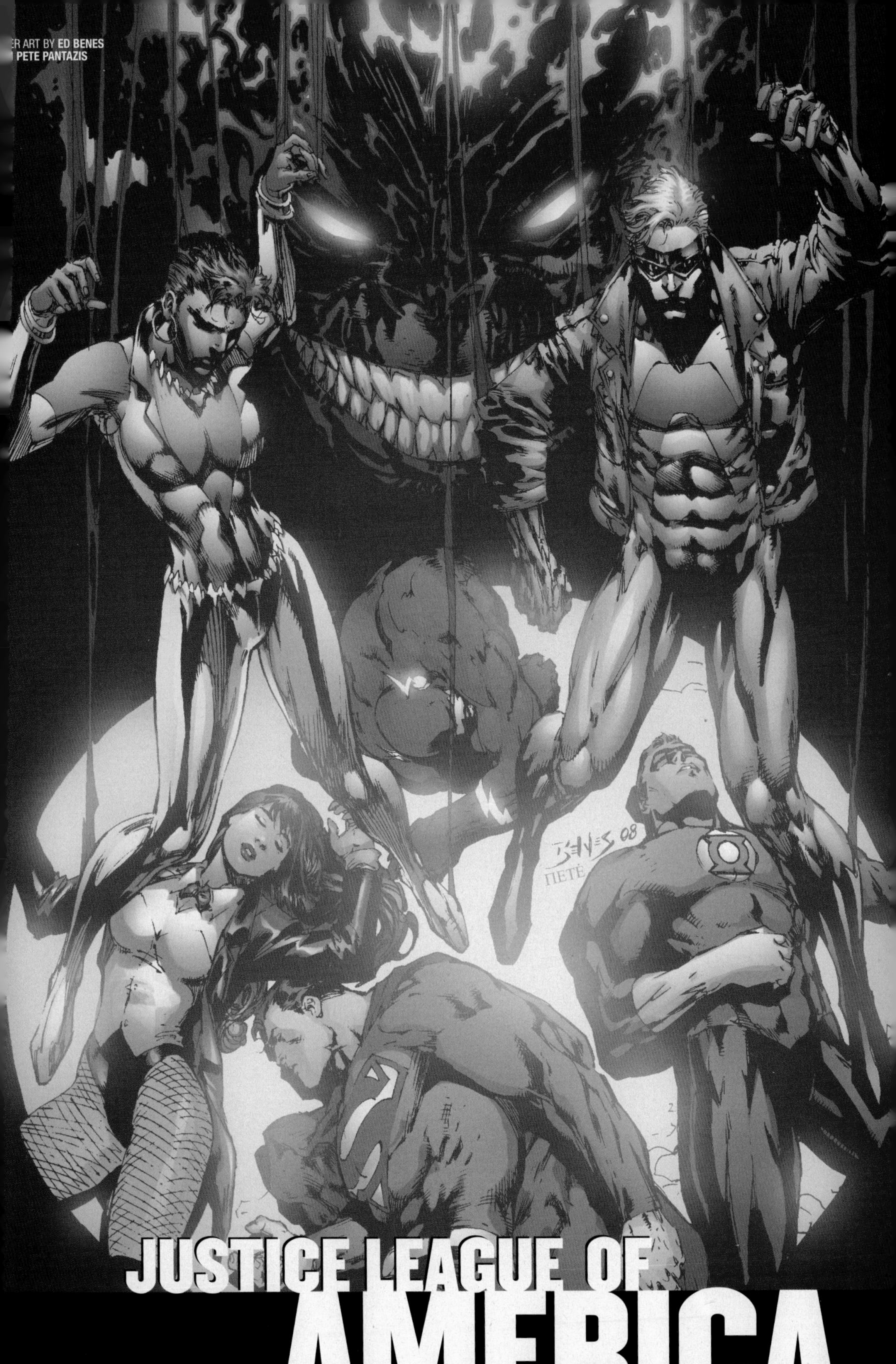

JUSTICE LEAGUE OF AMERICA

THE SECOND COMING
CHAPTER THREE: THE BLOOD-DIMMED TIDE

THE SECOND COMING
Chapter Three: The Blood-Dimmed Tide

Dwayne McDuffie
Writer

Alan Goldman
Penciller

Prentis Rollins
with
Rodney Ramos & Derek Fridolfs
Inkers

Rob Leigh
Letterer

Pete Pantazis
Colorist

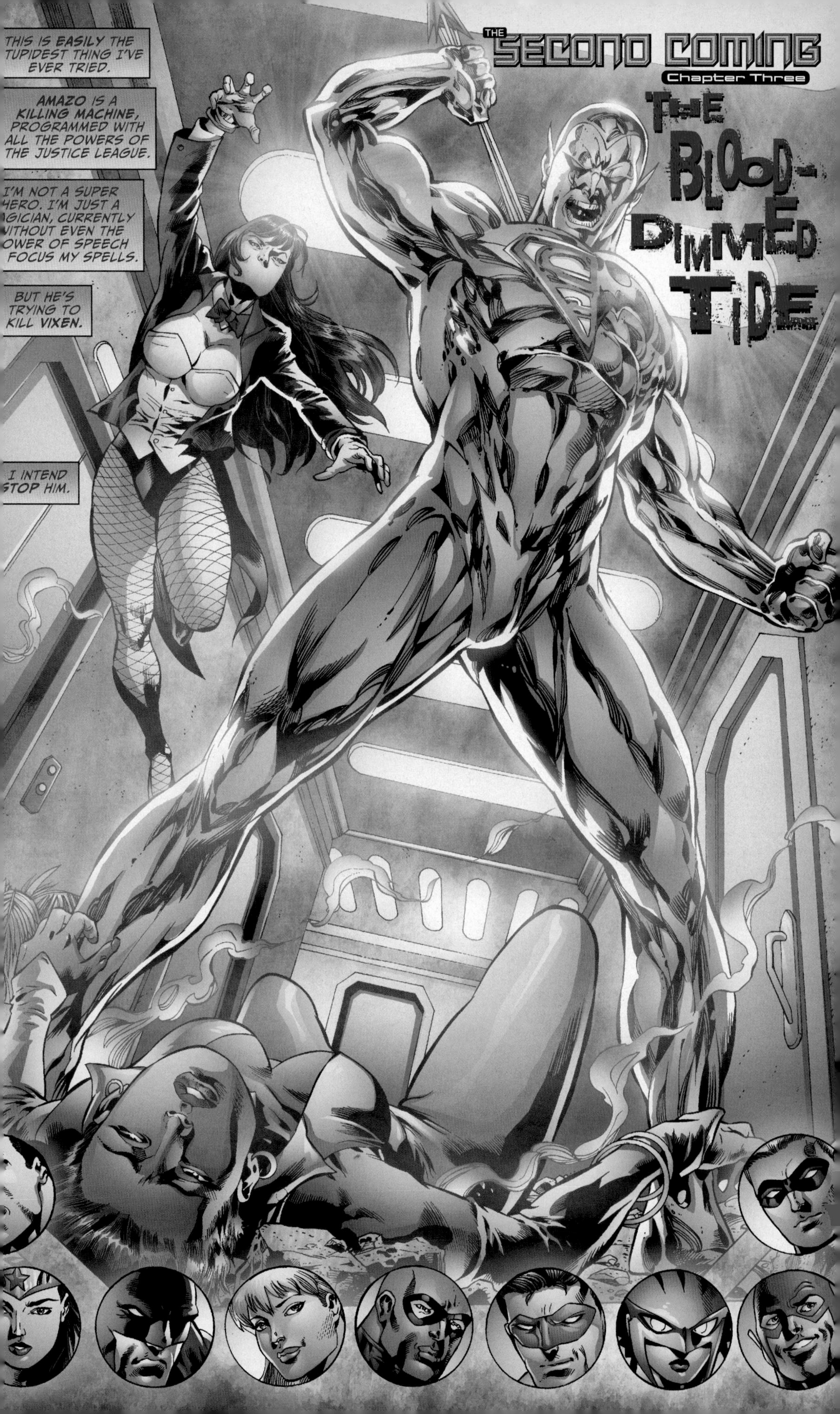
THE SECOND COMING
Chapter Three
THE BLOOD-DIMMED TIDE
THIS IS EASILY THE TUPIDEST THING I'VE EVER TRIED.
AMAZO IS A KILLING MACHINE, PROGRAMMED WITH ALL THE POWERS OF THE JUSTICE LEAGUE.
I'M NOT A SUPER HERO. I'M JUST A GICIAN, CURRENTLY WITHOUT EVEN THE OWER OF SPEECH FOCUS MY SPELLS.
BUT HE'S TRYING TO KILL VIXEN.
I INTEND STOP HIM.

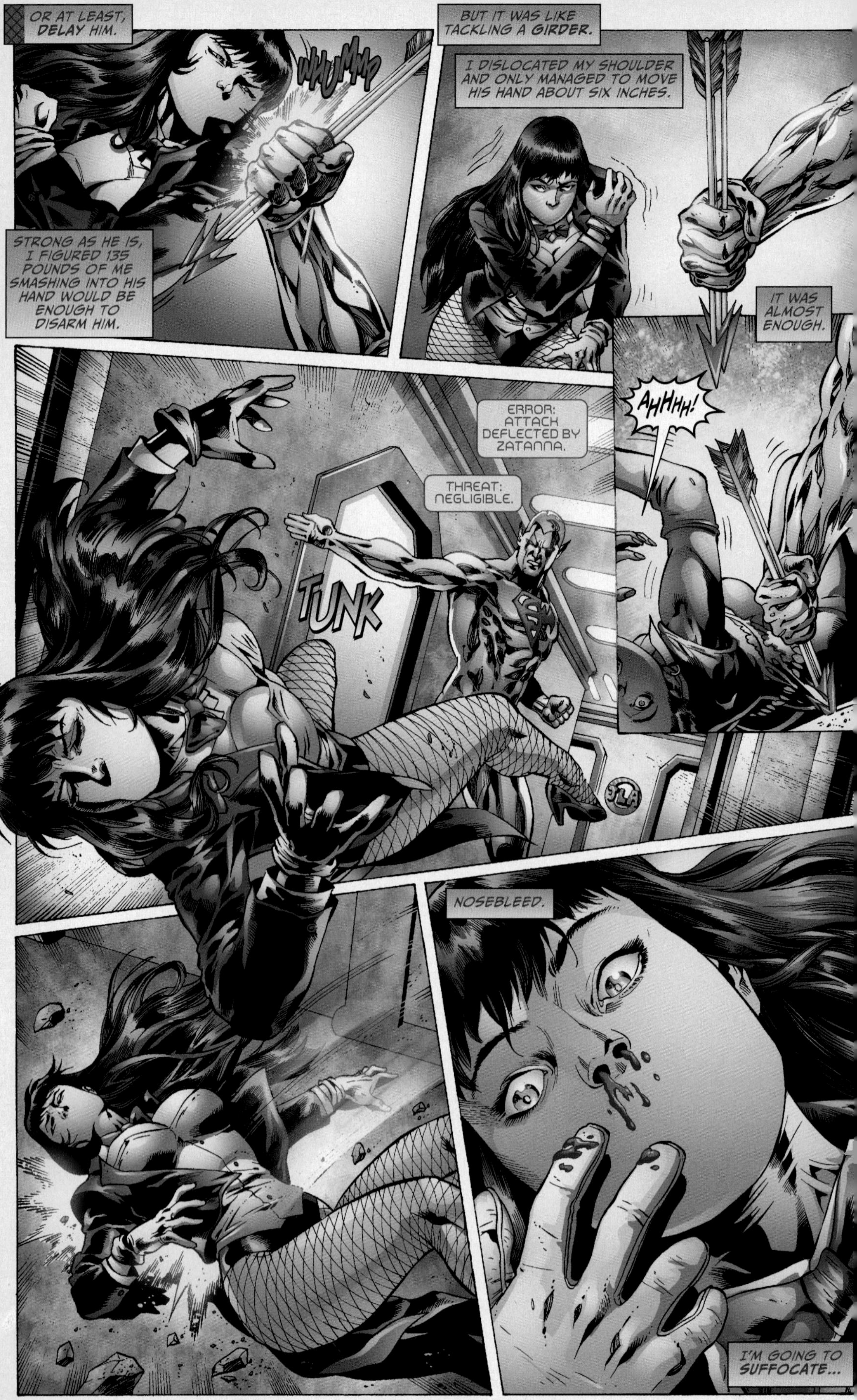
OR AT LEAST, DELAY HIM.
WHUMMP
STRONG AS HE IS, I FIGURED 135 POUNDS OF ME SMASHING INTO HIS HAND WOULD BE ENOUGH TO DISARM HIM.
BUT IT WAS LIKE TACKLING A GIRDER.
I DISLOCATED MY SHOULDER AND ONLY MANAGED TO MOVE HIS HAND ABOUT SIX INCHES.
IT WAS ALMOST ENOUGH.
AHHHH!
ERROR: ATTACK DEFLECTED BY ZATANNA.
THREAT: NEGLIGIBLE.
TUNK
NOSEBLEED.
I'M GOING TO SUFFOCATE...

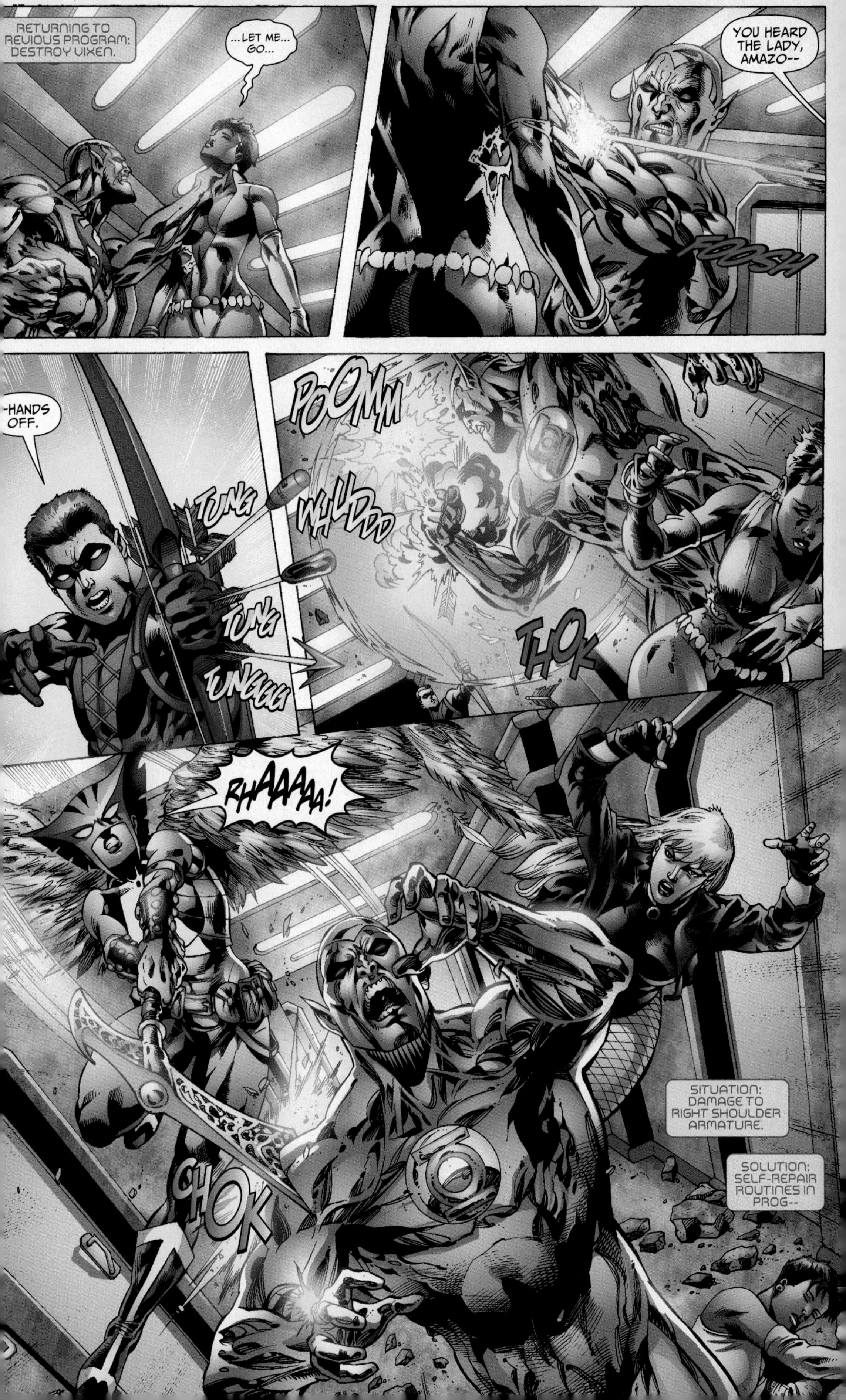

RETURNING TO REVIOUS PROGRAM: DESTROY VIXEN.
...LET ME... GO...
YOU HEARD THE LADY, AMAZO--
FOOSH
-HANDS OFF.
POOMM
TUNG
WHUDDD
TUNG
TUNGGG
THOK
RHAAAAAA!
SITUATION: DAMAGE TO RIGHT SHOULDER ARMATURE.
SOLUTION: SELF-REPAIR ROUTINES IN PROG--
CHOK

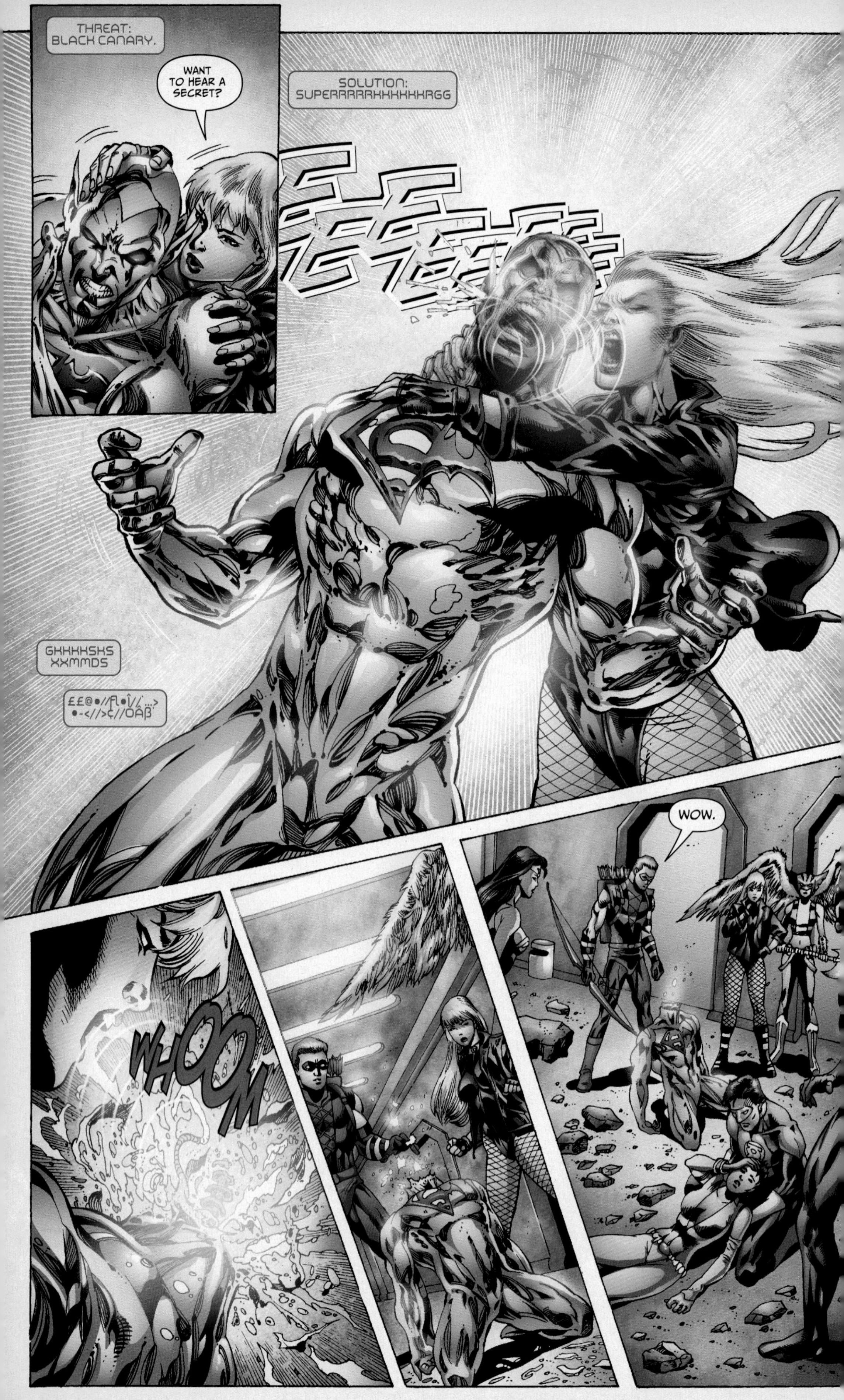
THREAT: BLACK CANARY.
WANT TO HEAR A SECRET?
SOLUTION: SUPERRRRRKKKKKKRGG
GKKKKSKS XXMMDS
££@•//ﬂ•Î/⁄...>
•-<//>ç//OÂβ
WHOOM
WOW.

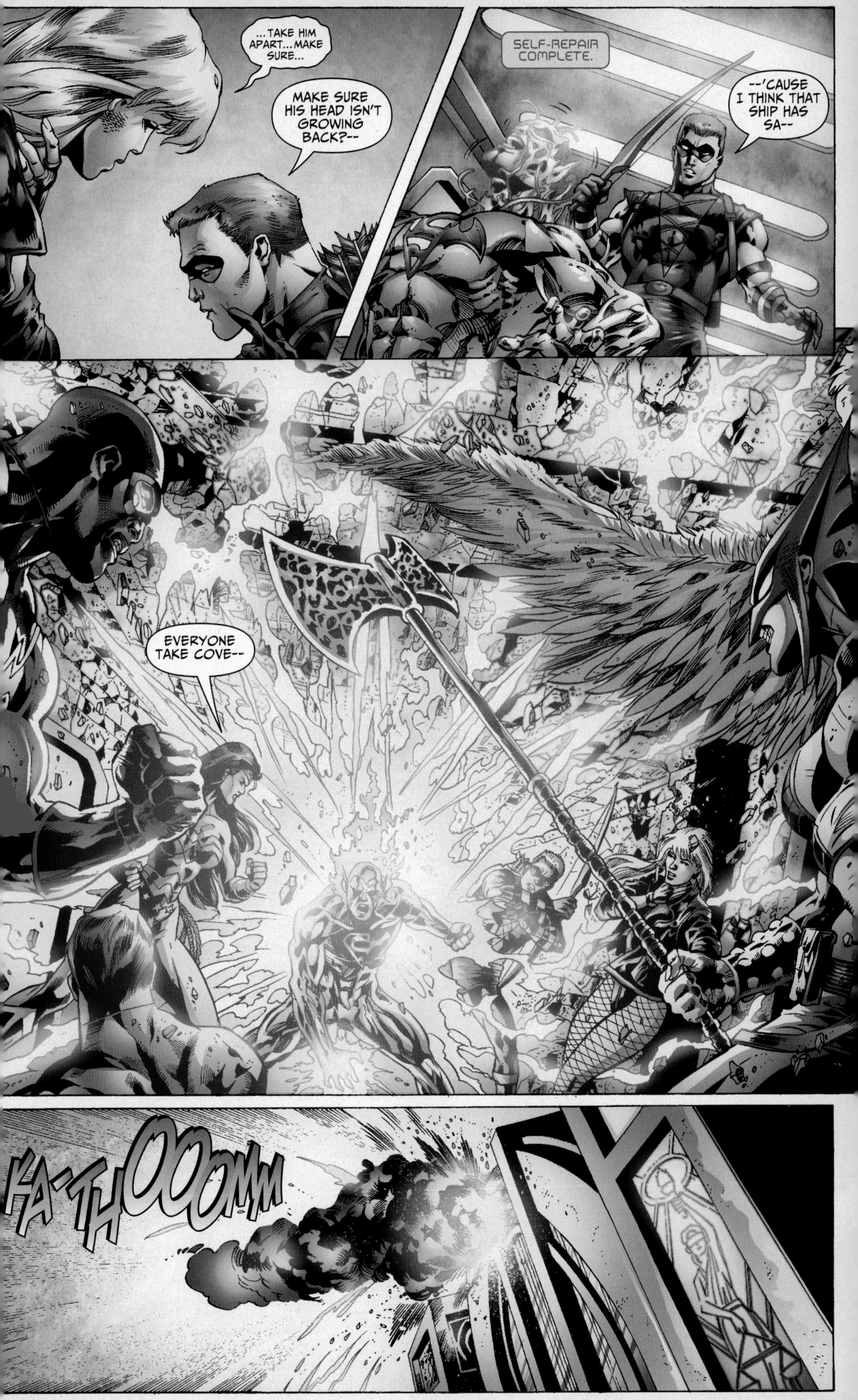
...TAKE HIM APART...MAKE SURE...
MAKE SURE HIS HEAD ISN'T GROWING BACK?--
SELF-REPAIR COMPLETE.
--'CAUSE I THINK THAT SHIP HAS SA--
EVERYONE TAKE COVE--
KA-THOOOMM

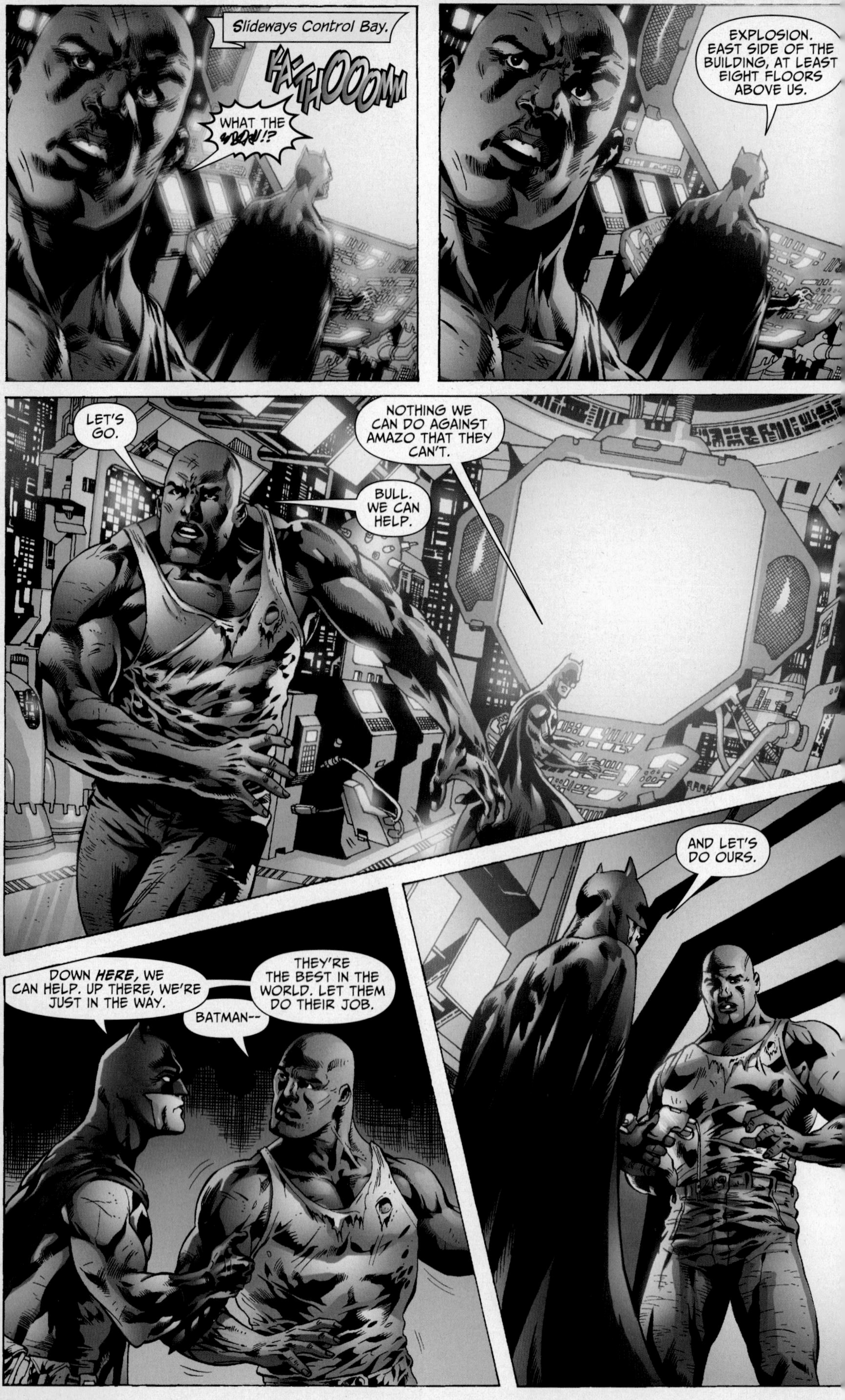
Slideways Control Bay.
KA-THOOOOMM
WHAT THE
EXPLOSION. EAST SIDE OF THE BUILDING, AT LEAST EIGHT FLOORS ABOVE US.
LET'S GO.
NOTHING WE CAN DO AGAINST AMAZO THAT THEY CAN'T.
BULL. WE CAN HELP.
DOWN HERE, WE CAN HELP. UP THERE, WE'RE JUST IN THE WAY.
BATMAN--
THEY'RE THE BEST IN THE WORLD. LET THEM DO THEIR JOB.
AND LET'S DO OURS.

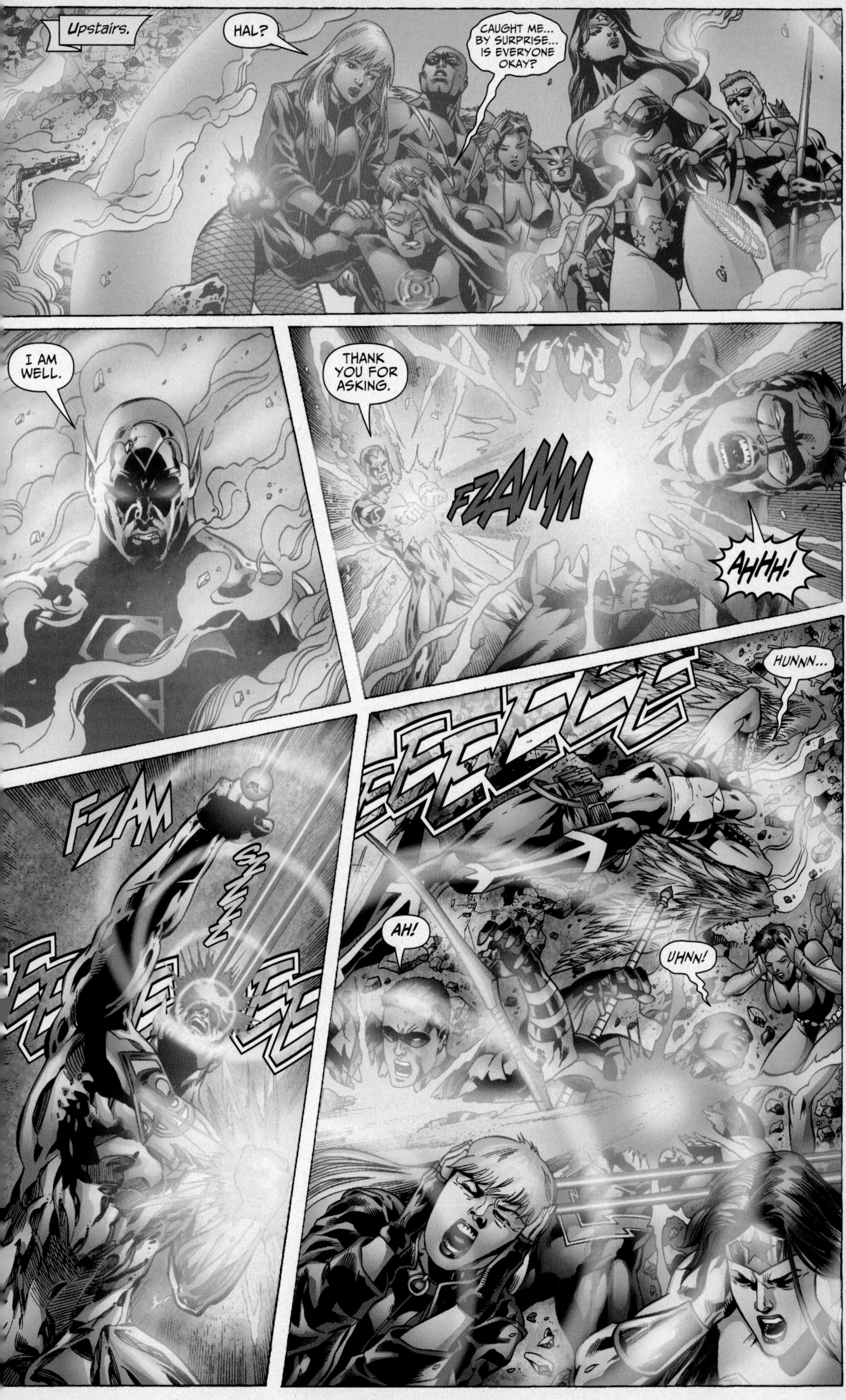
Upstairs.
HAL?
CAUGHT ME... BY SURPRISE... IS EVERYONE OKAY?
I AM WELL.
THANK YOU FOR ASKING.
FZAMM
AHHH!
HUNNN...
FZAM
EEEEEEE
AH!
UHNN!

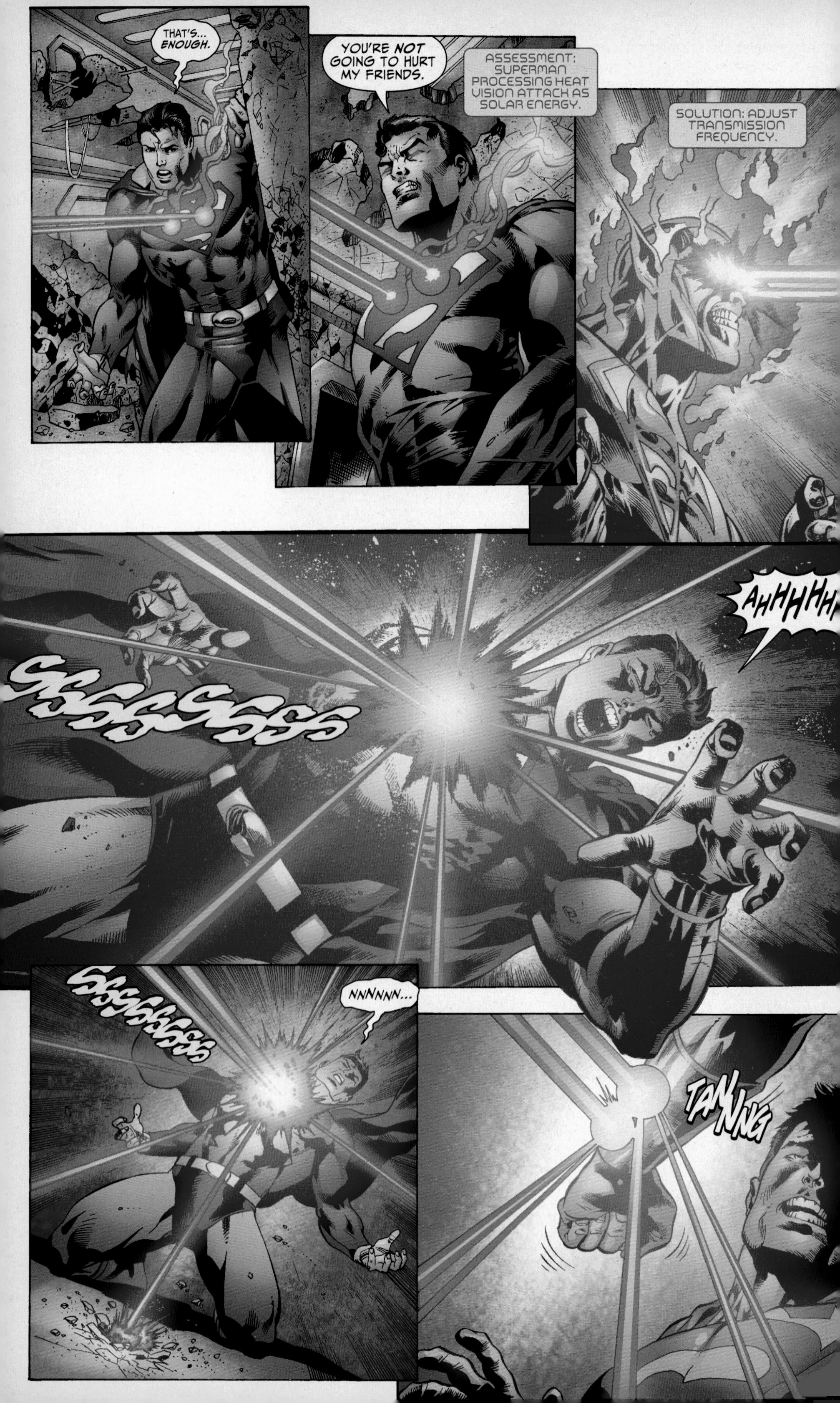
THAT'S... ENOUGH.
YOU'RE NOT GOING TO HURT MY FRIENDS.
ASSESSMENT: SUPERMAN PROCESSING HEAT VISION ATTACK AS SOLAR ENERGY.
SOLUTION: ADJUST TRANSMISSION FREQUENCY.
AHHHHH
SSSSSSSS
SSSSSSSSS
NNNNNN...
TANNNG

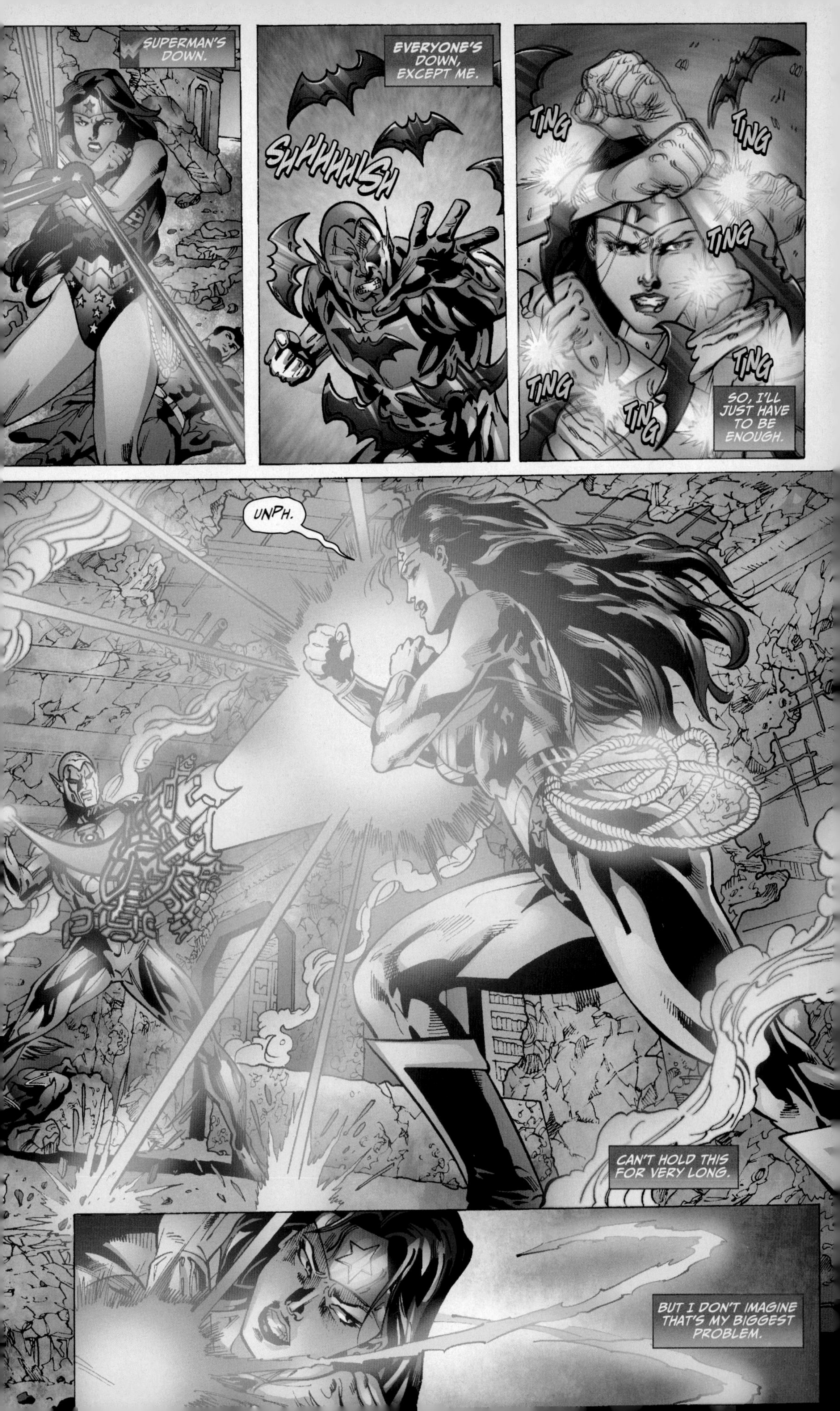
SUPERMAN'S DOWN.
EVERYONE'S DOWN, EXCEPT ME.
SHHHHHHSH
TING
TING
TING
TING
TING
TING
SO, I'LL JUST HAVE TO BE ENOUGH.
UNPH.
CAN'T HOLD THIS FOR VERY LONG.
BUT I DON'T IMAGINE THAT'S MY BIGGEST PROBLEM.

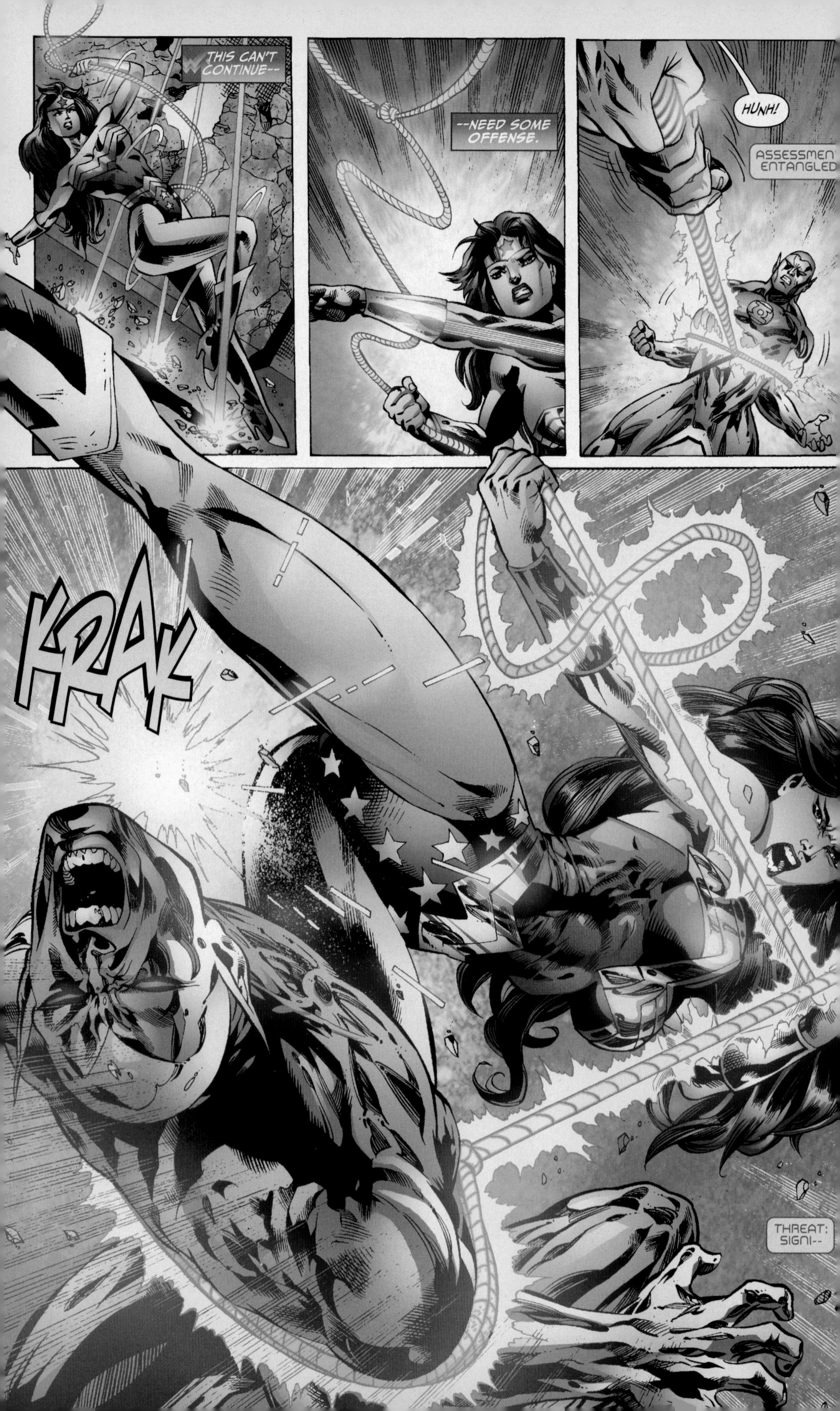
THIS CAN'T CONTINUE--
--NEED SOME OFFENSE.
HUNH!
ASSESSMEN
ENTANGLED
KRAK
THREAT: SIGNI--

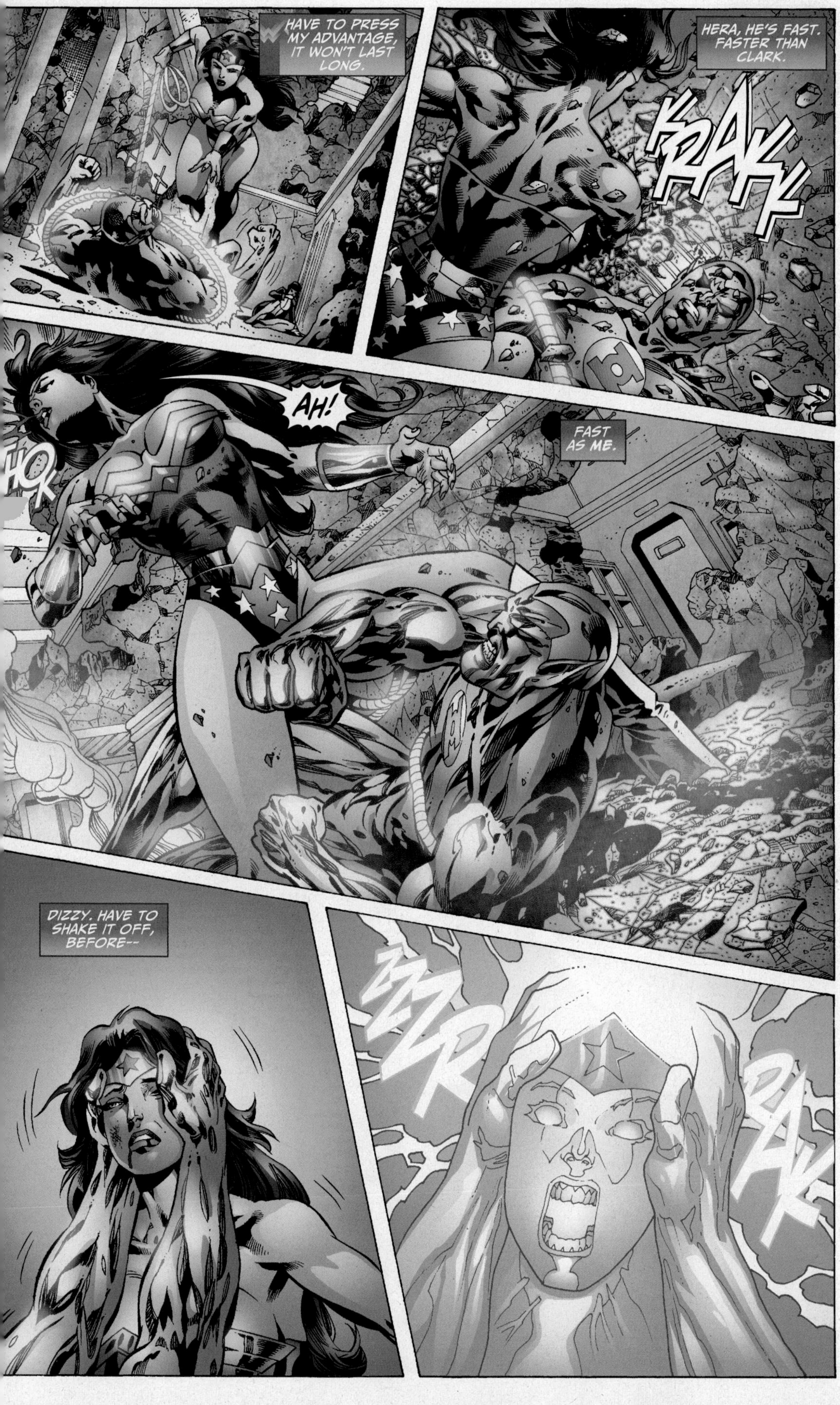
HAVE TO PRESS MY ADVANTAGE, IT WON'T LAST LONG.
HERA, HE'S FAST. FASTER THAN CLARK.
KRAKK
AH!
THOK
FAST AS ME.
DIZZY. HAVE TO SHAKE IT OFF, BEFORE--
ZZZZR
ZAK

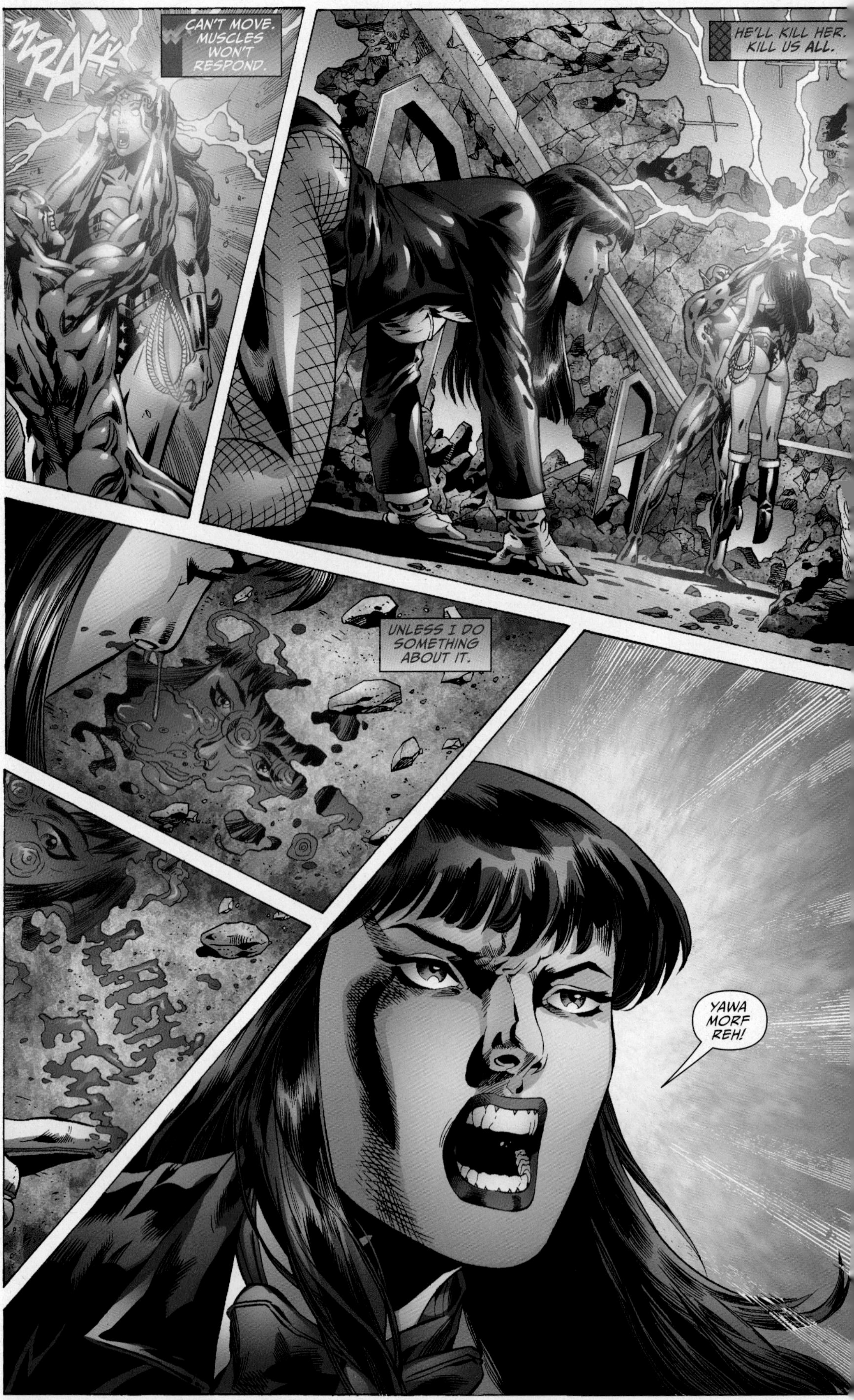
ZZRAKK
CAN'T MOVE. MUSCLES WON'T RESPOND.
HE'LL KILL HER. KILL US ALL.
UNLESS I DO SOMETHING ABOUT IT.
YAWA MORF REH!

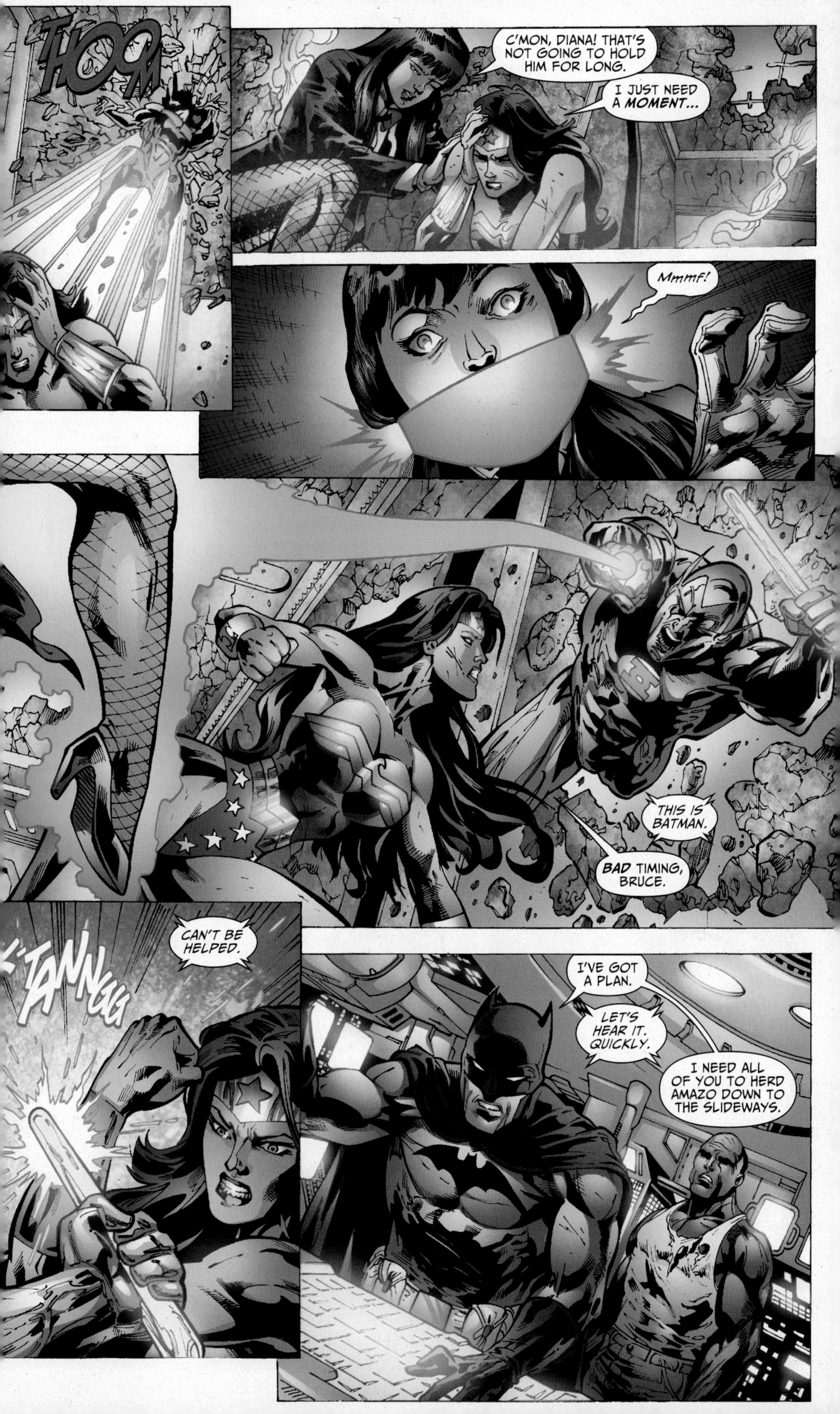
THOOM
C'MON, DIANA! THAT'S NOT GOING TO HOLD HIM FOR LONG.
I JUST NEED A MOMENT...
Mmmf!
THIS IS BATMAN.
BAD TIMING, BRUCE.
CAN'T BE HELPED.
TANNGG
I'VE GOT A PLAN.
LET'S HEAR IT. QUICKLY.
I NEED ALL OF YOU TO HERD AMAZO DOWN TO THE SLIDEWAYS.

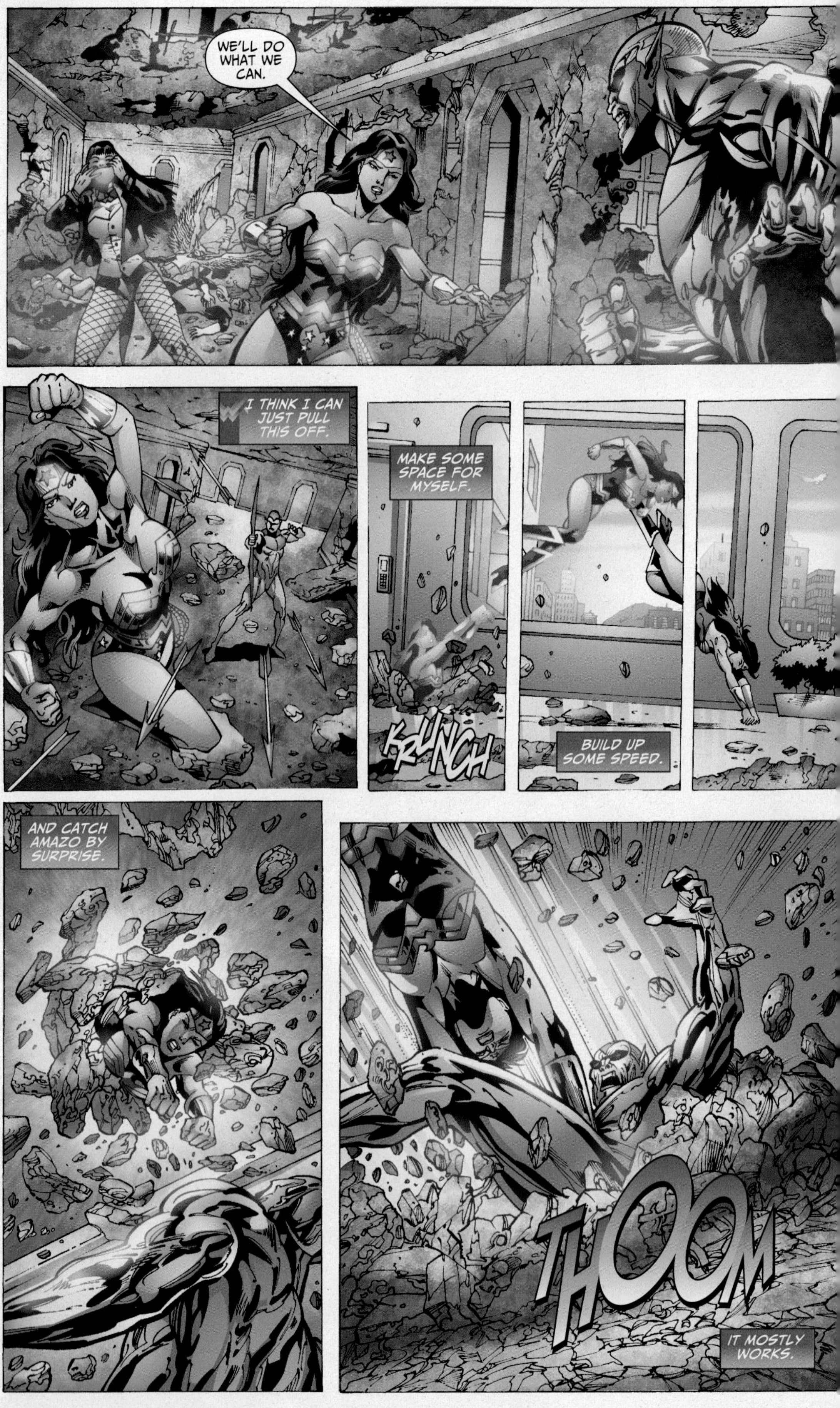
WE'LL DO WHAT WE CAN.
I THINK I CAN JUST PULL THIS OFF.
MAKE SOME SPACE FOR MYSELF.
KRUNCH
BUILD UP SOME SPEED.
AND CATCH AMAZO BY SURPRISE.
THOOM
IT MOSTLY WORKS.

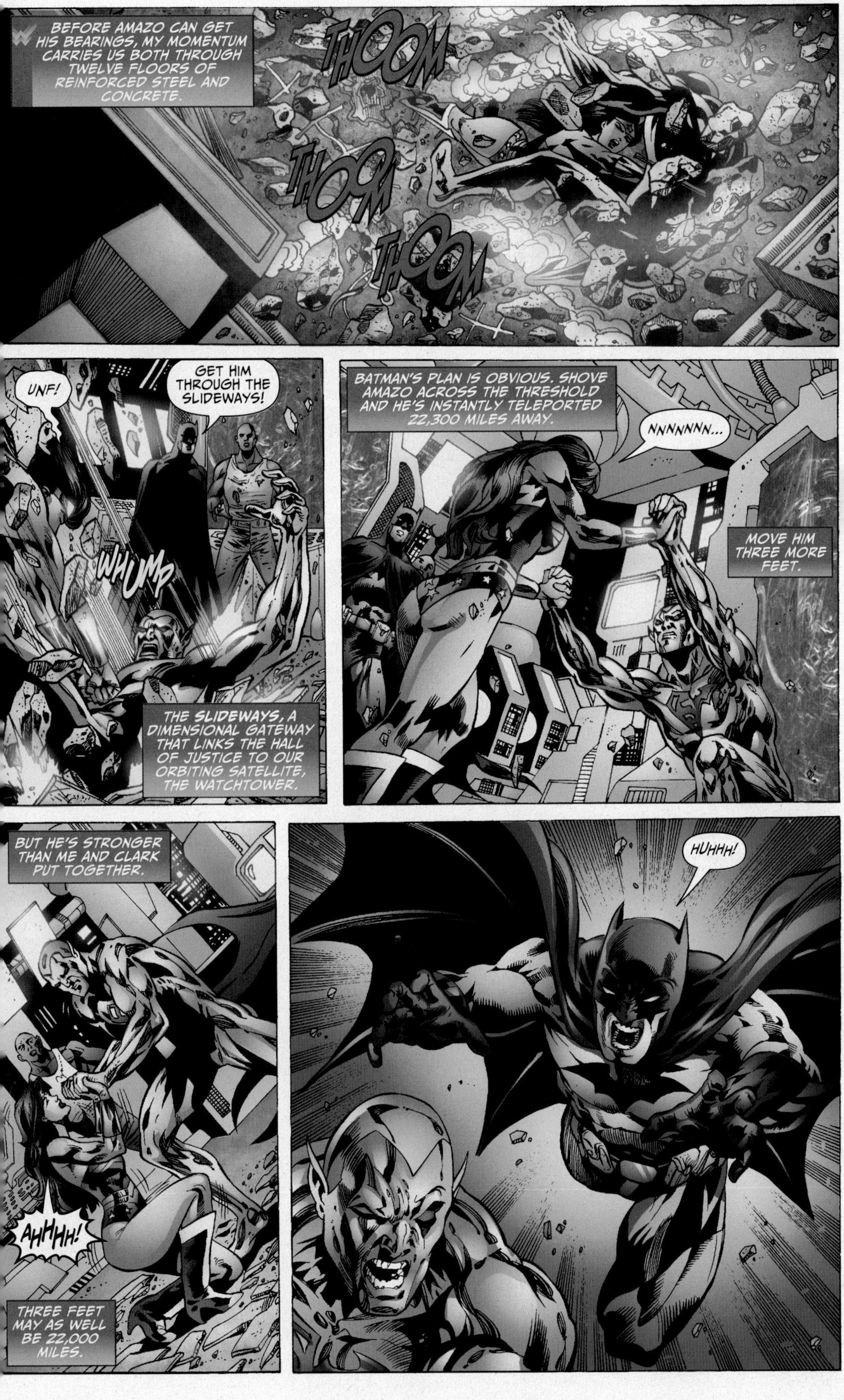
BEFORE AMAZO CAN GET HIS BEARINGS, MY MOMENTUM CARRIES US BOTH THROUGH TWELVE FLOORS OF REINFORCED STEEL AND CONCRETE.
THOOM
THOOM
THOOM
UNF!
GET HIM THROUGH THE SLIDEWAYS!
WHUMP
THE SLIDEWAYS, A DIMENSIONAL GATEWAY THAT LINKS THE HALL OF JUSTICE TO OUR ORBITING SATELLITE, THE WATCHTOWER.
BATMAN'S PLAN IS OBVIOUS. SHOVE AMAZO ACROSS THE THRESHOLD AND HE'S INSTANTLY TELEPORTED 22,300 MILES AWAY.
NNNNNNN...
MOVE HIM THREE MORE FEET.
BUT HE'S STRONGER THAN ME AND CLARK PUT TOGETHER.
AHHHH!
THREE FEET MAY AS WELL BE 22,000 MILES.
HUHHH!

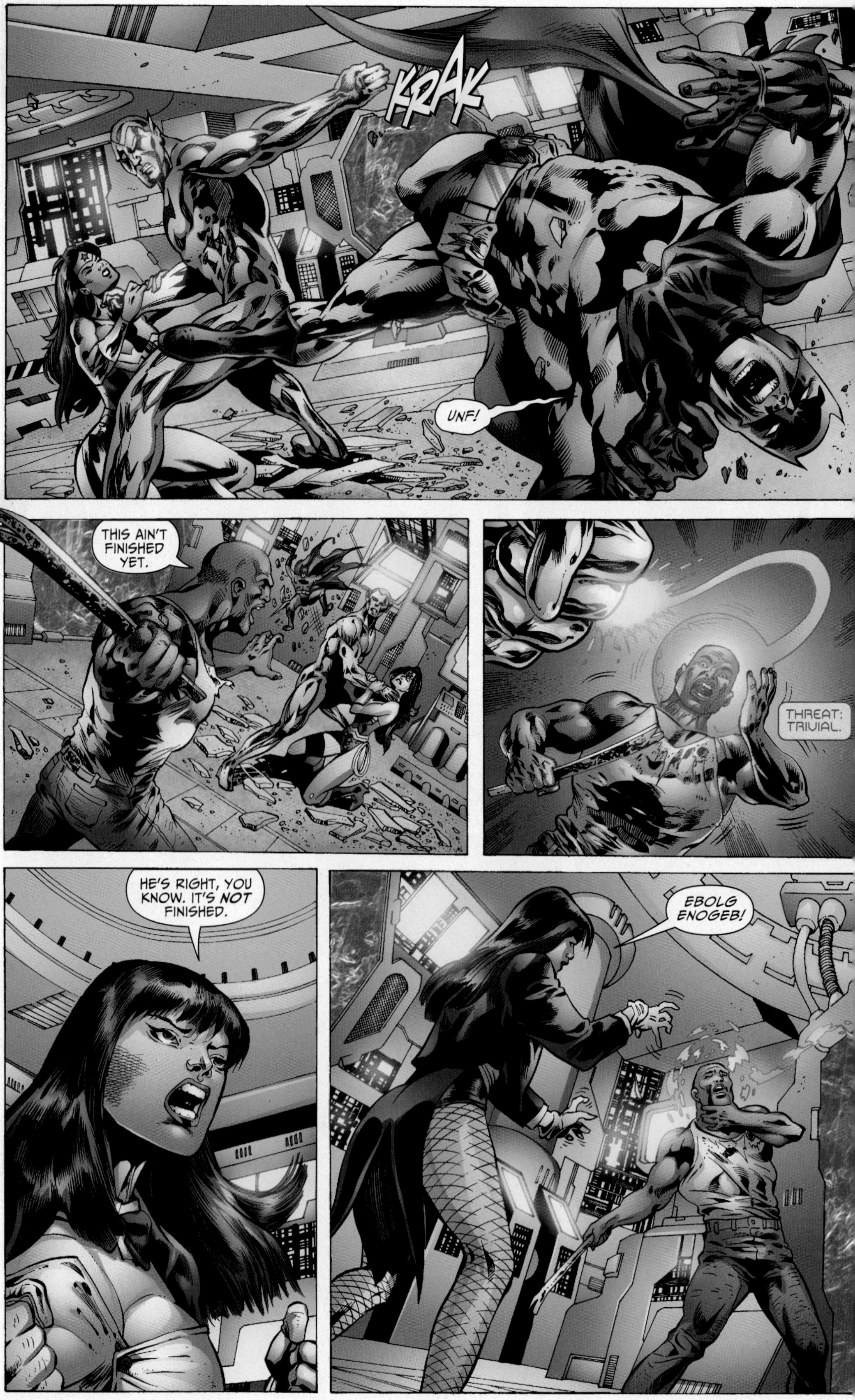
KRAK
UNF!
THIS AIN'T FINISHED YET.
THREAT: TRIVIAL.
HE'S RIGHT, YOU KNOW. IT'S **NOT** FINISHED.
EBOLG ENOGEB!

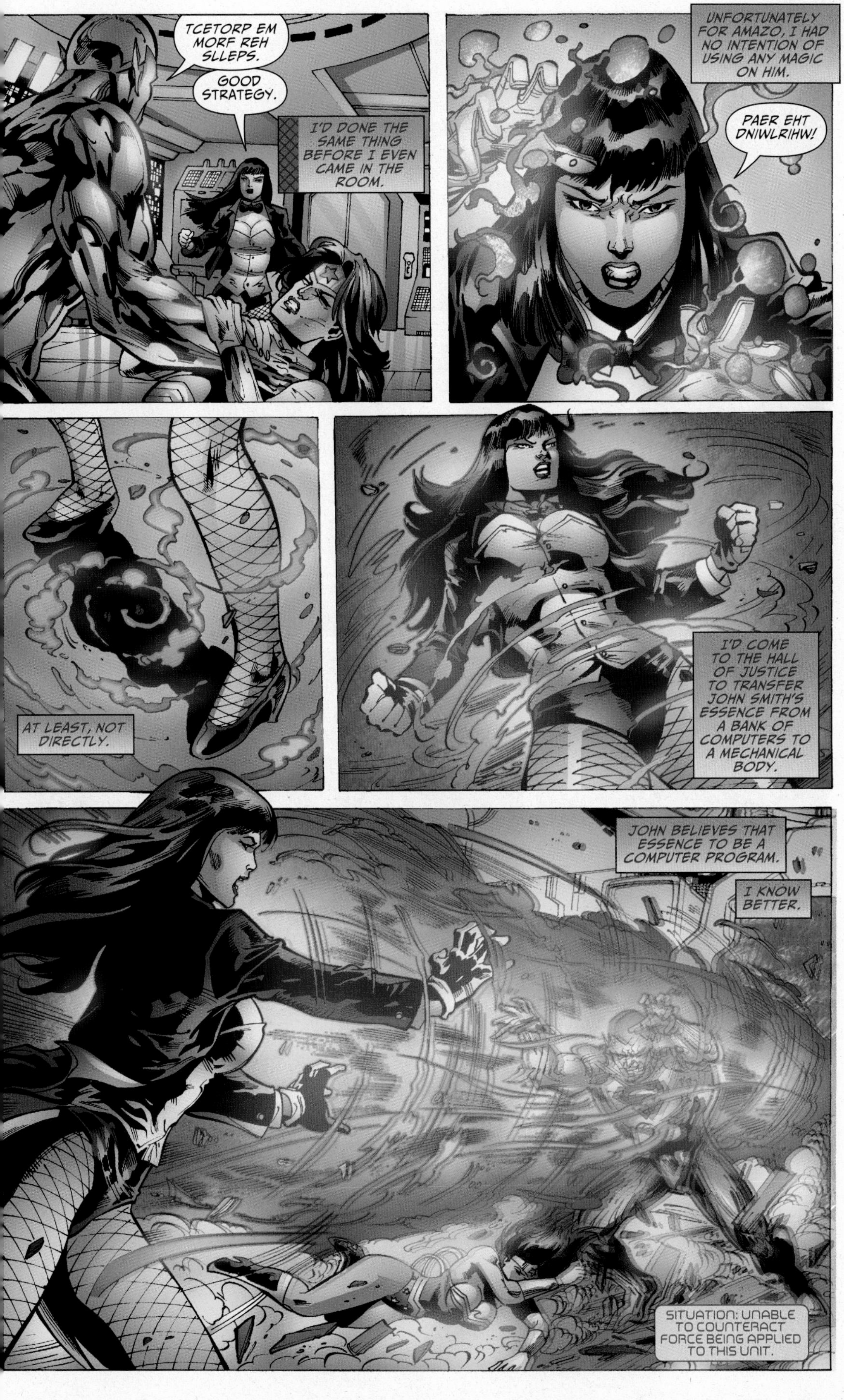
TCETORP EM MORF REH SLLEPS.
GOOD STRATEGY.
I'D DONE THE SAME THING BEFORE I EVEN CAME IN THE ROOM.
UNFORTUNATELY FOR AMAZO, I HAD NO INTENTION OF USING ANY MAGIC ON HIM.
PAER EHT DNIWLRIHW!
AT LEAST, NOT DIRECTLY.
I'D COME TO THE HALL OF JUSTICE TO TRANSFER JOHN SMITH'S ESSENCE FROM A BANK OF COMPUTERS TO A MECHANICAL BODY.
JOHN BELIEVES THAT ESSENCE TO BE A COMPUTER PROGRAM.
I KNOW BETTER.
SITUATION: UNABLE TO COUNTERACT FORCE BEING APPLIED TO THIS UNIT.

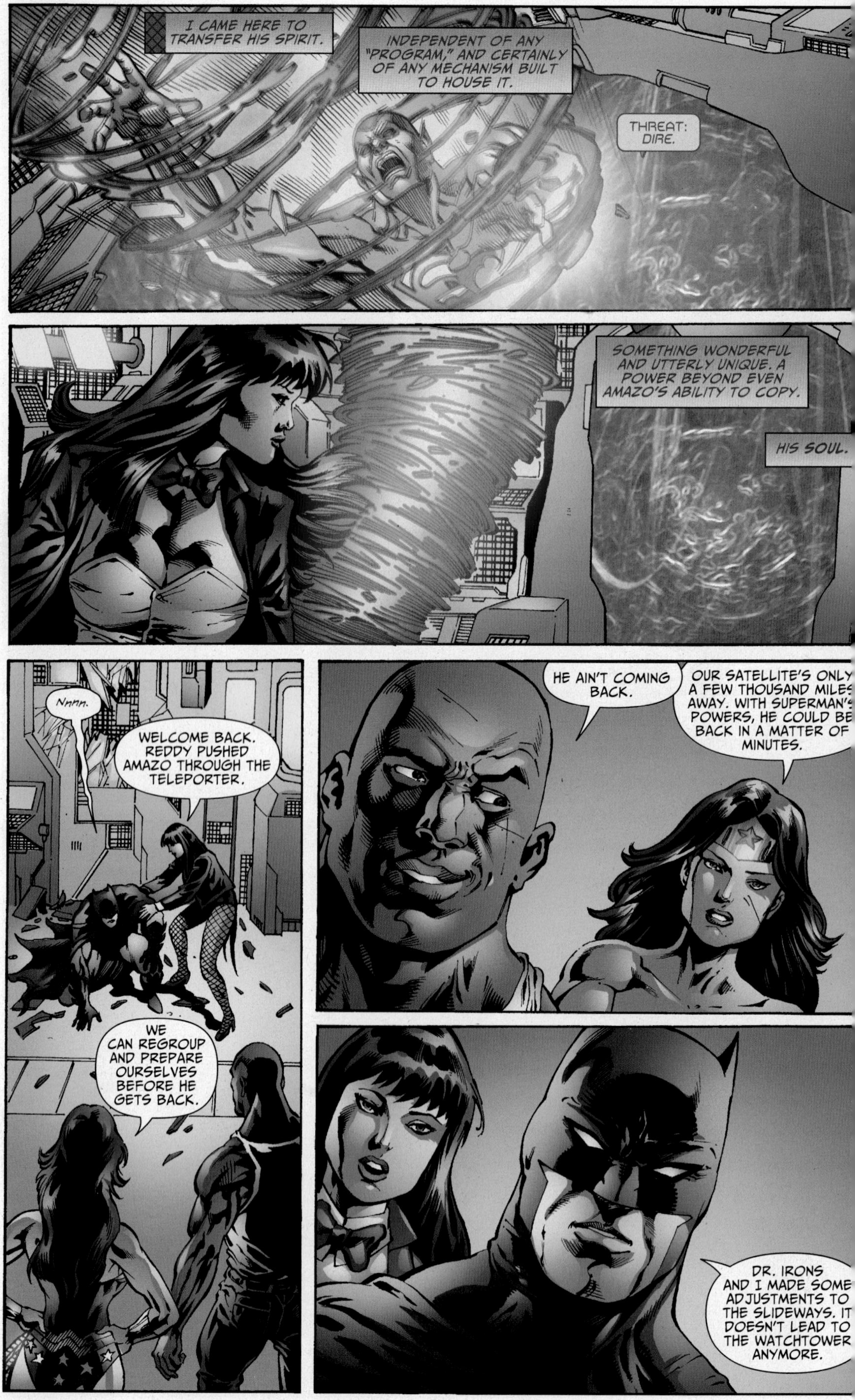
I CAME HERE TO TRANSFER HIS SPIRIT.
INDEPENDENT OF ANY "PROGRAM," AND CERTAINLY OF ANY MECHANISM BUILT TO HOUSE IT.
THREAT: DIRE.
SOMETHING WONDERFUL AND UTTERLY UNIQUE. A POWER BEYOND EVEN AMAZO'S ABILITY TO COPY.
HIS SOUL.
Nnnn.
WELCOME BACK. REDDY PUSHED AMAZO THROUGH THE TELEPORTER.
WE CAN REGROUP AND PREPARE OURSELVES BEFORE HE GETS BACK.
HE AIN'T COMING BACK.
OUR SATELLITE'S ONLY A FEW THOUSAND MILES AWAY. WITH SUPERMAN'S POWERS, HE COULD BE BACK IN A MATTER OF MINUTES.
DR. IRONS AND I MADE SOME ADJUSTMENTS TO THE SLIDEWAYS. IT DOESN'T LEAD TO THE WATCHTOWER ANYMORE.

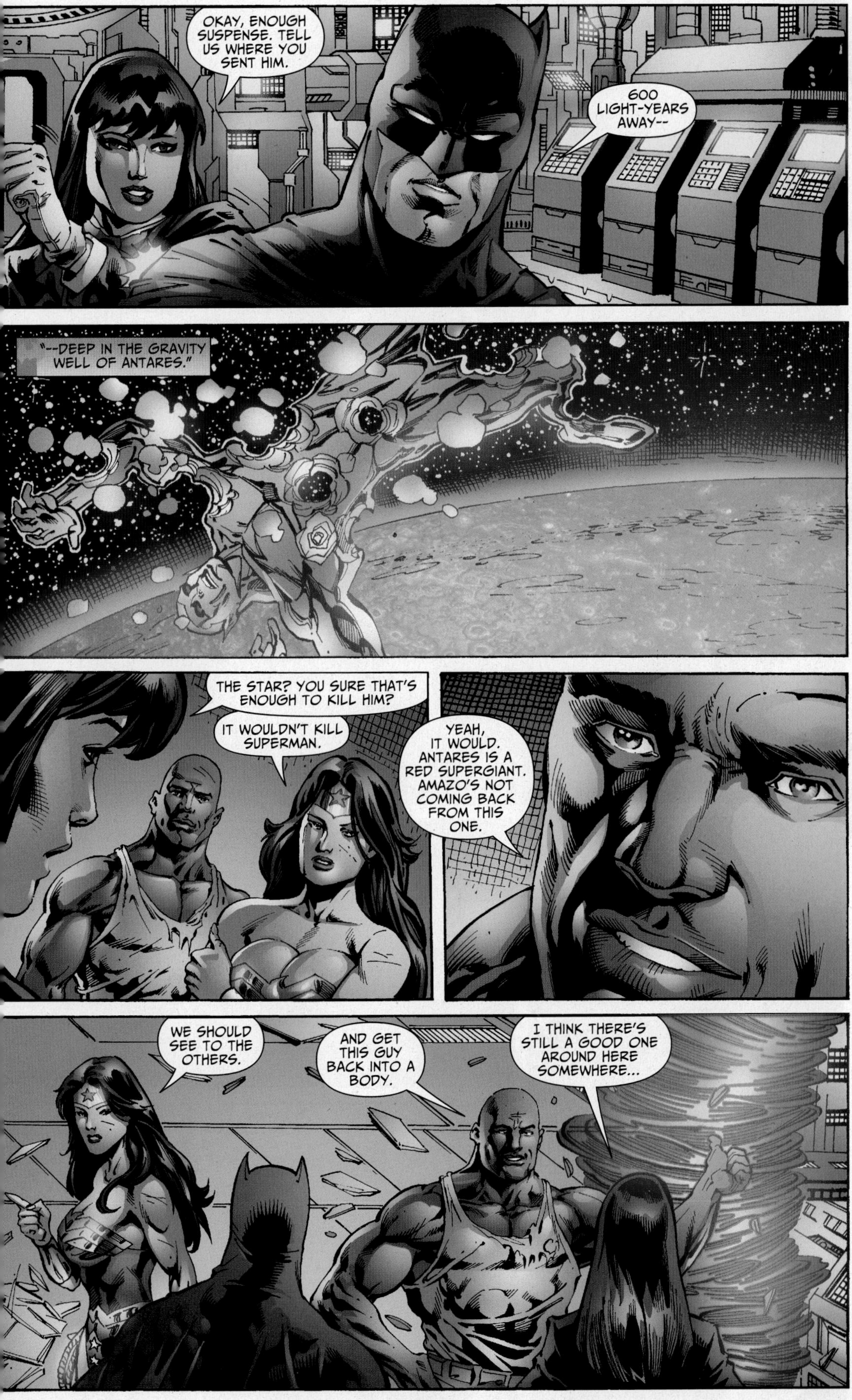
OKAY, ENOUGH SUSPENSE. TELL US WHERE YOU SENT HIM.
600 LIGHT-YEARS AWAY--
"--DEEP IN THE GRAVITY WELL OF ANTARES."
THE STAR? YOU SURE THAT'S ENOUGH TO KILL HIM?
IT WOULDN'T KILL SUPERMAN.
YEAH, IT WOULD. ANTARES IS A RED SUPERGIANT. AMAZO'S NOT COMING BACK FROM THIS ONE.
WE SHOULD SEE TO THE OTHERS.
AND GET THIS GUY BACK INTO A BODY.
I THINK THERE'S STILL A GOOD ONE AROUND HERE SOMEWHERE...

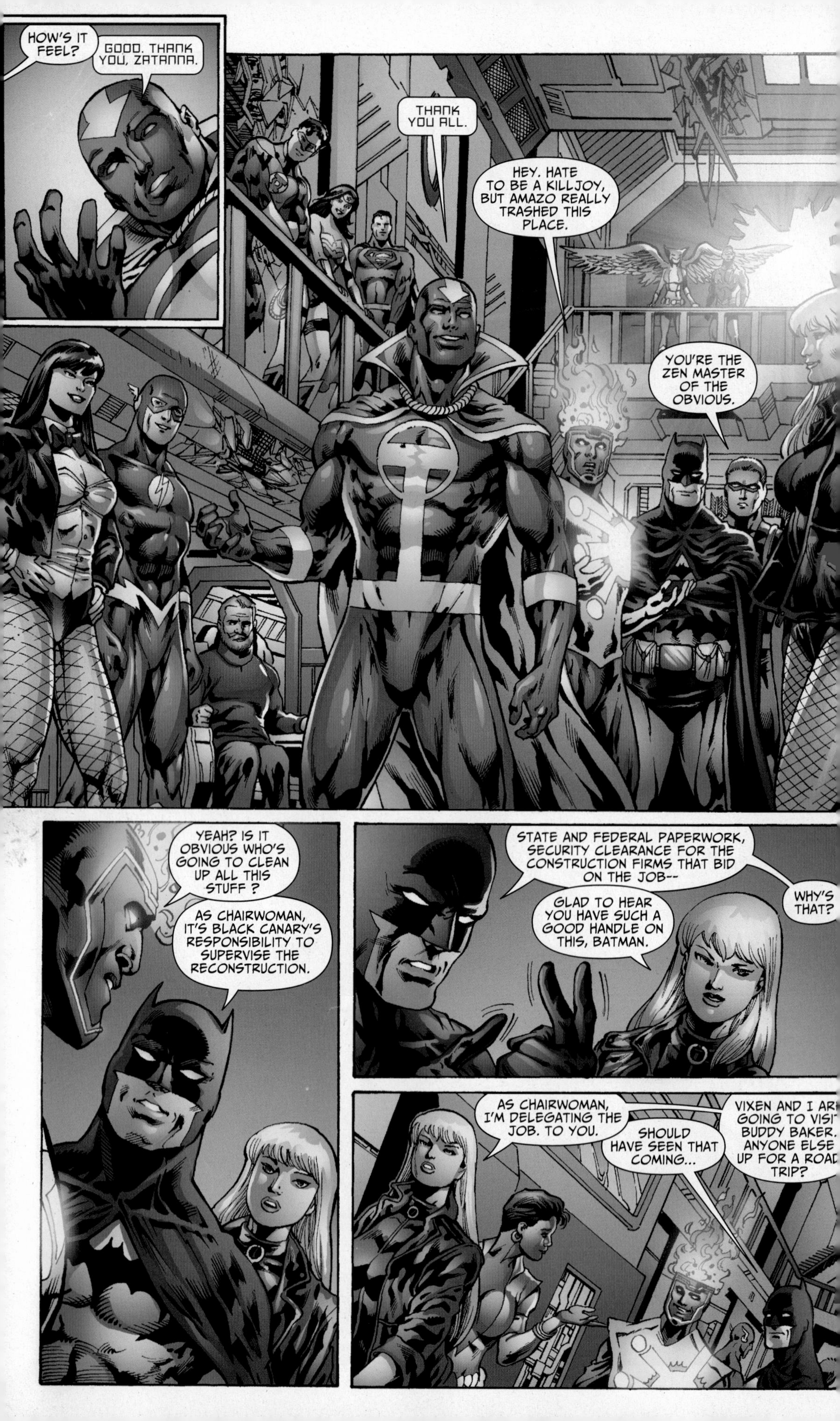
HOW'S IT FEEL?
GOOD. THANK YOU, ZATANNA.
THANK YOU ALL.
HEY. HATE TO BE A KILLJOY, BUT AMAZO REALLY TRASHED THIS PLACE.
YOU'RE THE ZEN MASTER OF THE OBVIOUS.
YEAH? IS IT OBVIOUS WHO'S GOING TO CLEAN UP ALL THIS STUFF ?
AS CHAIRWOMAN, IT'S BLACK CANARY'S RESPONSIBILITY TO SUPERVISE THE RECONSTRUCTION.
STATE AND FEDERAL PAPERWORK, SECURITY CLEARANCE FOR THE CONSTRUCTION FIRMS THAT BID ON THE JOB--
GLAD TO HEAR YOU HAVE SUCH A GOOD HANDLE ON THIS, BATMAN.
WHY'S THAT?
AS CHAIRWOMAN, I'M DELEGATING THE JOB. TO YOU.
SHOULD HAVE SEEN THAT COMING...
VIXEN AND I AR GOING TO VISIT BUDDY BAKER. ANYONE ELSE UP FOR A ROAD TRIP?

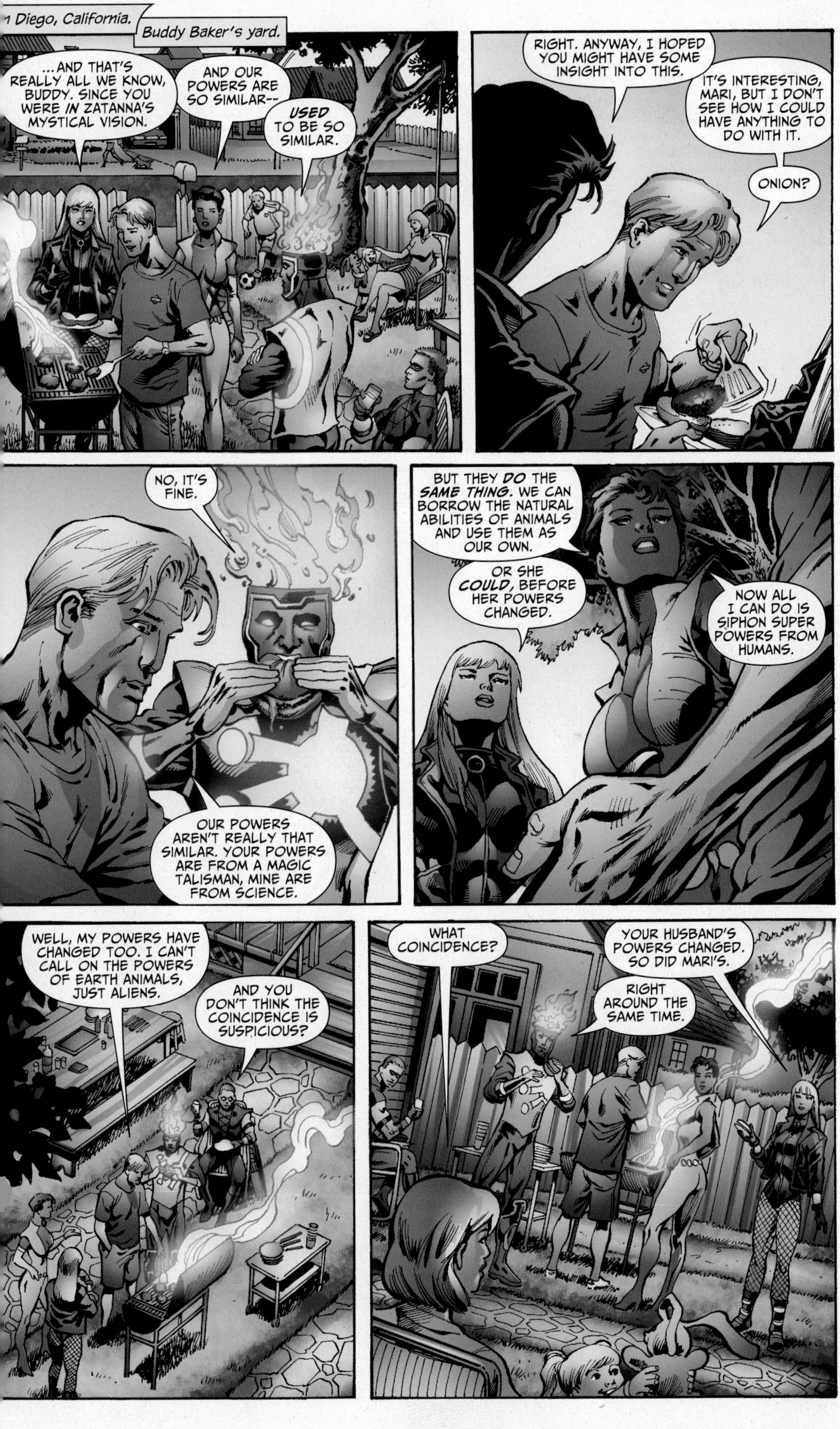

n Diego, California.
Buddy Baker's yard.
...AND THAT'S REALLY ALL WE KNOW, BUDDY. SINCE YOU WERE *IN* ZATANNA'S MYSTICAL VISION.
AND OUR POWERS ARE SO SIMILAR--
USED TO BE SO SIMILAR.
RIGHT. ANYWAY, I HOPED YOU MIGHT HAVE SOME INSIGHT INTO THIS.
IT'S INTERESTING, MARI, BUT I DON'T SEE HOW I COULD HAVE ANYTHING TO DO WITH IT.
ONION?
NO, IT'S FINE.
OUR POWERS AREN'T REALLY THAT SIMILAR. YOUR POWERS ARE FROM A MAGIC TALISMAN, MINE ARE FROM SCIENCE.
BUT THEY *DO* THE *SAME THING*. WE CAN BORROW THE NATURAL ABILITIES OF ANIMALS AND USE THEM AS OUR OWN.
OR SHE *COULD*, BEFORE HER POWERS CHANGED.
NOW ALL I CAN DO IS SIPHON SUPER POWERS FROM HUMANS.
WELL, MY POWERS HAVE CHANGED TOO. I CAN'T CALL ON THE POWERS OF EARTH ANIMALS, JUST ALIENS.
AND YOU DON'T THINK THE COINCIDENCE IS SUSPICIOUS?
WHAT COINCIDENCE?
YOUR HUSBAND'S POWERS CHANGED. SO DID MARI'S.
RIGHT AROUND THE SAME TIME.

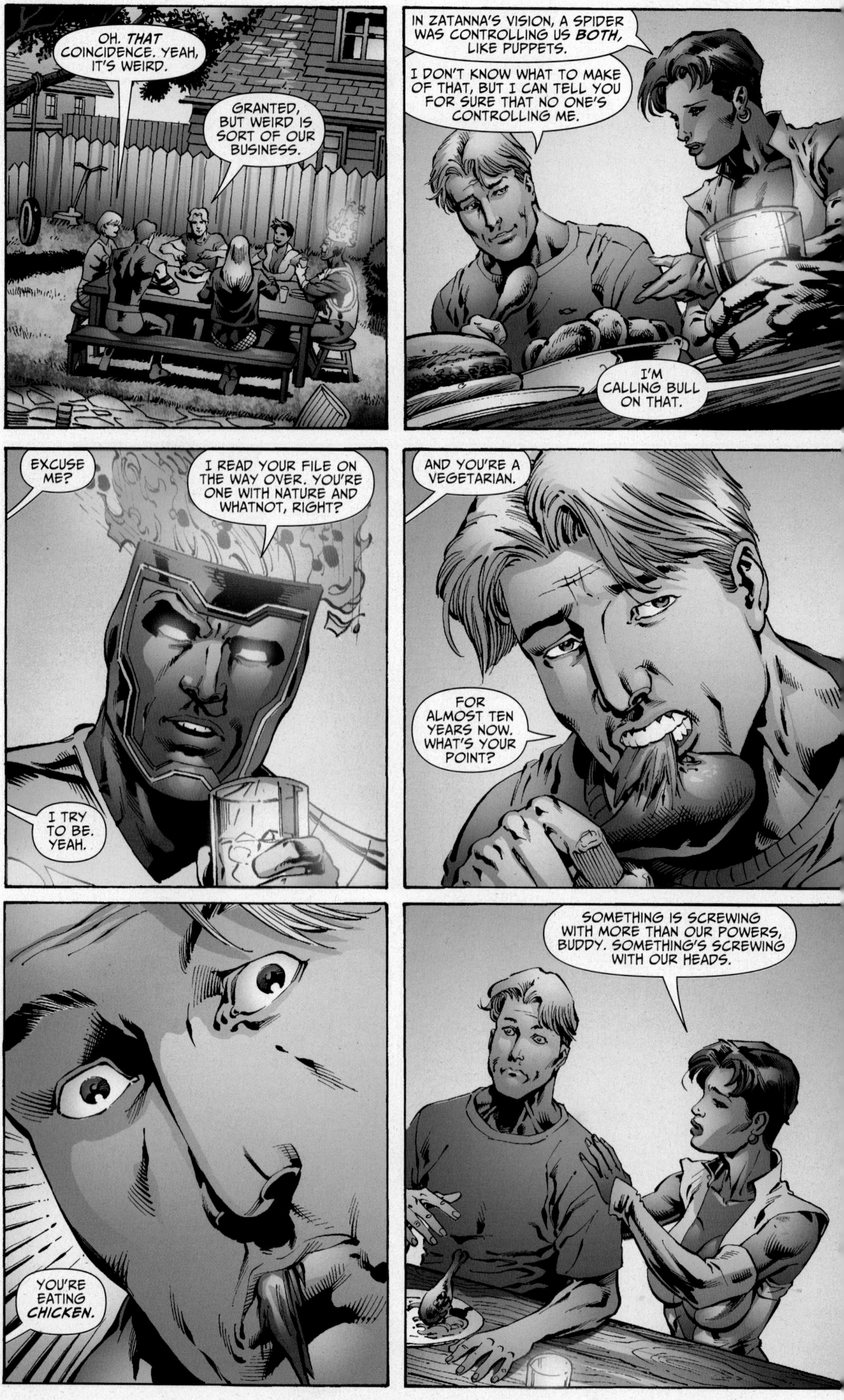
OH. *THAT* COINCIDENCE. YEAH, IT'S WEIRD.
GRANTED, BUT WEIRD IS SORT OF OUR BUSINESS.
IN ZATANNA'S VISION, A SPIDER WAS CONTROLLING US *BOTH,* LIKE PUPPETS.
I DON'T KNOW WHAT TO MAKE OF THAT, BUT I CAN TELL YOU FOR SURE THAT NO ONE'S CONTROLLING ME.
I'M CALLING BULL ON THAT.
EXCUSE ME?
I READ YOUR FILE ON THE WAY OVER. YOU'RE ONE WITH NATURE AND WHATNOT, RIGHT?
I TRY TO BE. YEAH.
AND YOU'RE A VEGETARIAN.
FOR ALMOST TEN YEARS NOW. WHAT'S YOUR POINT?
YOU'RE EATING *CHICKEN.*
SOMETHING IS SCREWING WITH MORE THAN OUR POWERS, BUDDY. SOMETHING'S SCREWING WITH OUR HEADS.

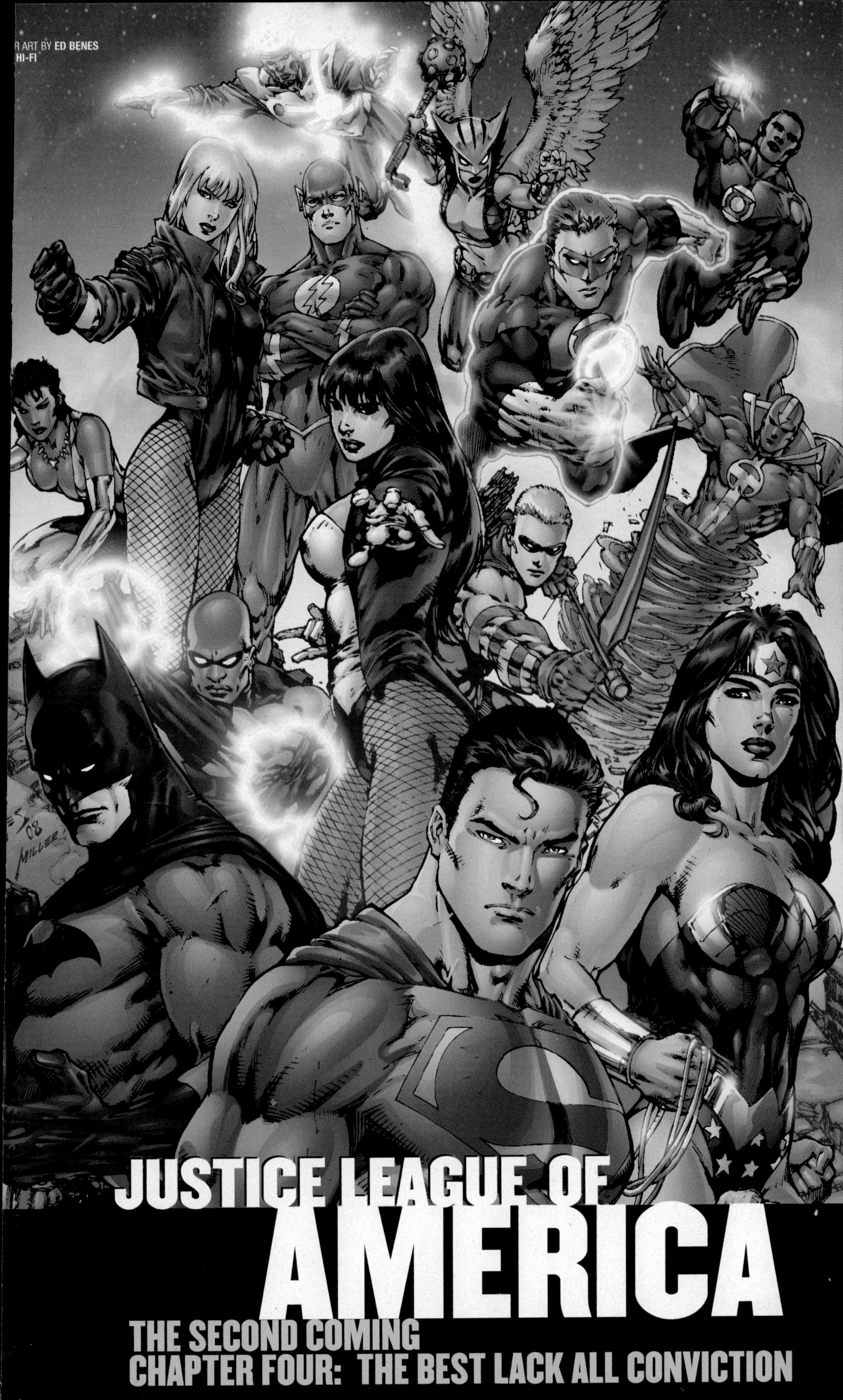
R ART BY ED BENES
HI-FI
JUSTICE LEAGUE OF
AMERICA
THE SECOND COMING
CHAPTER FOUR: THE BEST LACK ALL CONVICTION

Ed Benes
Doug Mahnke
Darick Robertson
Shane Davis
Ian Churchill
Ivan Reis
Pencillers

Ed Benes
Christian Alamy
Darick Robertson
Rob Stull
Ian Churchill
Joe Prado
Inkers

Rob Leigh
Letterer

Pete Pantazis
Colorist

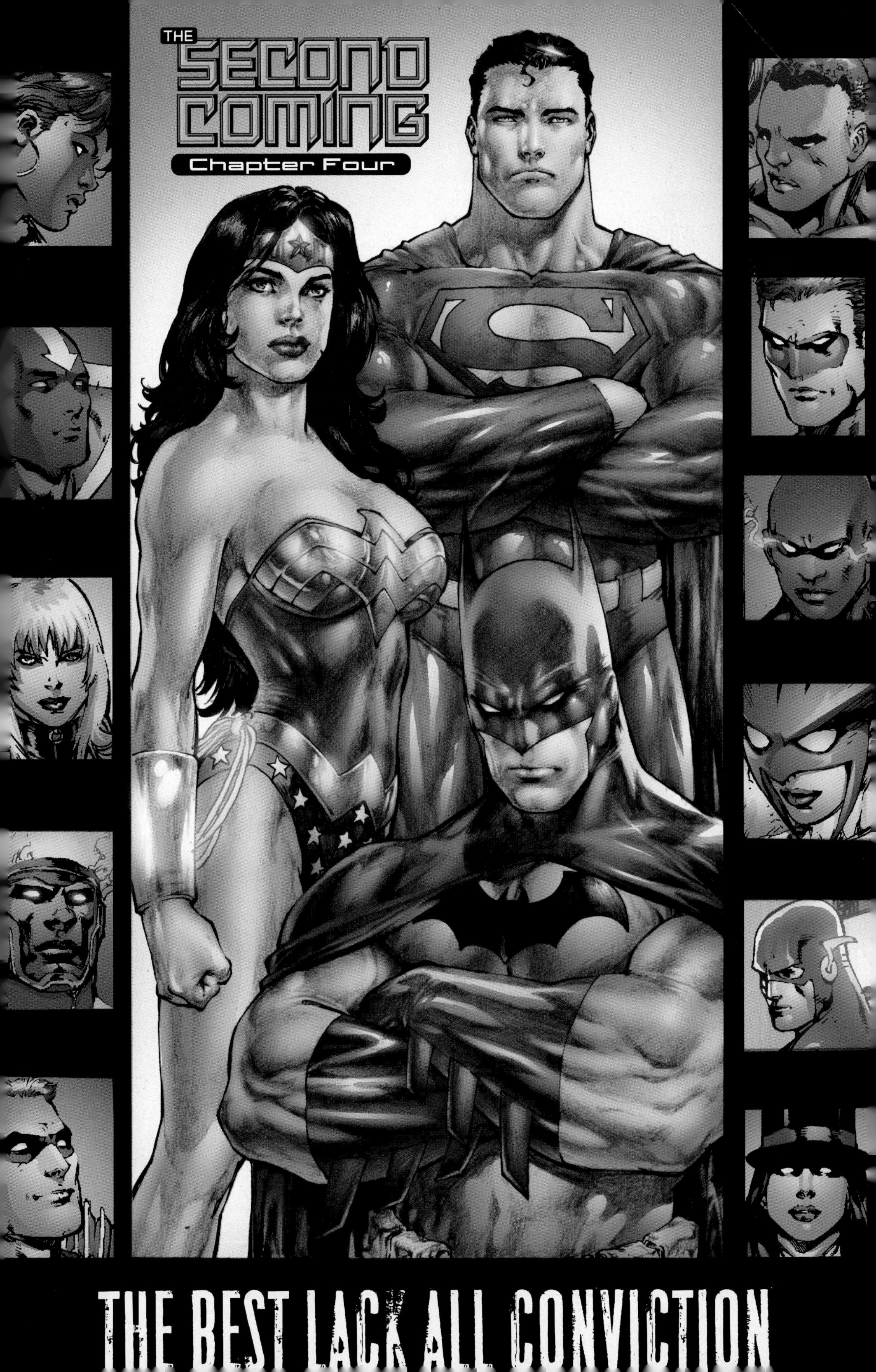
THE
SECOND
COMING
Chapter Four
THE BEST LACK ALL CONVICTION

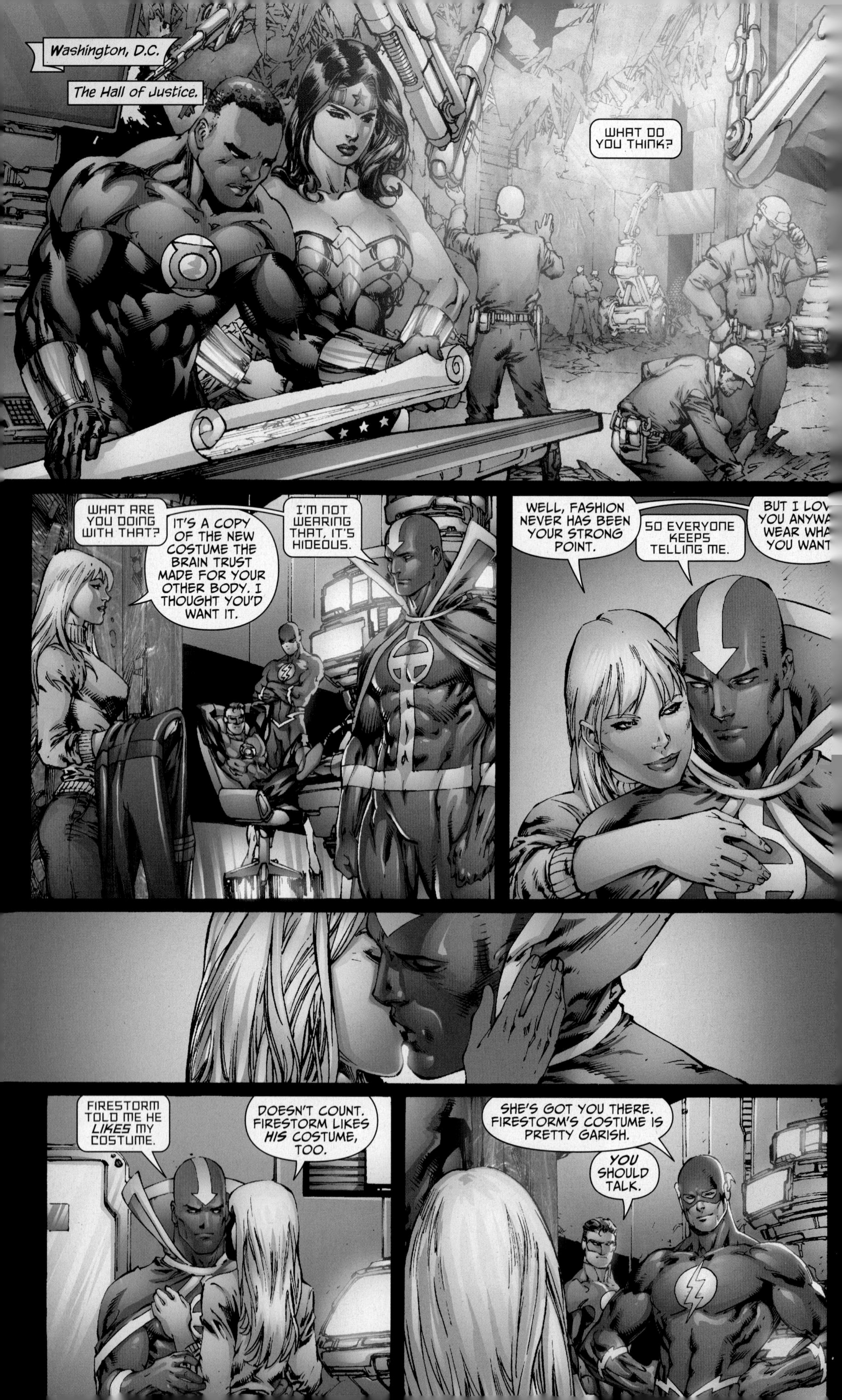
Washington, D.C.
The Hall of Justice.
WHAT DO YOU THINK?
WHAT ARE YOU DOING WITH THAT?
IT'S A COPY OF THE NEW COSTUME THE BRAIN TRUST MADE FOR YOUR OTHER BODY. I THOUGHT YOU'D WANT IT.
I'M NOT WEARING THAT, IT'S HIDEOUS.
WELL, FASHION NEVER HAS BEEN YOUR STRONG POINT.
SO EVERYONE KEEPS TELLING ME.
BUT I LOV YOU ANYWA WEAR WHA YOU WANT
FIRESTORM TOLD ME HE LIKES MY COSTUME.
DOESN'T COUNT. FIRESTORM LIKES HIS COSTUME, TOO.
SHE'S GOT YOU THERE. FIRESTORM'S COSTUME IS PRETTY GARISH.
YOU SHOULD TALK.

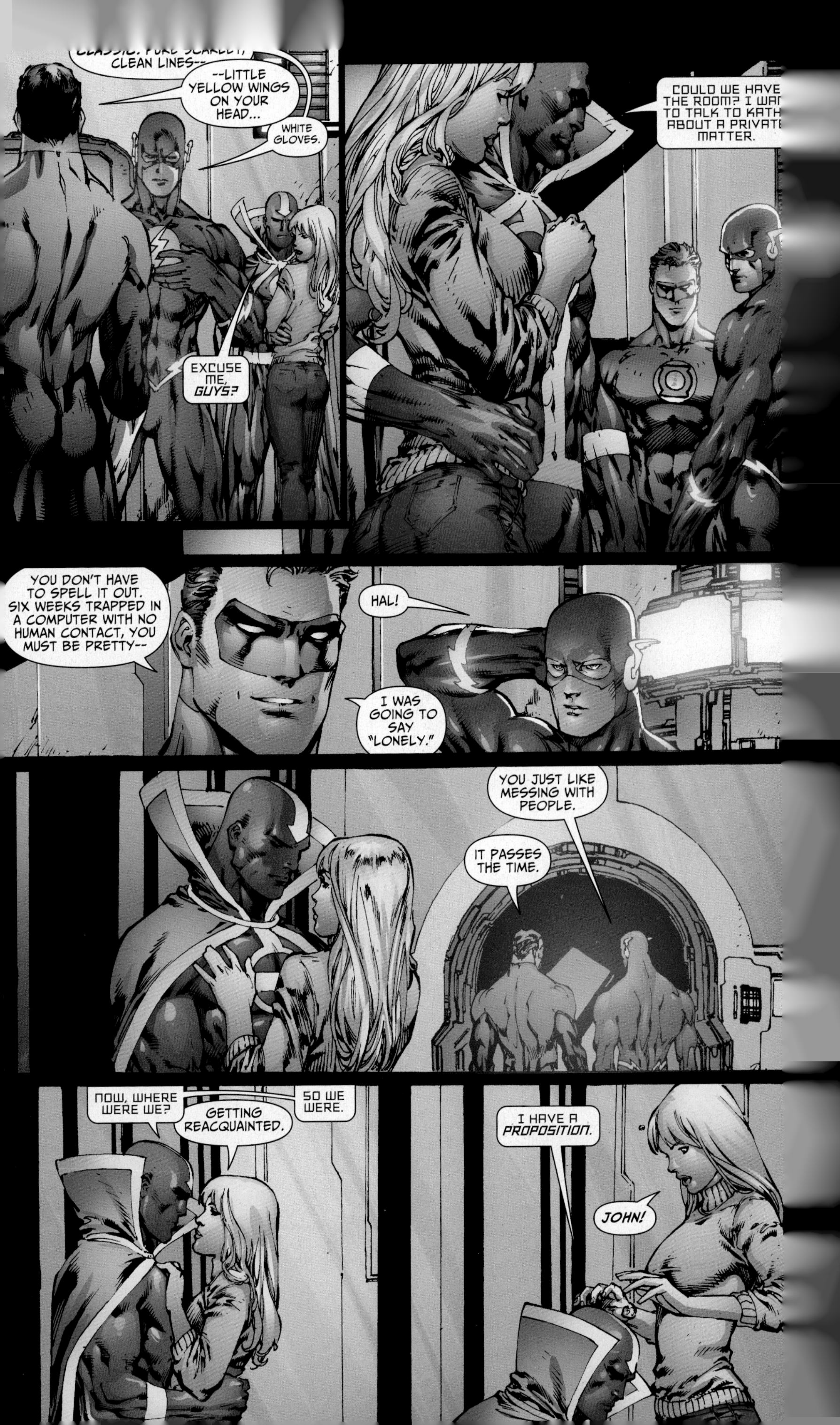

CLEAN LINES--
--LITTLE YELLOW WINGS ON YOUR HEAD...
WHITE GLOVES.
EXCUSE ME, *GUYS?*
COULD WE HAVE THE ROOM? I WAN TO TALK TO KATH ABOUT A PRIVATE MATTER.
YOU DON'T HAVE TO SPELL IT OUT. SIX WEEKS TRAPPED IN A COMPUTER WITH NO HUMAN CONTACT, YOU MUST BE PRETTY--
HAL!
I WAS GOING TO SAY "LONELY."
YOU JUST LIKE MESSING WITH PEOPLE.
IT PASSES THE TIME.
NOW, WHERE WERE WE?
SO WE WERE.
GETTING REACQUAINTED.
I HAVE A *PROPOSITION*.
JOHN!

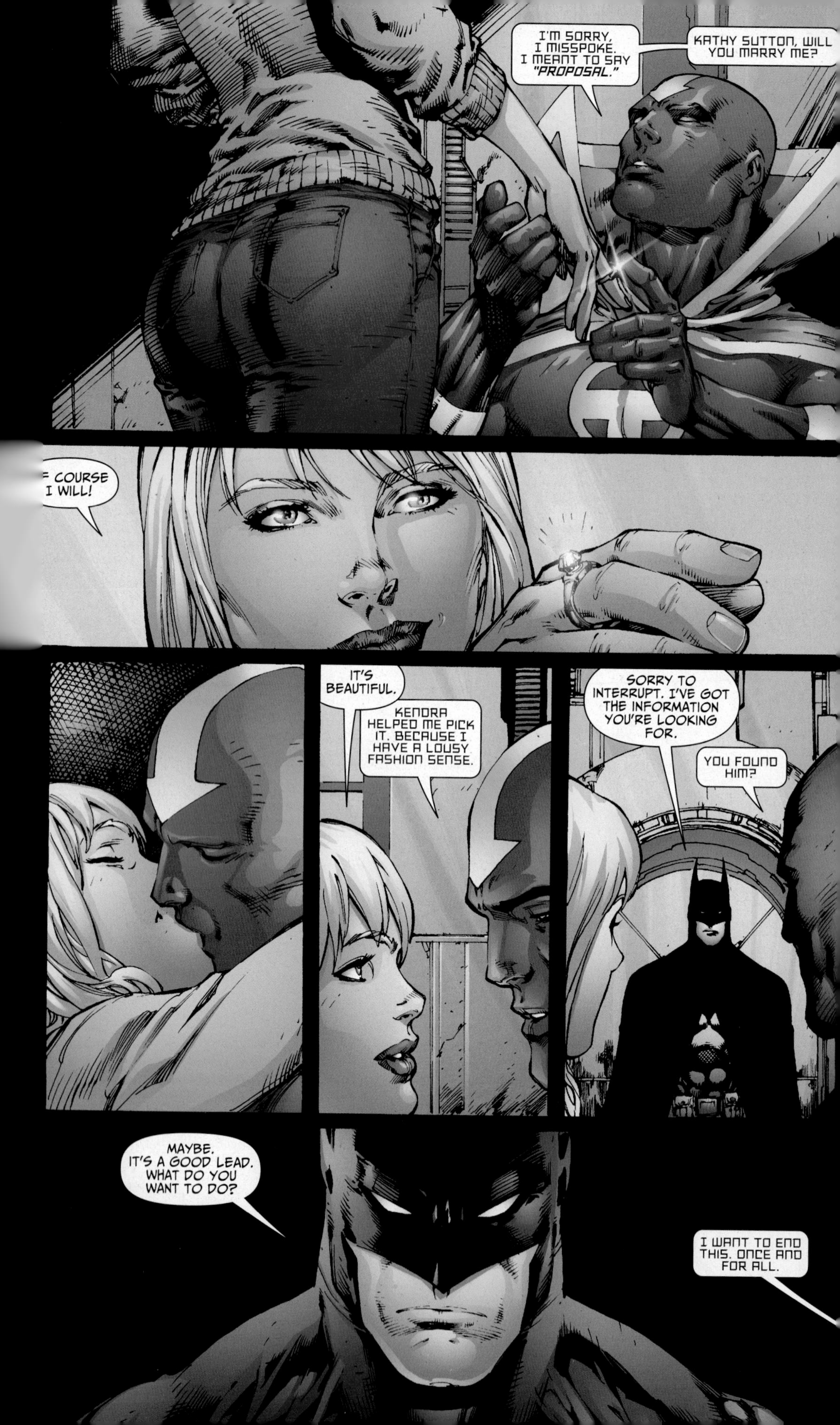
I'M SORRY, I MISSPOKE. I MEANT TO SAY "PROPOSAL."
KATHY SUTTON, WILL YOU MARRY ME?
F COURSE I WILL!
IT'S BEAUTIFUL.
KENDRA HELPED ME PICK IT. BECAUSE I HAVE A LOUSY FASHION SENSE.
SORRY TO INTERRUPT. I'VE GOT THE INFORMATION YOU'RE LOOKING FOR.
YOU FOUND HIM?
MAYBE. IT'S A GOOD LEAD. WHAT DO YOU WANT TO DO?
I WANT TO END THIS. ONCE AND FOR ALL.

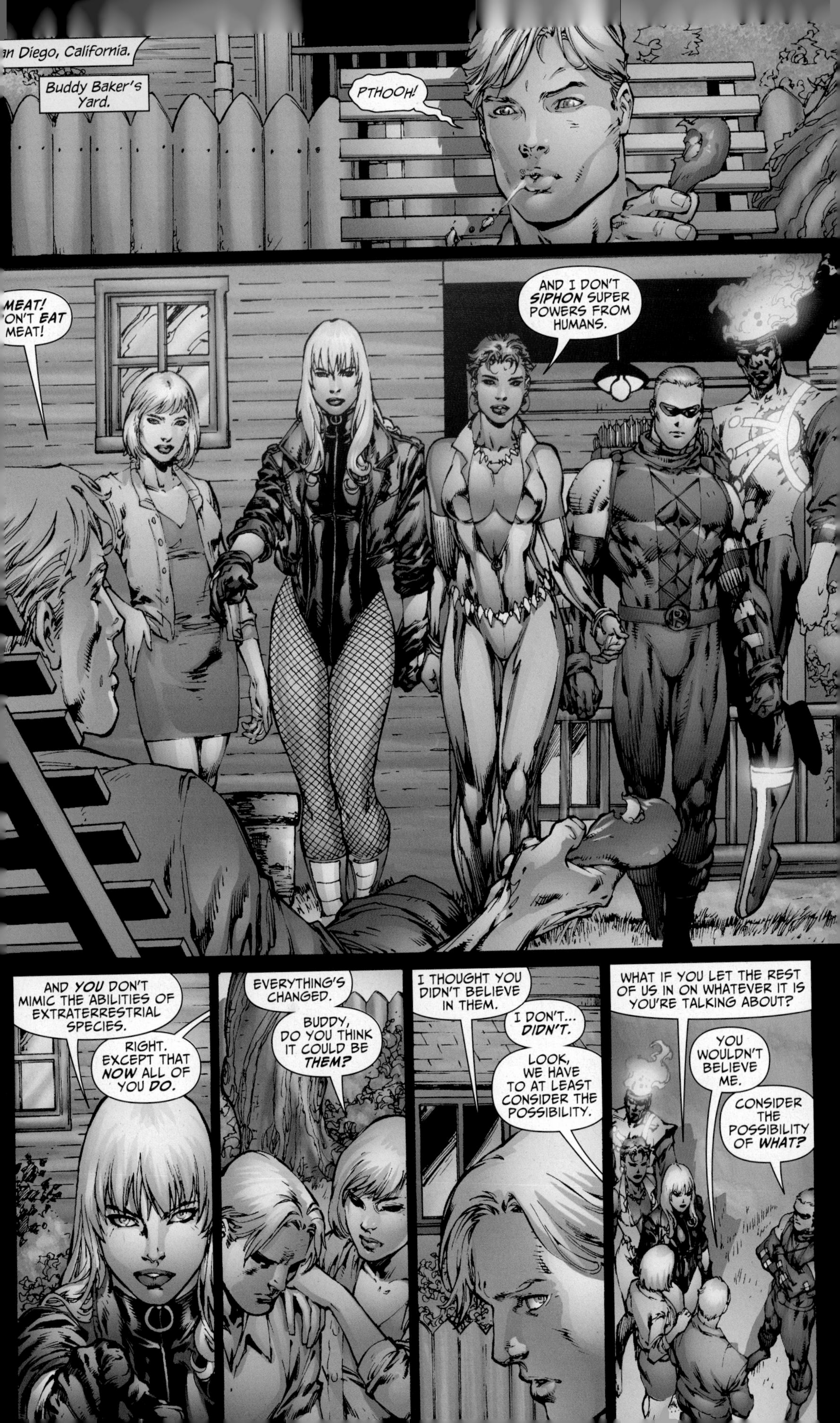

an Diego, California.
Buddy Baker's Yard.
PTHOOH!
MEAT! ON'T EAT MEAT!
AND I DON'T SIPHON SUPER POWERS FROM HUMANS.
AND YOU DON'T MIMIC THE ABILITIES OF EXTRATERRESTRIAL SPECIES.
RIGHT. EXCEPT THAT NOW ALL OF YOU DO.
EVERYTHING'S CHANGED.
BUDDY, DO YOU THINK IT COULD BE THEM?
I THOUGHT YOU DIDN'T BELIEVE IN THEM.
I DON'T... DIDN'T.
LOOK, WE HAVE TO AT LEAST CONSIDER THE POSSIBILITY.
WHAT IF YOU LET THE REST OF US IN ON WHATEVER IT IS YOU'RE TALKING ABOUT?
YOU WOULDN'T BELIEVE ME.
CONSIDER THE POSSIBILITY OF WHAT?

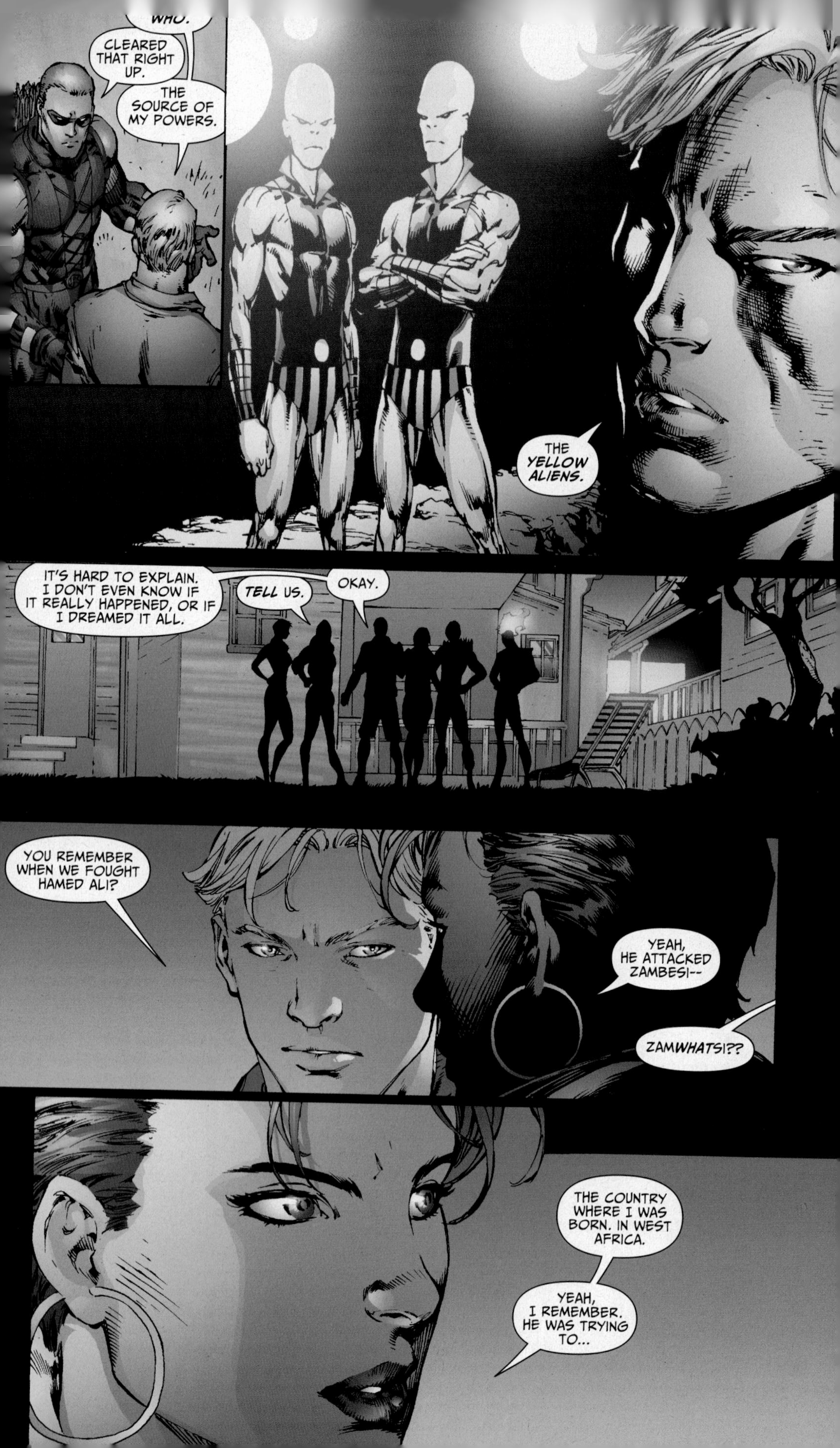
WHO.
CLEARED THAT RIGHT UP.
THE SOURCE OF MY POWERS.
THE YELLOW ALIENS.
IT'S HARD TO EXPLAIN. I DON'T EVEN KNOW IF IT REALLY HAPPENED, OR IF I DREAMED IT ALL.
TELL US.
OKAY.
YOU REMEMBER WHEN WE FOUGHT HAMED ALI?
YEAH, HE ATTACKED ZAMBESI--
ZAMWHATSI??
THE COUNTRY WHERE I WAS BORN. IN WEST AFRICA.
YEAH, I REMEMBER. HE WAS TRYING TO...

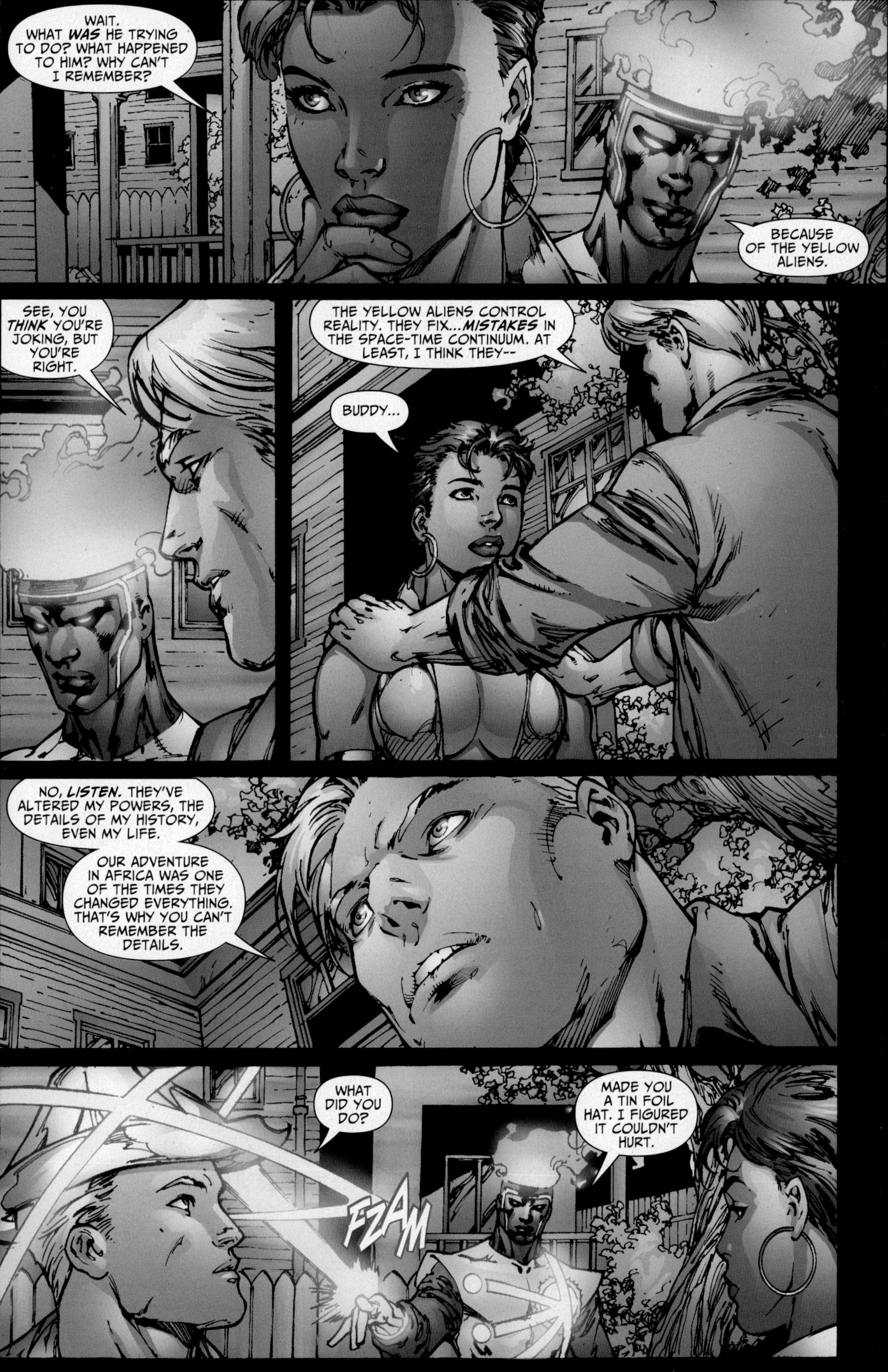
WAIT. WHAT WAS HE TRYING TO DO? WHAT HAPPENED TO HIM? WHY CAN'T I REMEMBER?
BECAUSE OF THE YELLOW ALIENS.
SEE, YOU THINK YOU'RE JOKING, BUT YOU'RE RIGHT.
THE YELLOW ALIENS CONTROL REALITY. THEY FIX...MISTAKES IN THE SPACE-TIME CONTINUUM. AT LEAST, I THINK THEY--
BUDDY...
NO, LISTEN. THEY'VE ALTERED MY POWERS, THE DETAILS OF MY HISTORY, EVEN MY LIFE.
OUR ADVENTURE IN AFRICA WAS ONE OF THE TIMES THEY CHANGED EVERYTHING. THAT'S WHY YOU CAN'T REMEMBER THE DETAILS.
WHAT DID YOU DO?
FZAM
MADE YOU A TIN FOIL HAT. I FIGURED IT COULDN'T HURT.

JUSTICE LEAGUE of AMERICA

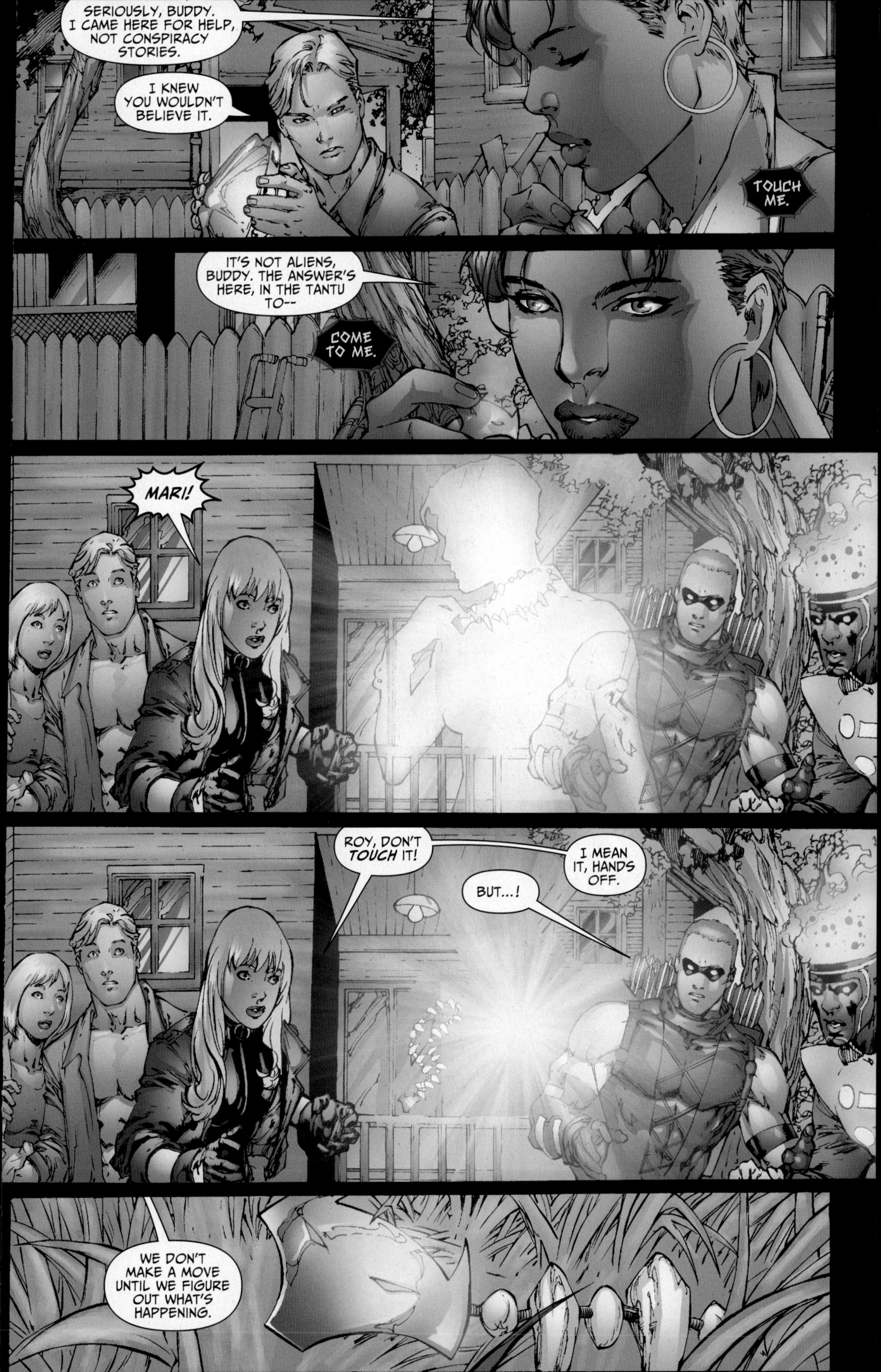

SERIOUSLY, BUDDY. I CAME HERE FOR HELP, NOT CONSPIRACY STORIES.
I KNEW YOU WOULDN'T BELIEVE IT.
TOUCH ME.
IT'S NOT ALIENS, BUDDY. THE ANSWER'S HERE, IN THE TANTU TO--
COME TO ME.
MARI!
ROY, DON'T TOUCH IT!
I MEAN IT, HANDS OFF.
BUT...!
WE DON'T MAKE A MOVE UNTIL WE FIGURE OUT WHAT'S HAPPENING.

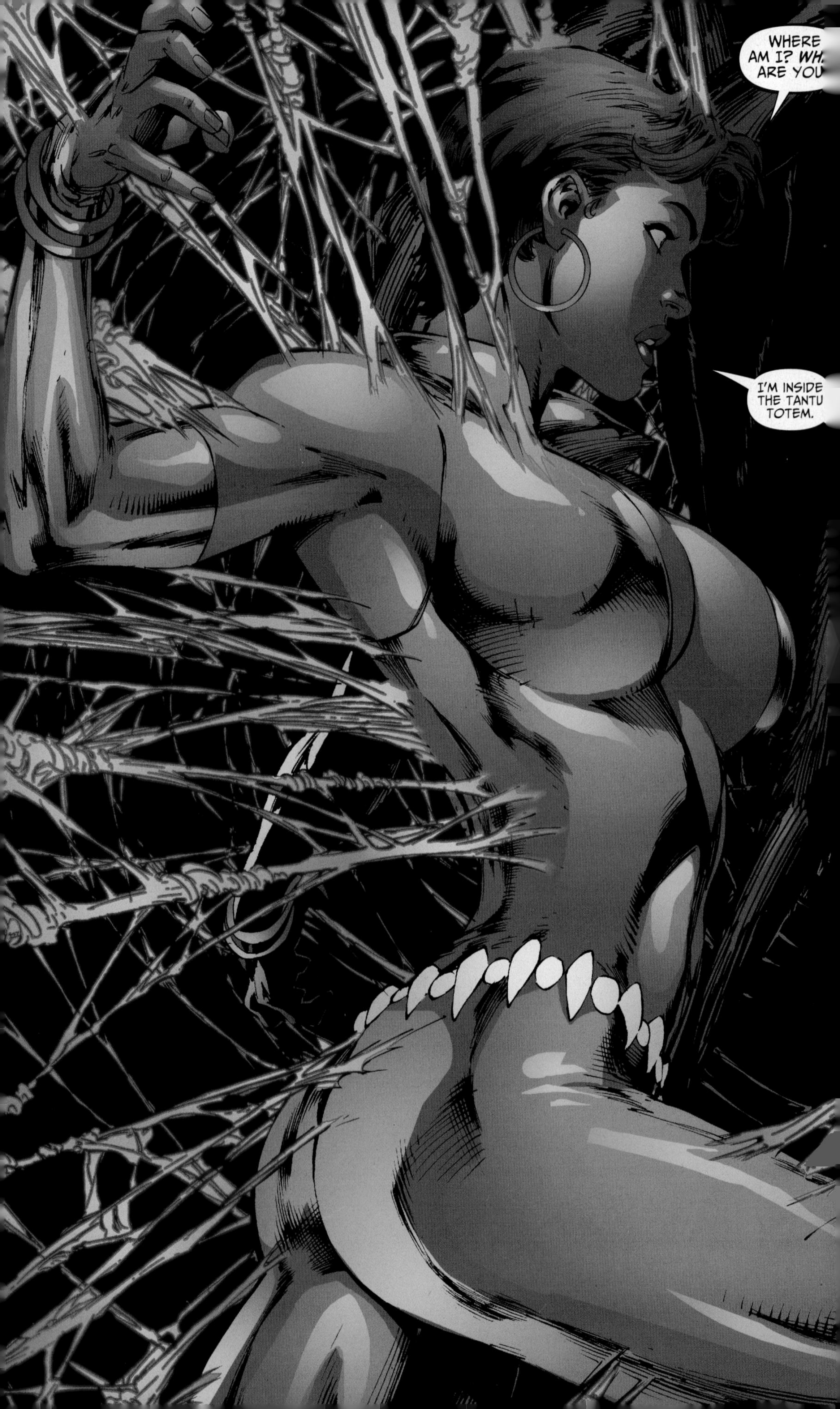
WHERE AM I? WH ARE YOU
I'M INSIDE THE TANTU TOTEM.

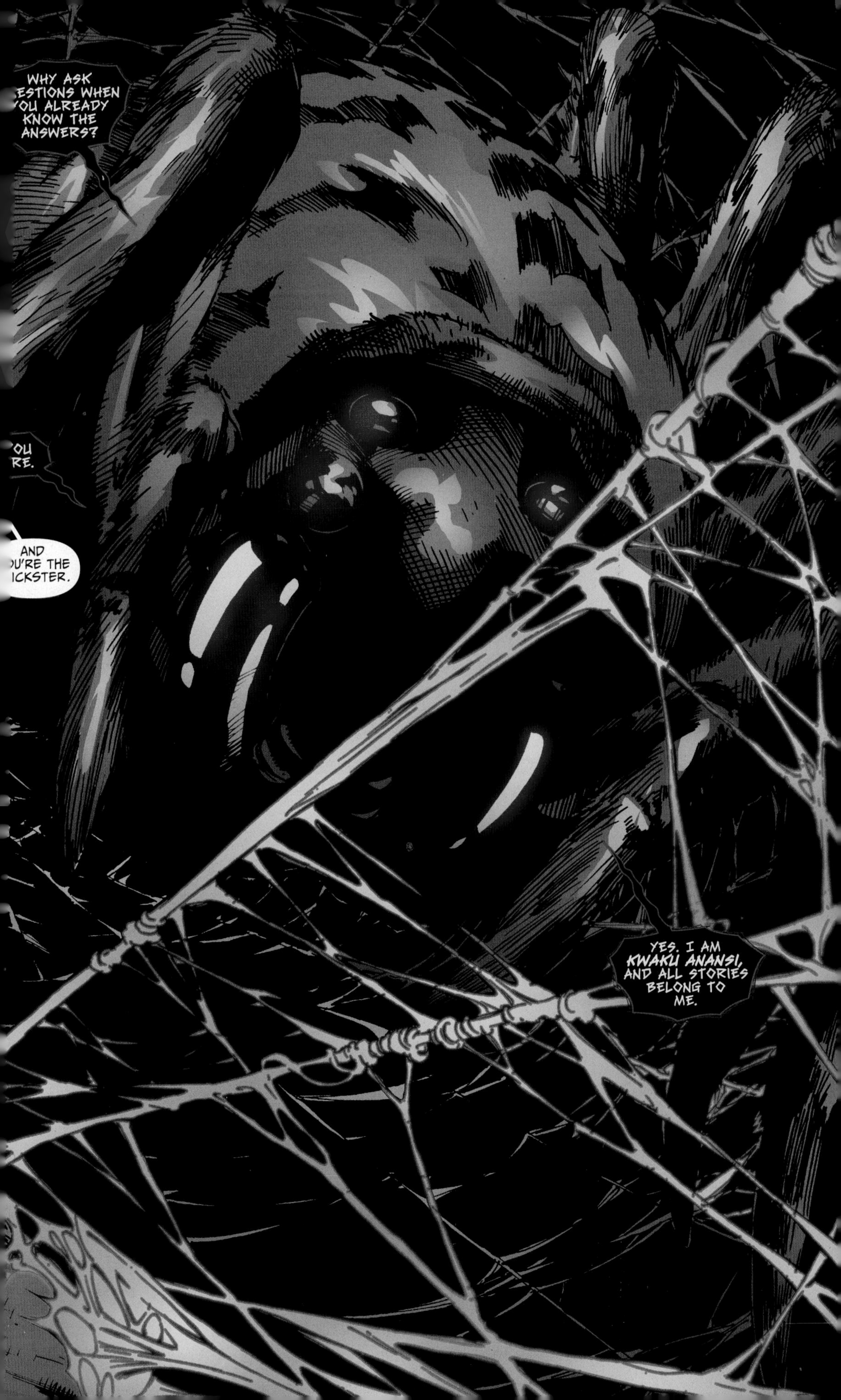
WHY ASK
ESTIONS WHEN
OU ALREADY
KNOW THE
ANSWERS?
OU
RE.
AND
U'RE THE
ICKSTER.
YES. I AM
KWAKU ANANSI,
AND ALL STORIES
BELONG TO
ME.

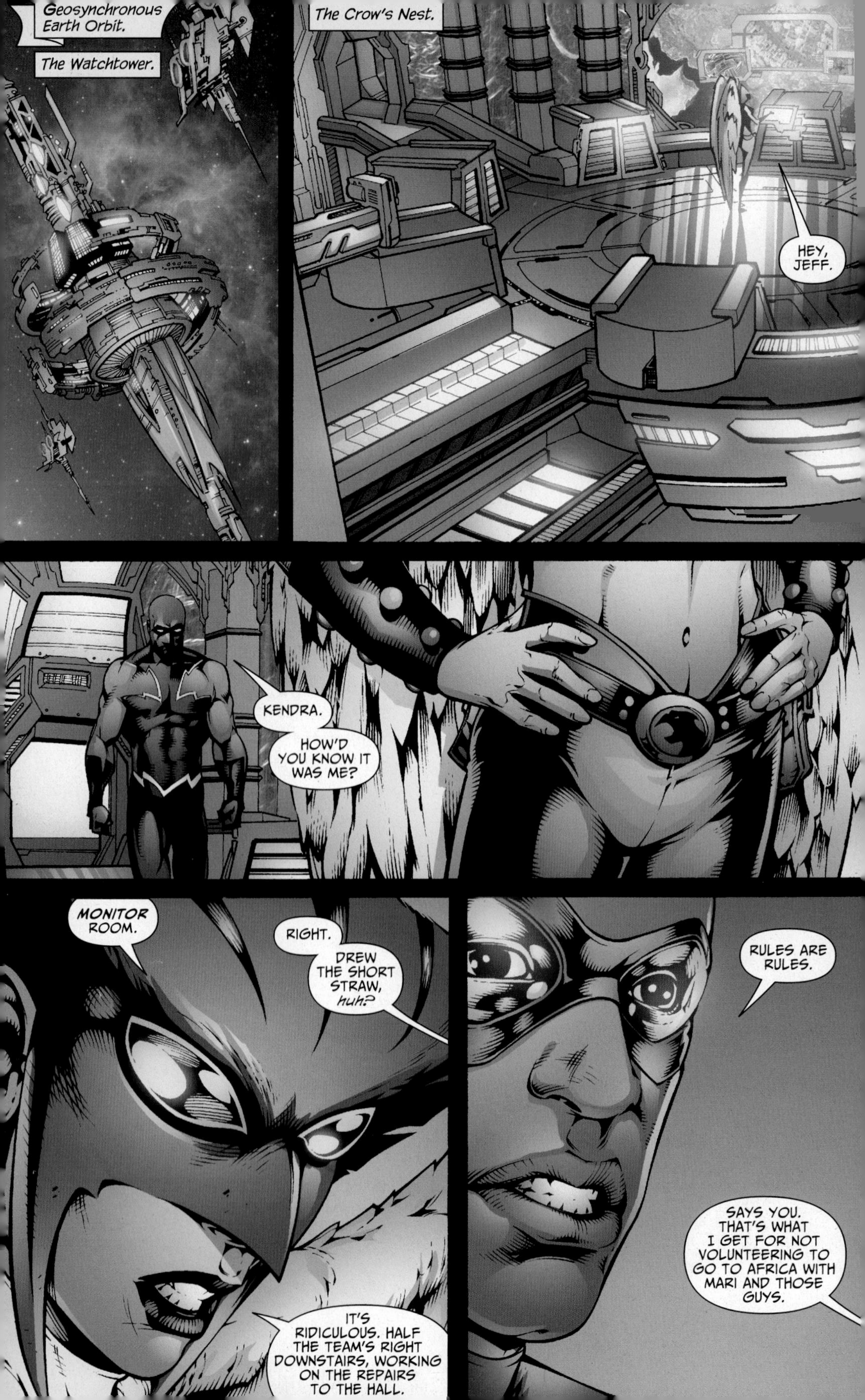
Geosynchronous Earth Orbit.
The Watchtower.
The Crow's Nest.
HEY, JEFF.
KENDRA.
HOW'D YOU KNOW IT WAS ME?
MONITOR ROOM.
RIGHT.
DREW THE SHORT STRAW, huh?
IT'S RIDICULOUS. HALF THE TEAM'S RIGHT DOWNSTAIRS, WORKING ON THE REPAIRS TO THE HALL.
RULES ARE RULES.
SAYS YOU. THAT'S WHAT I GET FOR NOT VOLUNTEERING TO GO TO AFRICA WITH MARI AND THOSE GUYS.

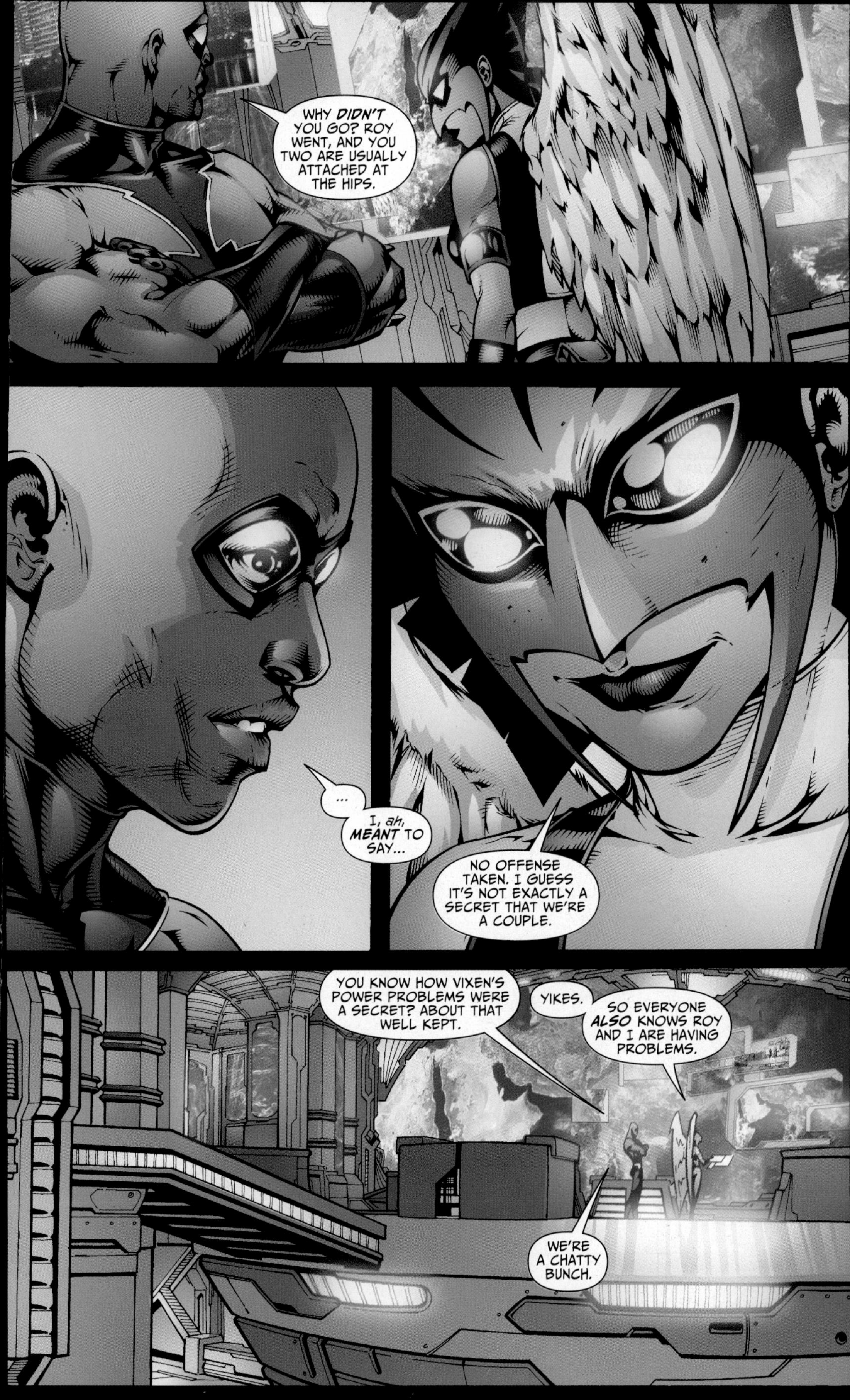

WHY *DIDN'T* YOU GO? ROY WENT, AND YOU TWO ARE USUALLY ATTACHED AT THE HIPS.
... I, *ah,* **MEANT** TO SAY...
NO OFFENSE TAKEN. I GUESS IT'S NOT EXACTLY A SECRET THAT WE'RE A COUPLE.
YOU KNOW HOW VIXEN'S POWER PROBLEMS WERE A SECRET? ABOUT THAT WELL KEPT.
YIKES.
SO EVERYONE **ALSO** KNOWS ROY AND I ARE HAVING PROBLEMS.
WE'RE A CHATTY BUNCH.

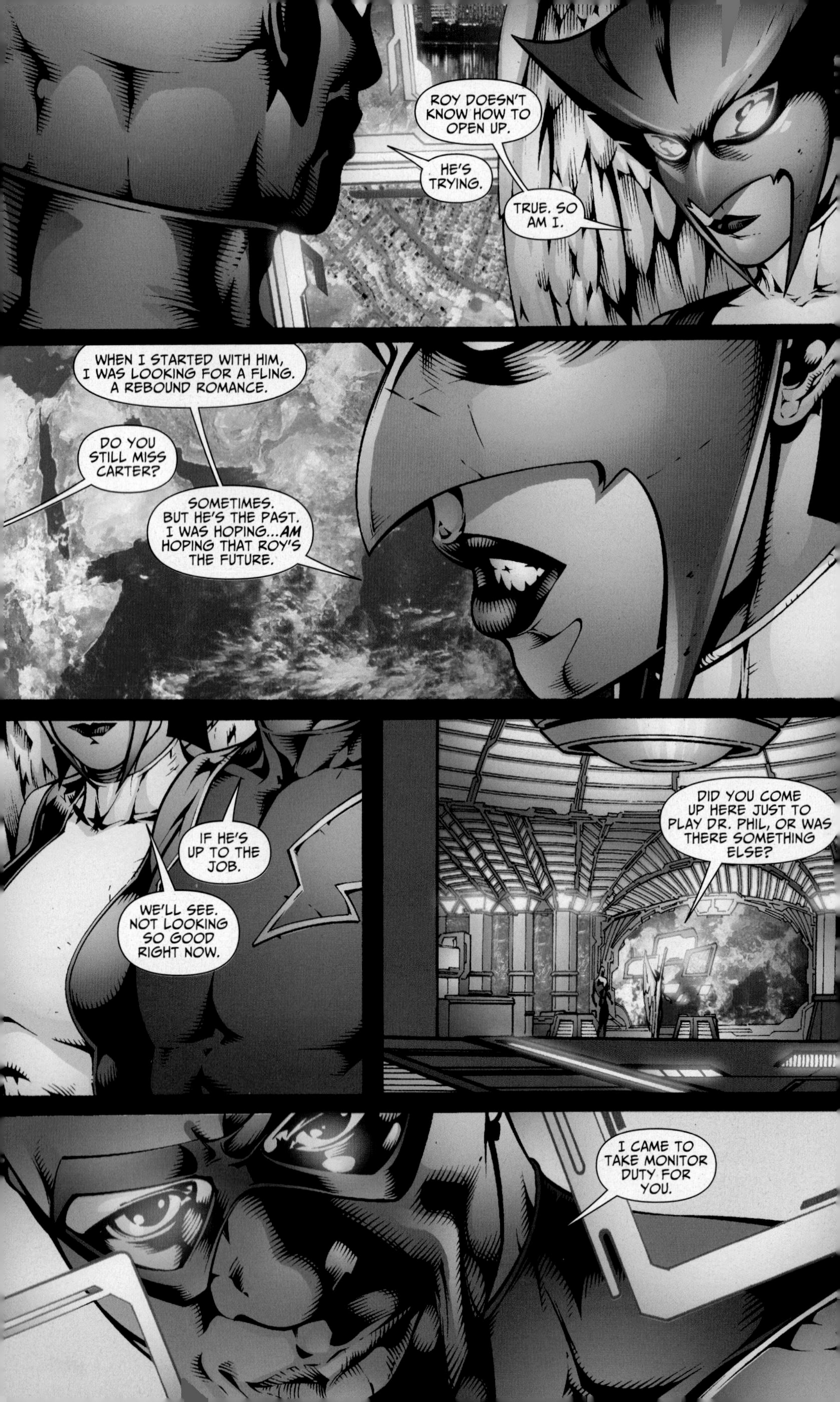
ROY DOESN'T KNOW HOW TO OPEN UP.
HE'S TRYING.
TRUE. SO AM I.
WHEN I STARTED WITH HIM, I WAS LOOKING FOR A FLING. A REBOUND ROMANCE.
DO YOU STILL MISS CARTER?
SOMETIMES. BUT HE'S THE PAST. I WAS HOPING...AM HOPING THAT ROY'S THE FUTURE.
IF HE'S UP TO THE JOB.
WE'LL SEE. NOT LOOKING SO GOOD RIGHT NOW.
DID YOU COME UP HERE JUST TO PLAY DR. PHIL, OR WAS THERE SOMETHING ELSE?
I CAME TO TAKE MONITOR DUTY FOR YOU.

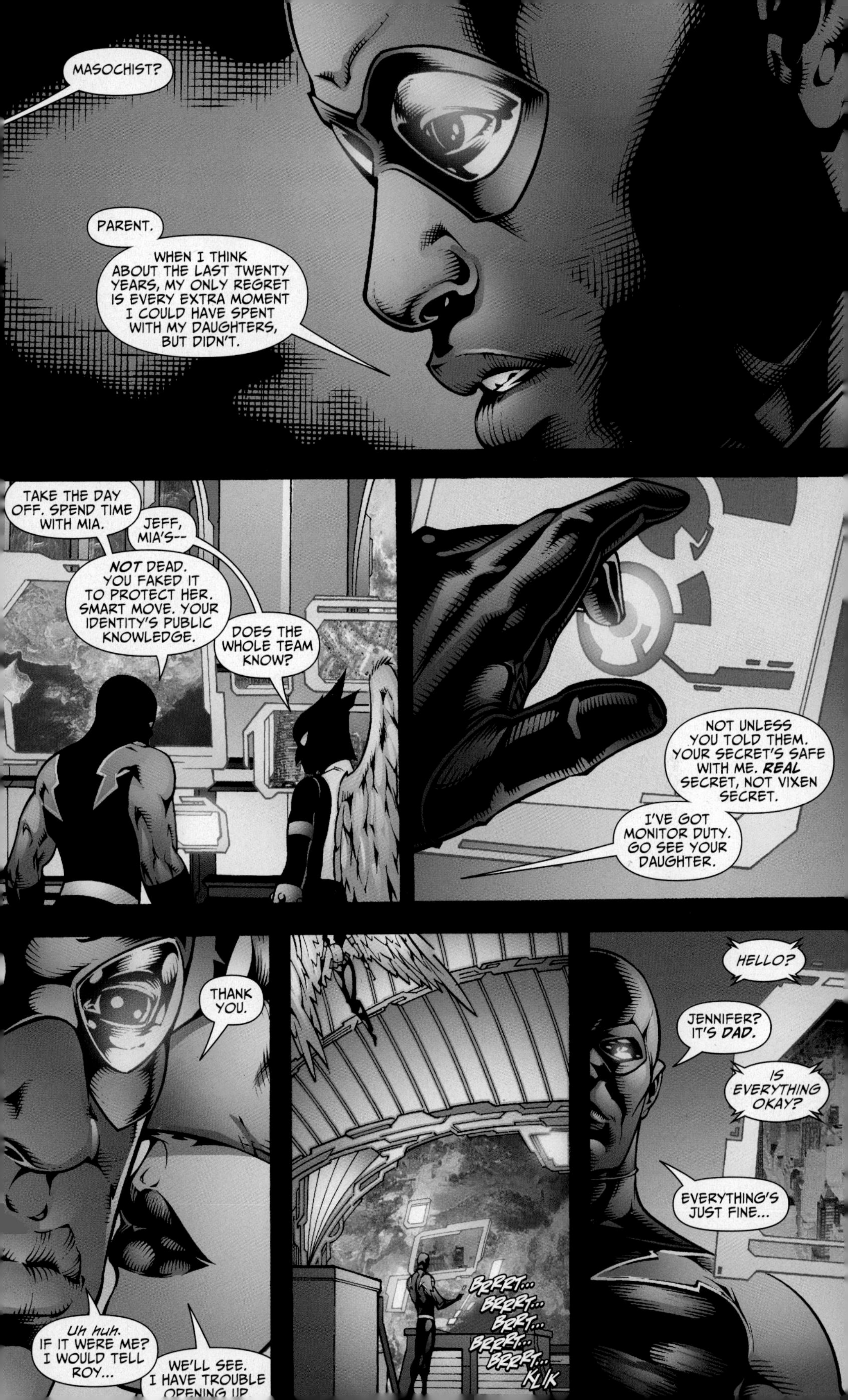
MASOCHIST?
PARENT.
WHEN I THINK ABOUT THE LAST TWENTY YEARS, MY ONLY REGRET IS EVERY EXTRA MOMENT I COULD HAVE SPENT WITH MY DAUGHTERS, BUT DIDN'T.
TAKE THE DAY OFF. SPEND TIME WITH MIA.
JEFF, MIA'S--
NOT DEAD. YOU FAKED IT TO PROTECT HER. SMART MOVE. YOUR IDENTITY'S PUBLIC KNOWLEDGE.
DOES THE WHOLE TEAM KNOW?
NOT UNLESS YOU TOLD THEM. YOUR SECRET'S SAFE WITH ME. *REAL* SECRET, NOT VIXEN SECRET.
I'VE GOT MONITOR DUTY. GO SEE YOUR DAUGHTER.
THANK YOU.
Uh huh. IF IT WERE ME? I WOULD TELL ROY...
WE'LL SEE. I HAVE TROUBLE OPENING UP
BRRRT... BRRRT... BRRT... BRRRT... BRRRT... KLIK
HELLO?
JENNIFER? IT'S *DAD*.
IS EVERYTHING OKAY?
EVERYTHING'S JUST FINE...

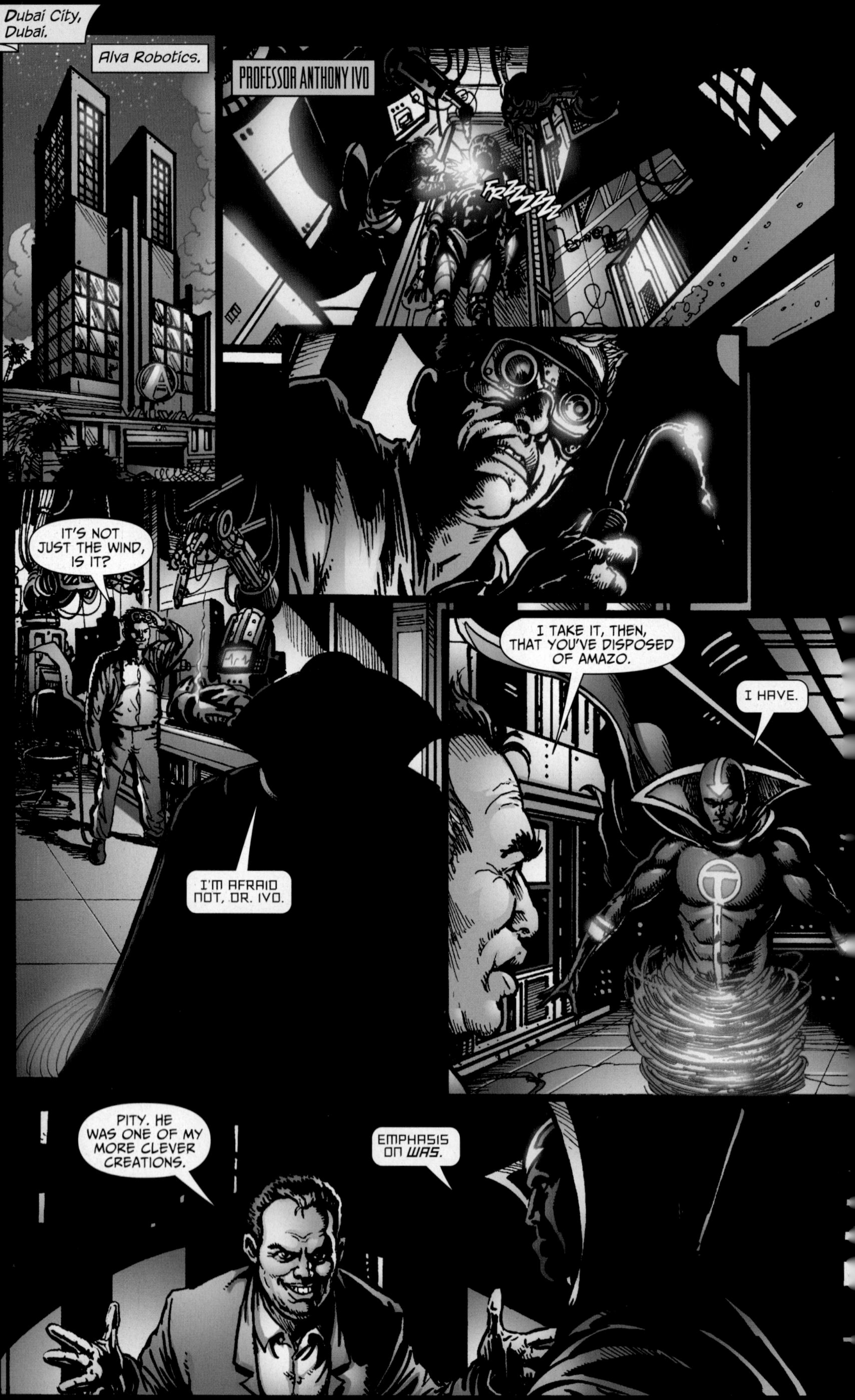
Dubai City, Dubai.
Alva Robotics.
PROFESSOR ANTHONY IVO
FRZZZZZ
IT'S NOT JUST THE WIND, IS IT?
I'M AFRAID NOT, DR. IVO.
I TAKE IT, THEN, THAT YOU'VE DISPOSED OF AMAZO.
I HAVE.
PITY. HE WAS ONE OF MY MORE CLEVER CREATIONS.
EMPHASIS ON WAS.

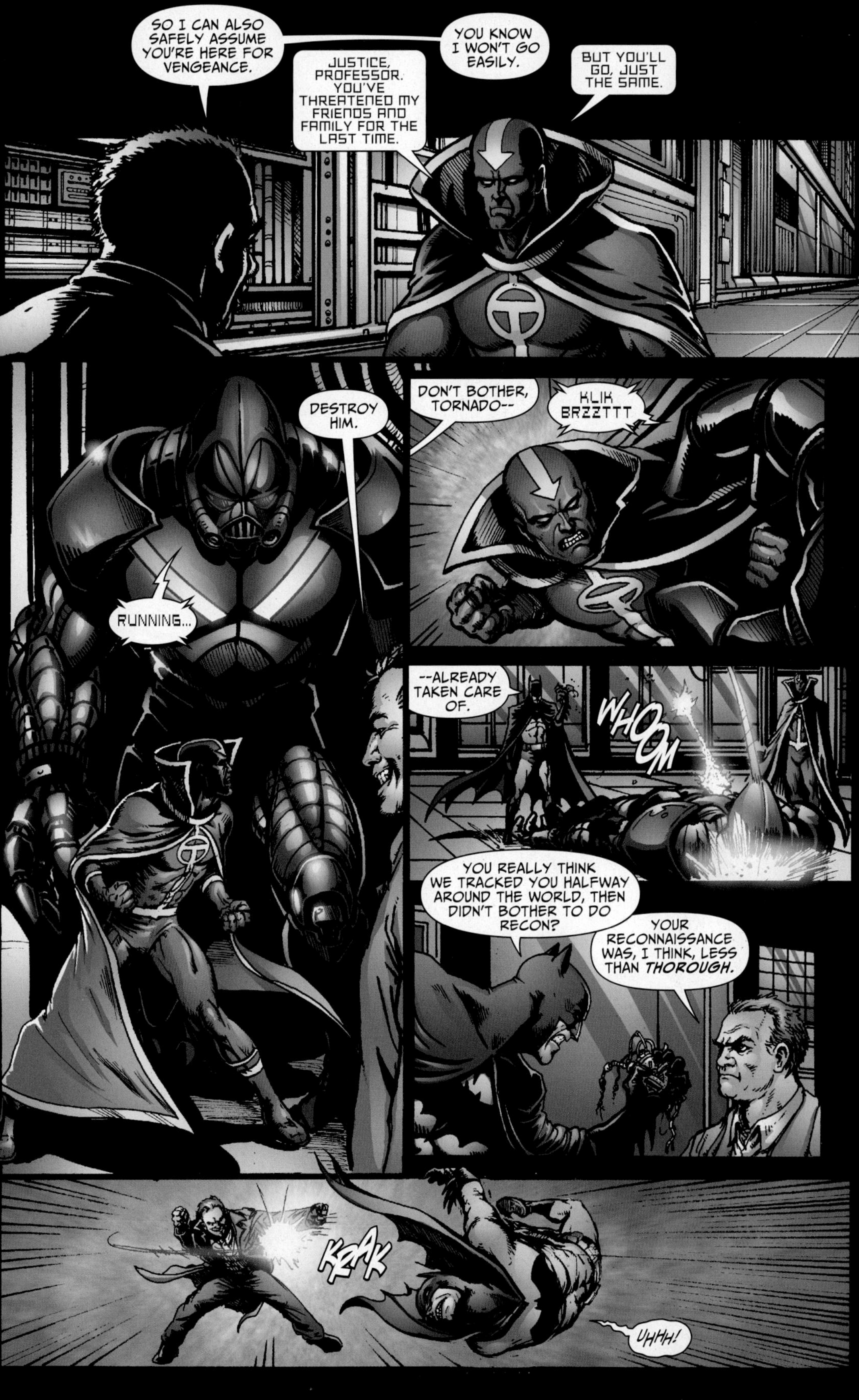

SO I CAN ALSO SAFELY ASSUME YOU'RE HERE FOR VENGEANCE.
JUSTICE, PROFESSOR. YOU'VE THREATENED MY FRIENDS AND FAMILY FOR THE LAST TIME.
YOU KNOW I WON'T GO EASILY.
BUT YOU'LL GO, JUST THE SAME.
DESTROY HIM.
RUNNING...
DON'T BOTHER, TORNADO--
KLIK BRZZTTT
--ALREADY TAKEN CARE OF.
WHOOM
YOU REALLY THINK WE TRACKED YOU HALFWAY AROUND THE WORLD, THEN DIDN'T BOTHER TO DO RECON?
YOUR RECONNAISSANCE WAS, I THINK, LESS THAN THOROUGH.
KRAK
UHHH!

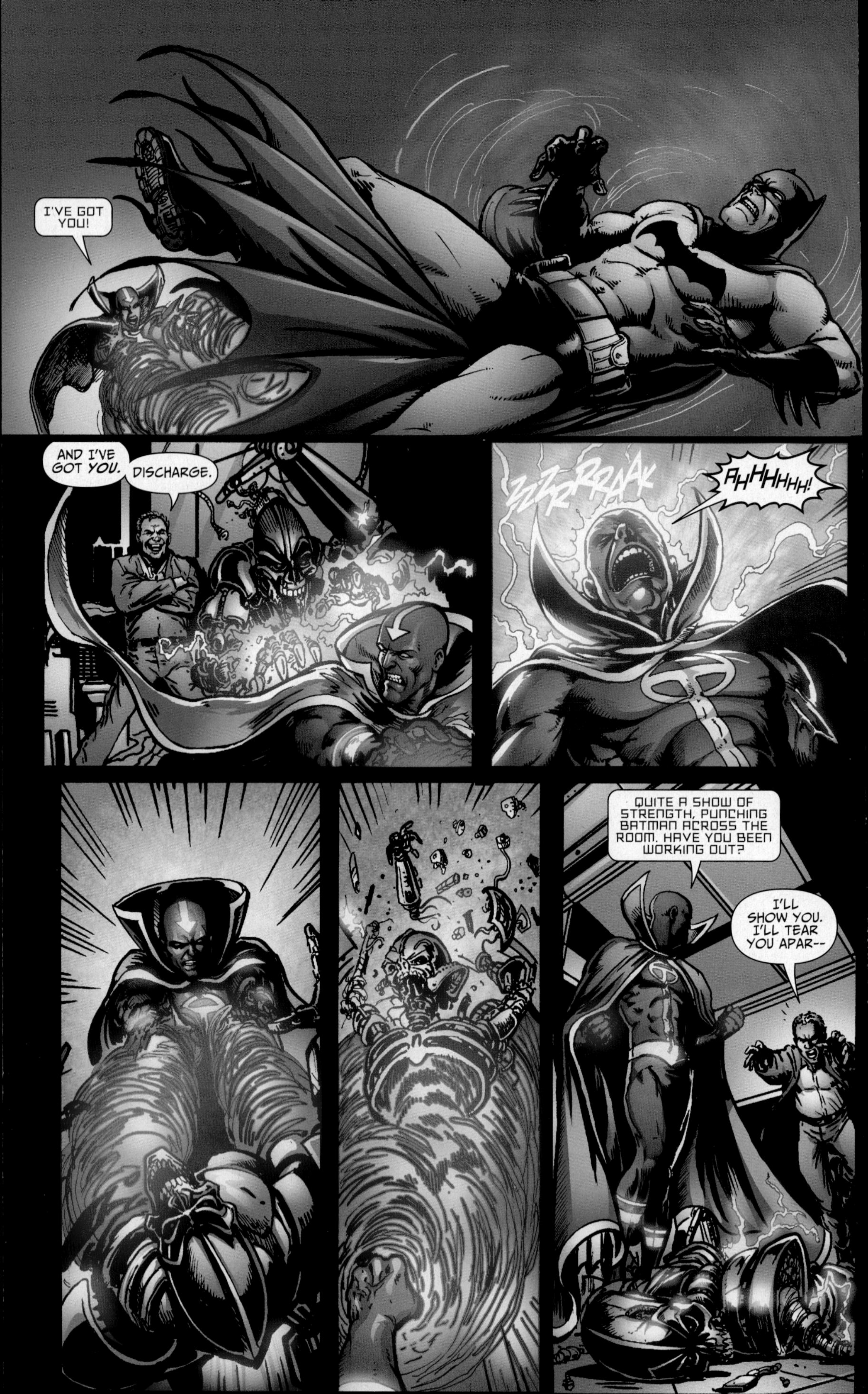
I'VE GOT YOU!
AND I'VE GOT *YOU*.
DISCHARGE.
ZZZRRRRAAK
AHHHHHH!
QUITE A SHOW OF STRENGTH, PUNCHING BATMAN ACROSS THE ROOM. HAVE YOU BEEN WORKING OUT?
I'LL SHOW YOU. I'LL TEAR YOU APAR--

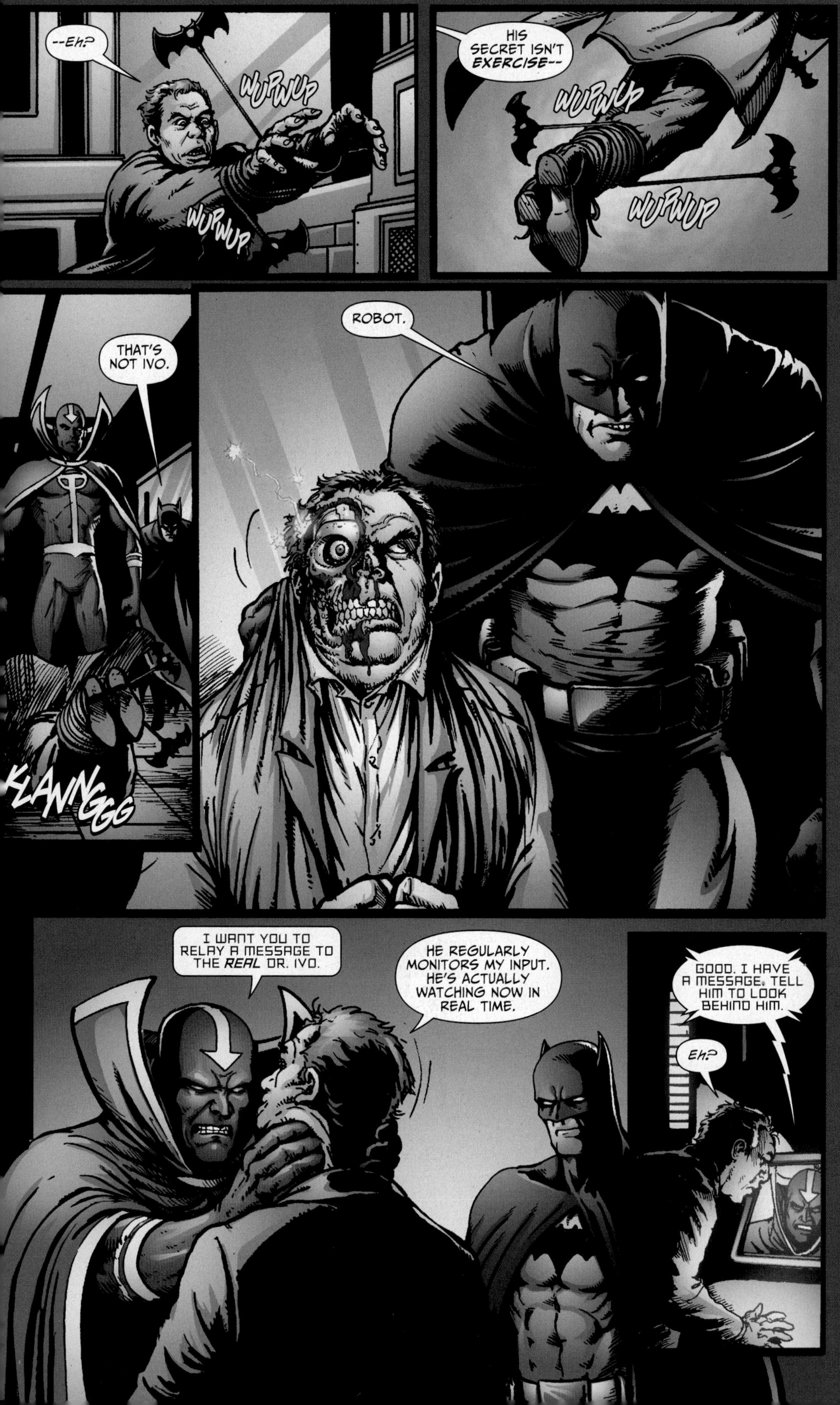
--Eh?
WUPWUP
WUPWUP
HIS SECRET ISN'T *EXERCISE*--
WUPWUP
WUPWUP
THAT'S NOT IVO.
KLANNGGG
ROBOT.
I WANT YOU TO RELAY A MESSAGE TO THE *REAL* DR. IVO.
HE REGULARLY MONITORS MY INPUT. HE'S ACTUALLY WATCHING NOW IN REAL TIME.
GOOD. I HAVE A MESSAGE. TELL HIM TO LOOK BEHIND HIM.
Eh?

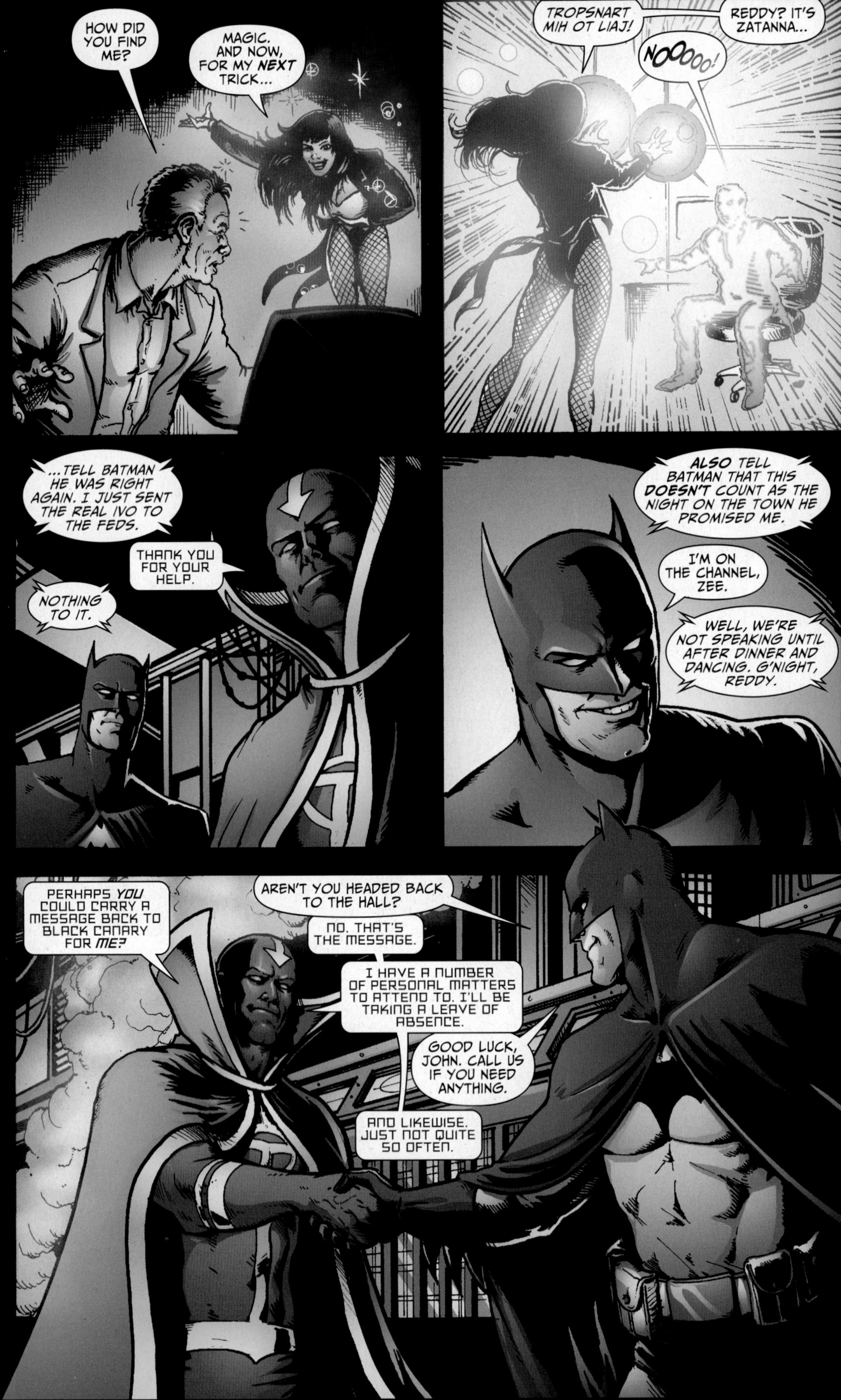
HOW DID YOU FIND ME?
MAGIC. AND NOW, FOR MY NEXT TRICK...
TROPSNART MIH OT LIAJ!
REDDY? IT'S ZATANNA...
NOOOOO!
...TELL BATMAN HE WAS RIGHT AGAIN. I JUST SENT THE REAL IVO TO THE FEDS.
THANK YOU FOR YOUR HELP.
NOTHING TO IT.
ALSO TELL BATMAN THAT THIS DOESN'T COUNT AS THE NIGHT ON THE TOWN HE PROMISED ME.
I'M ON THE CHANNEL, ZEE.
WELL, WE'RE NOT SPEAKING UNTIL AFTER DINNER AND DANCING. G'NIGHT, REDDY.
PERHAPS YOU COULD CARRY A MESSAGE BACK TO BLACK CANARY FOR ME?
AREN'T YOU HEADED BACK TO THE HALL?
NO. THAT'S THE MESSAGE.
I HAVE A NUMBER OF PERSONAL MATTERS TO ATTEND TO. I'LL BE TAKING A LEAVE OF ABSENCE.
GOOD LUCK, JOHN. CALL US IF YOU NEED ANYTHING.
AND LIKEWISE. JUST NOT QUITE SO OFTEN.

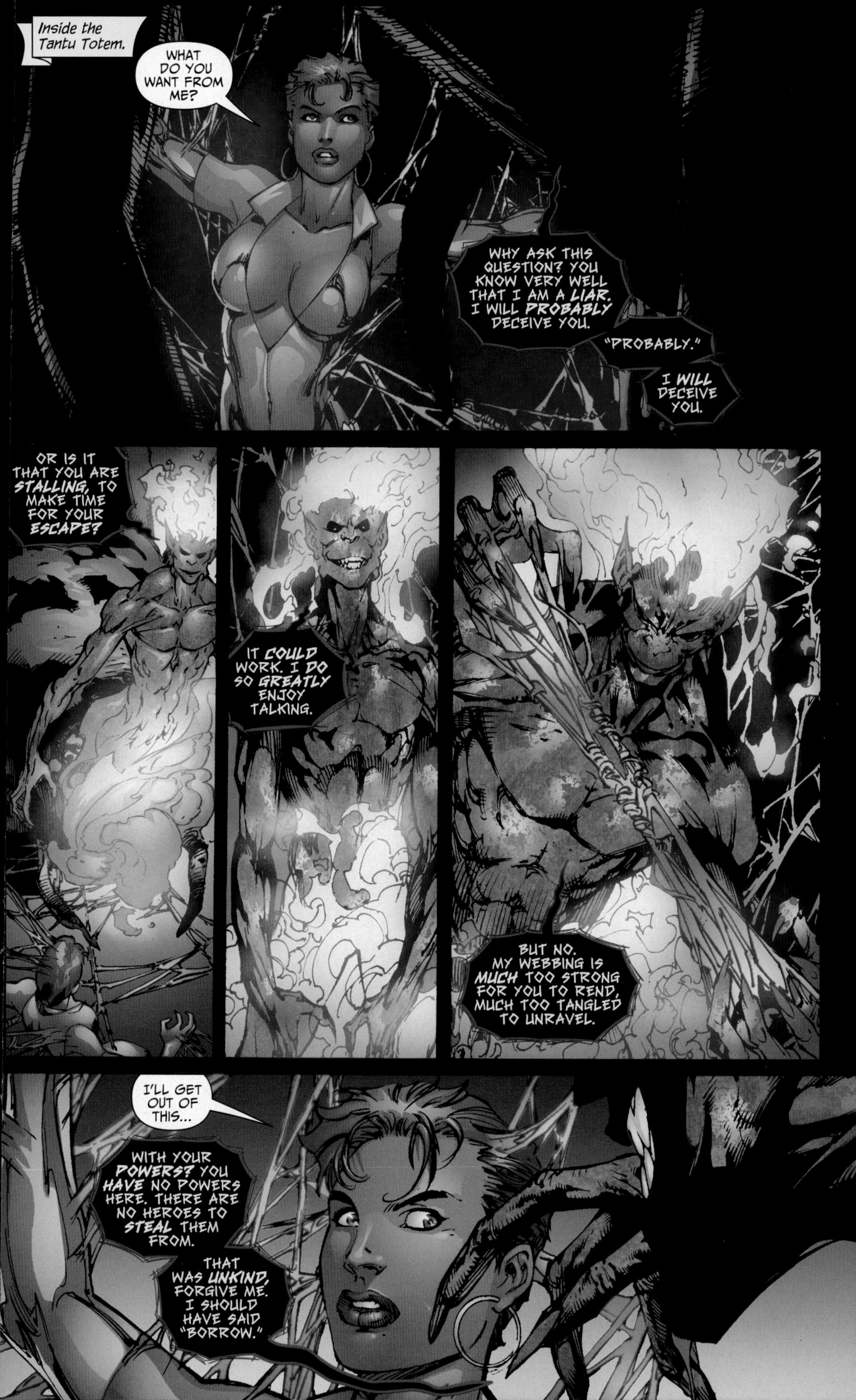
Inside the Tantu Totem.
WHAT DO YOU WANT FROM ME?
WHY ASK THIS QUESTION? YOU KNOW VERY WELL THAT I AM A LIAR. I WILL PROBABLY DECEIVE YOU.
"PROBABLY."
I WILL DECEIVE YOU.
OR IS IT THAT YOU ARE STALLING, TO MAKE TIME FOR YOUR ESCAPE?
IT COULD WORK. I DO SO GREATLY ENJOY TALKING.
BUT NO. MY WEBBING IS MUCH TOO STRONG FOR YOU TO REND, MUCH TOO TANGLED TO UNRAVEL.
I'LL GET OUT OF THIS...
WITH YOUR POWERS? YOU HAVE NO POWERS HERE. THERE ARE NO HEROES TO STEAL THEM FROM.
THAT WAS UNKIND, FORGIVE ME. I SHOULD HAVE SAID "BORROW."

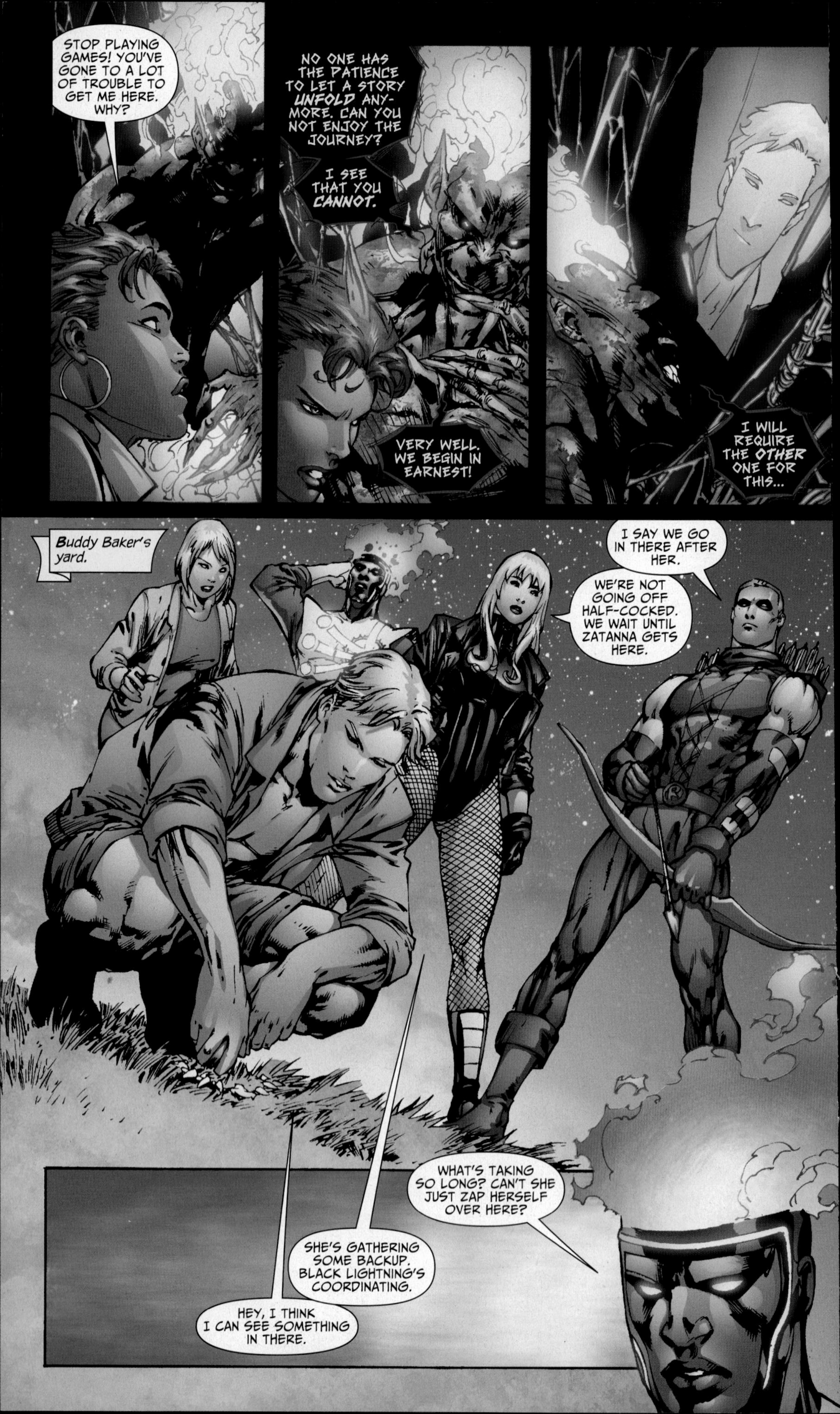
STOP PLAYING GAMES! YOU'VE GONE TO A LOT OF TROUBLE TO GET ME HERE. WHY?
NO ONE HAS THE PATIENCE TO LET A STORY UNFOLD ANY-MORE. CAN YOU NOT ENJOY THE JOURNEY?
I SEE THAT YOU CANNOT.
VERY WELL. WE BEGIN IN EARNEST!
I WILL REQUIRE THE OTHER ONE FOR THIS...
Buddy Baker's yard.
I SAY WE GO IN THERE AFTER HER.
WE'RE NOT GOING OFF HALF-COCKED. WE WAIT UNTIL ZATANNA GETS HERE.
WHAT'S TAKING SO LONG? CAN'T SHE JUST ZAP HERSELF OVER HERE?
SHE'S GATHERING SOME BACKUP. BLACK LIGHTNING'S COORDINATING.
HEY, I THINK I CAN SEE SOMETHING IN THERE.

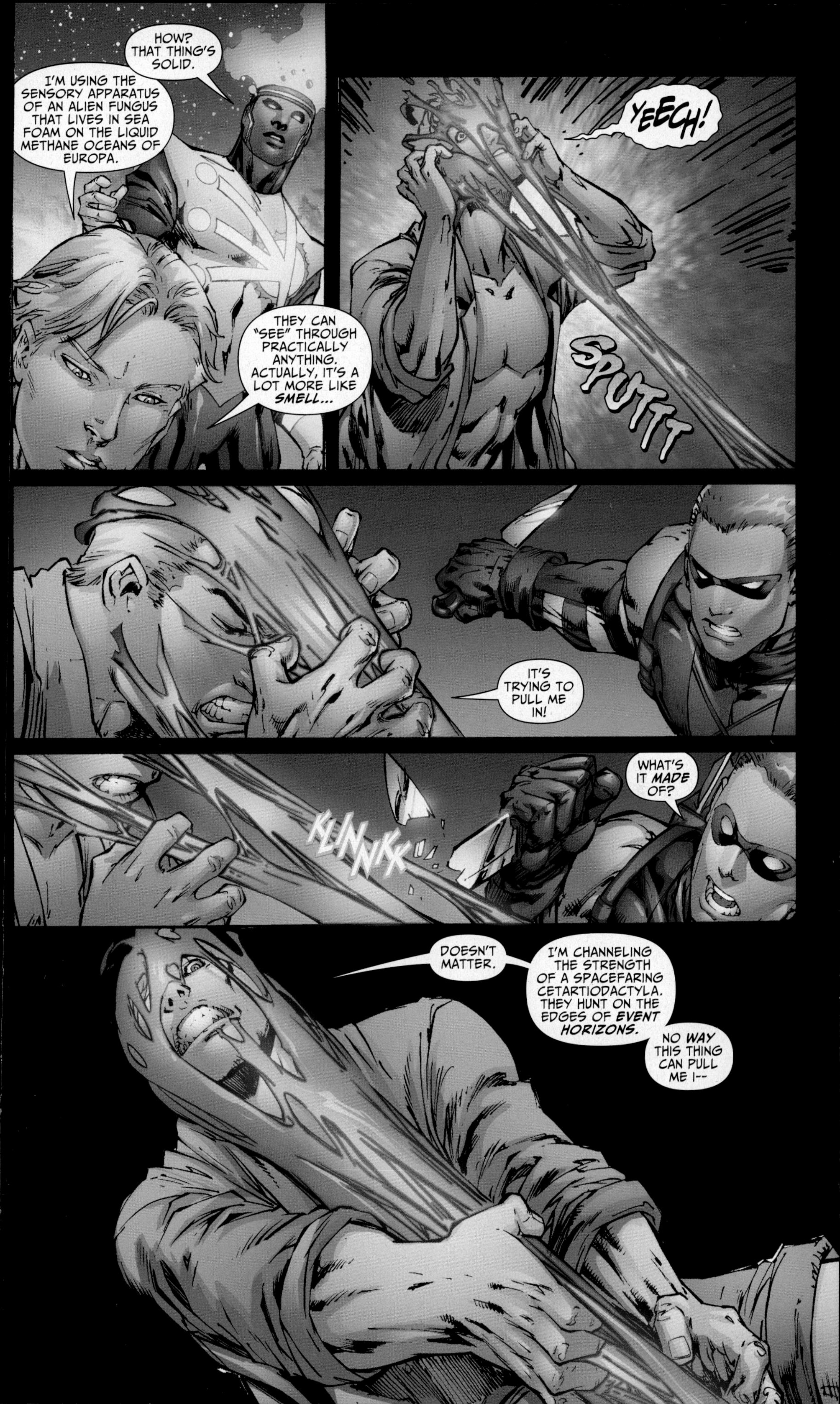

HOW? THAT THING'S SOLID.
I'M USING THE SENSORY APPARATUS OF AN ALIEN FUNGUS THAT LIVES IN SEA FOAM ON THE LIQUID METHANE OCEANS OF EUROPA.
THEY CAN "SEE" THROUGH PRACTICALLY ANYTHING. ACTUALLY, IT'S A LOT MORE LIKE SMELL...
YEECH!
SPUTTT
IT'S TRYING TO PULL ME IN!
KLINNKK
WHAT'S IT MADE OF?
DOESN'T MATTER.
I'M CHANNELING THE STRENGTH OF A SPACEFARING CETARTIODACTYLA. THEY HUNT ON THE EDGES OF EVENT HORIZONS.
NO WAY THIS THING CAN PULL ME I--

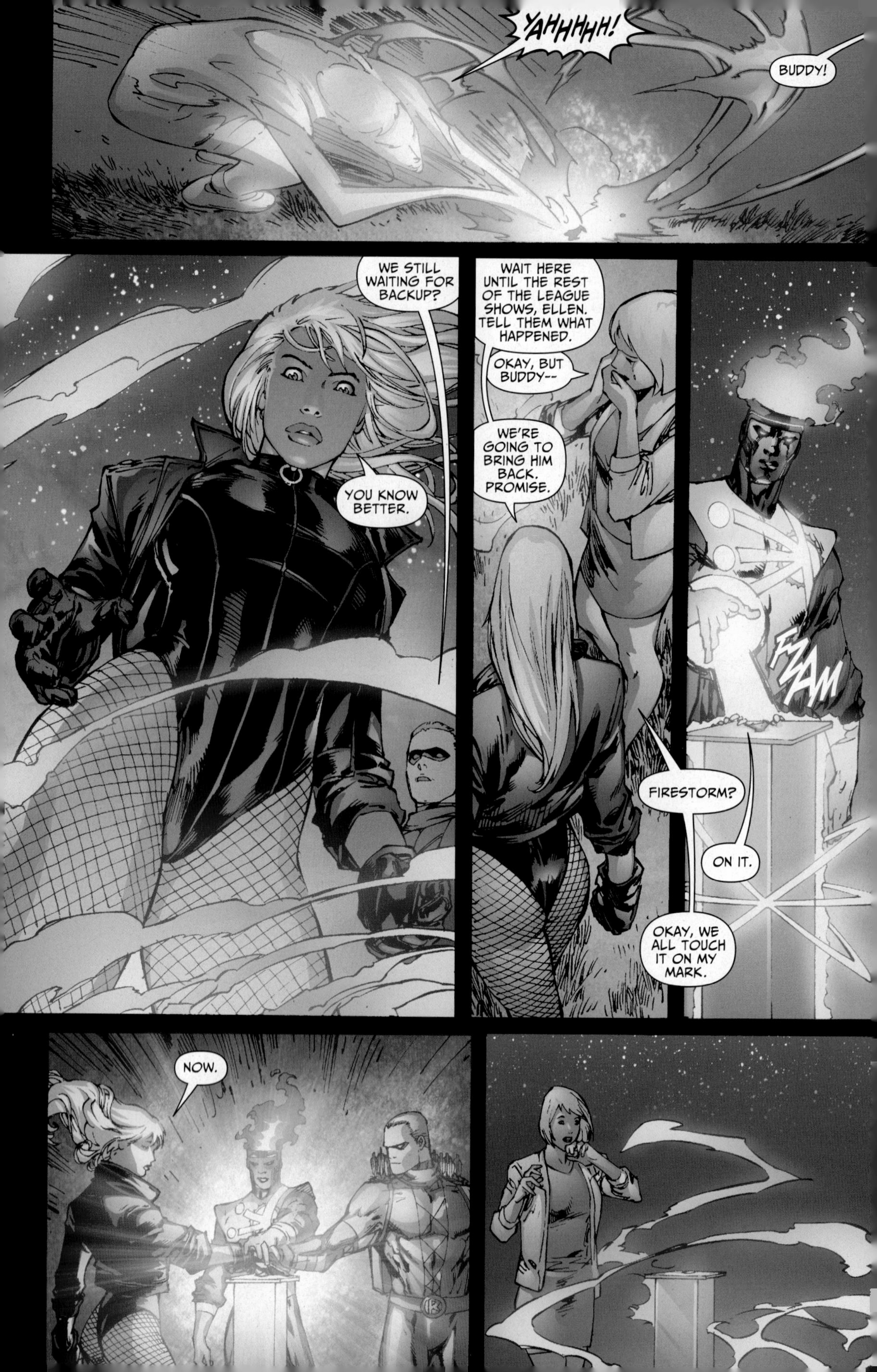
YAHHHHH!
BUDDY!
WE STILL WAITING FOR BACKUP?
YOU KNOW BETTER.
WAIT HERE UNTIL THE REST OF THE LEAGUE SHOWS, ELLEN. TELL THEM WHAT HAPPENED.
OKAY, BUT BUDDY--
WE'RE GOING TO BRING HIM BACK. PROMISE.
FWAM
FIRESTORM?
ON IT.
OKAY, WE ALL TOUCH IT ON MY MARK.
NOW.

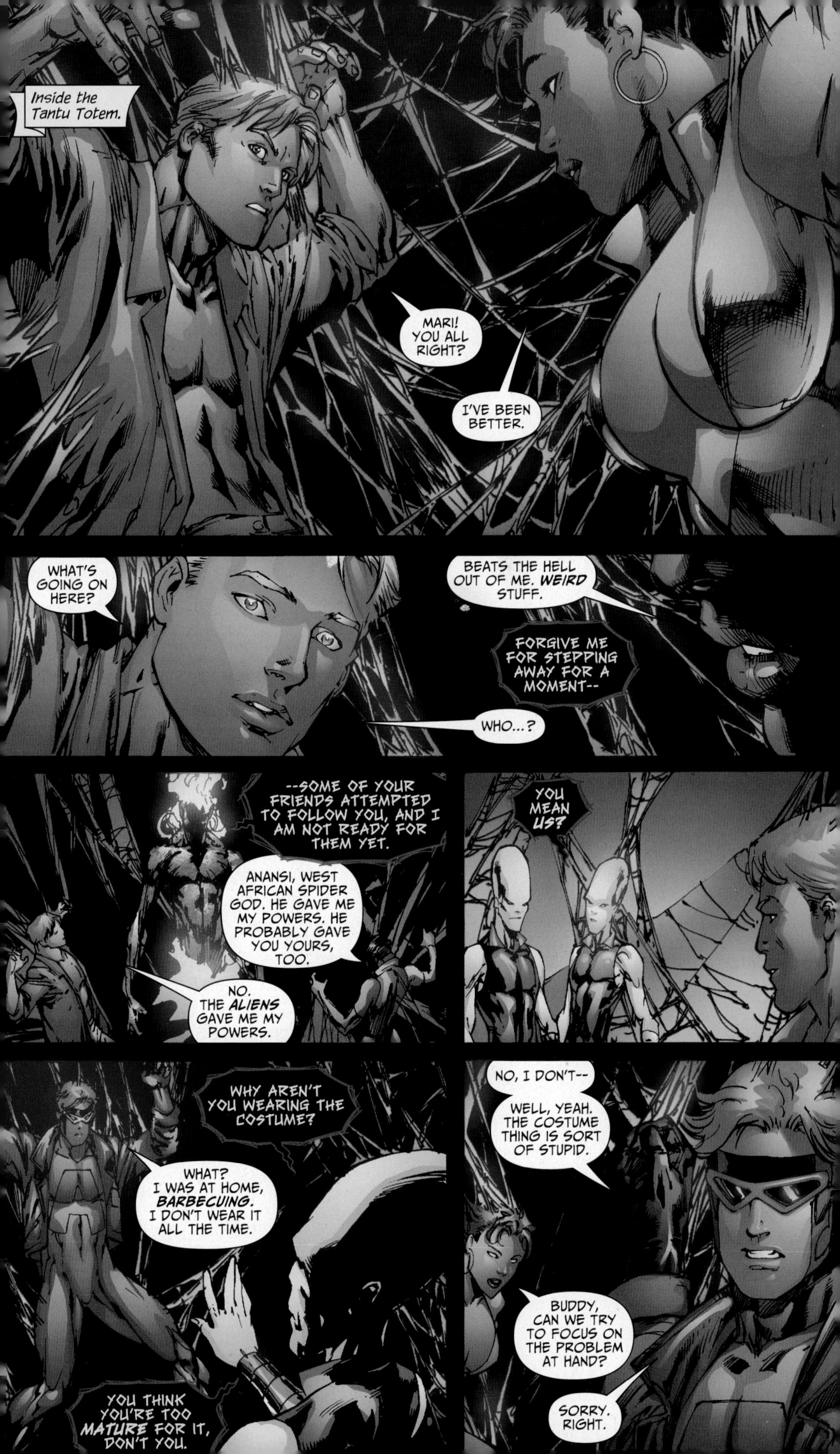

Inside the Tantu Totem.
MARI! YOU ALL RIGHT?
I'VE BEEN BETTER.
WHAT'S GOING ON HERE?
BEATS THE HELL OUT OF ME. WEIRD STUFF.
FORGIVE ME FOR STEPPING AWAY FOR A MOMENT--
WHO...?
--SOME OF YOUR FRIENDS ATTEMPTED TO FOLLOW YOU, AND I AM NOT READY FOR THEM YET.
ANANSI, WEST AFRICAN SPIDER GOD. HE GAVE ME MY POWERS. HE PROBABLY GAVE YOU YOURS, TOO.
NO. THE ALIENS GAVE ME MY POWERS.
YOU MEAN US?
WHY AREN'T YOU WEARING THE COSTUME?
WHAT? I WAS AT HOME, BARBECUING. I DON'T WEAR IT ALL THE TIME.
YOU THINK YOU'RE TOO MATURE FOR IT, DON'T YOU.
NO, I DON'T--
WELL, YEAH. THE COSTUME THING IS SORT OF STUPID.
BUDDY, CAN WE TRY TO FOCUS ON THE PROBLEM AT HAND?
SORRY. RIGHT.

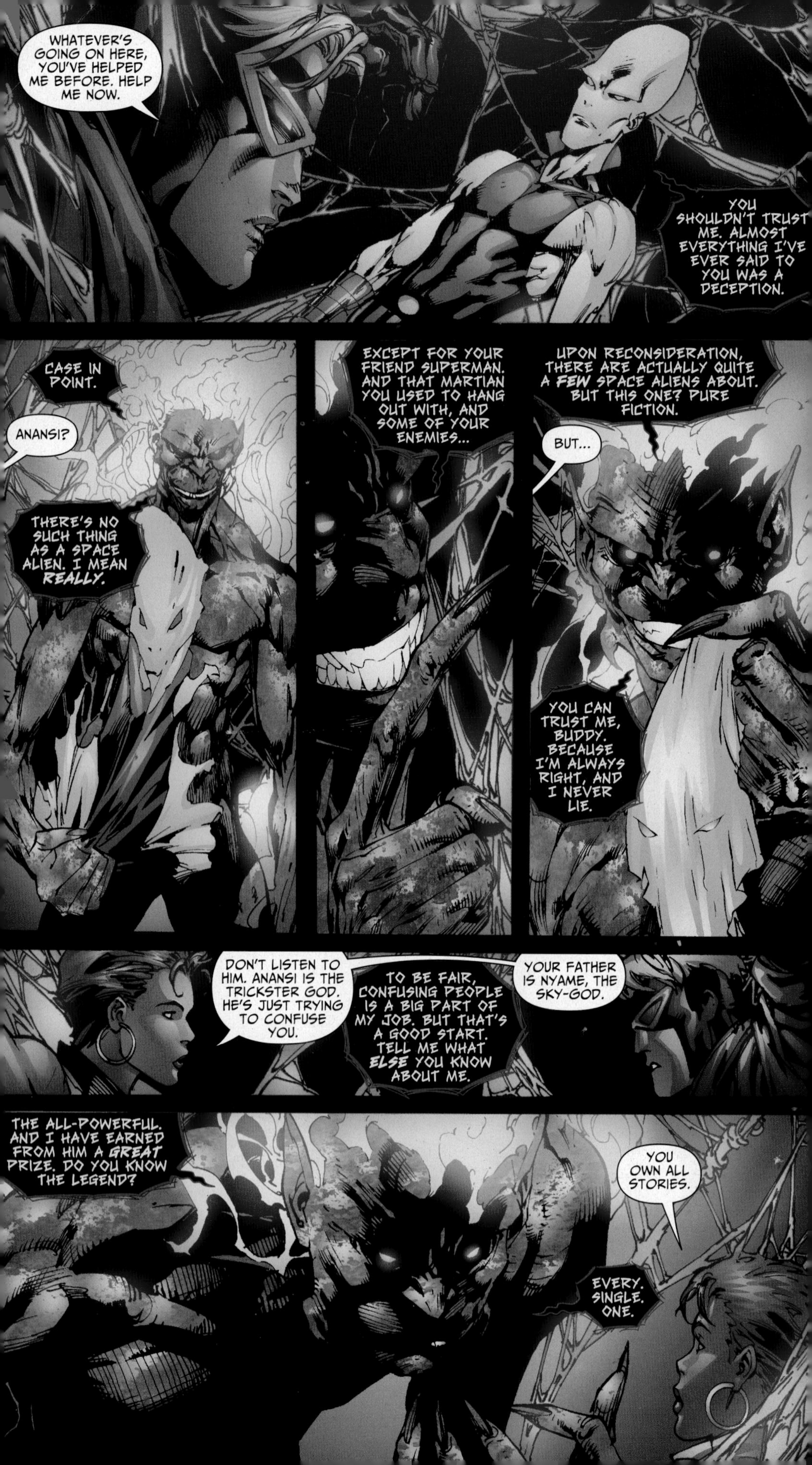

WHATEVER'S GOING ON HERE, YOU'VE HELPED ME BEFORE. HELP ME NOW.
YOU SHOULDN'T TRUST ME. ALMOST EVERYTHING I'VE EVER SAID TO YOU WAS A DECEPTION.
CASE IN POINT.
ANANSI?
THERE'S NO SUCH THING AS A SPACE ALIEN. I MEAN *REALLY*.
EXCEPT FOR YOUR FRIEND SUPERMAN. AND THAT MARTIAN YOU USED TO HANG OUT WITH, AND SOME OF YOUR ENEMIES...
UPON RECONSIDERATION, THERE ARE ACTUALLY QUITE A *FEW* SPACE ALIENS ABOUT. BUT THIS ONE? PURE FICTION.
BUT...
YOU CAN TRUST ME, BUDDY. BECAUSE I'M ALWAYS RIGHT, AND I NEVER LIE.
DON'T LISTEN TO HIM. ANANSI IS THE TRICKSTER GOD. HE'S JUST TRYING TO CONFUSE YOU.
YOUR FATHER IS NYAME, THE SKY-GOD.
TO BE FAIR, CONFUSING PEOPLE IS A BIG PART OF MY JOB. BUT THAT'S A GOOD START. TELL ME WHAT *ELSE* YOU KNOW ABOUT ME.
THE ALL-POWERFUL. AND I HAVE EARNED FROM HIM A *GREAT* PRIZE. DO YOU KNOW THE LEGEND?
YOU OWN ALL STORIES.
EVERY. SINGLE. ONE.

THE CONTRADICTORY *HISTORIES* OF HAPLESS BUDDY BAKER. THE MANY *VERSIONS* OF A SIMPLE CHILDREN'S FABLE. THE INCONSISTENCIES IN THE *MEMORIES* OF TWO WITNESSES TO THE SAME EVENT.

THE *RIFT* IN THE BLEED. THE POTENTIALLY CATASTROPHIC *DIVERGENCES* THAT LEAVE THE MULTIVERSE IN CONSTANT CRISIS.

I AM THE *LIE* THAT REVEALS THE *TRUTH*, MARI JIWE McCABE.

I OWN *ALL* TALES.

AT ONE POINT, I THOUGHT *YOU* MIGHT BE WHAT I REQUIRE, BUT YOUR LIFE IS SIMPLY *METAFICTION*, MEANINGLESS IN THIS CONTEXT.

AH, BUT BEAUTIFUL MARI.

YOUR LIFE IS A WEB OF *DECEPTION*, BUT ALSO A SINGLE, GRAND NARRATIVE. PRECISELY WHAT I NEED TO *REASSERT* MY CONTROL.

YOU CAN'T *CONTROL* ME.

NOT WHAT I SAID, BUT OF *COURSE* I CAN. I WILL DEMONSTRATE.

"YOUR FRIENDS ARRIVE, INTENDING TO RESCUE YOU."

WE'RE IN.

BUDDY! MARI!

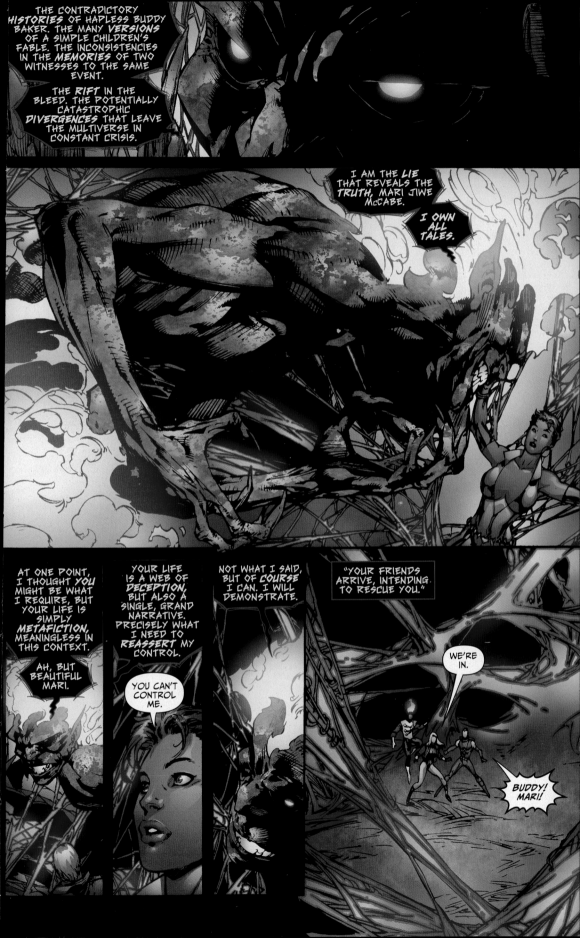

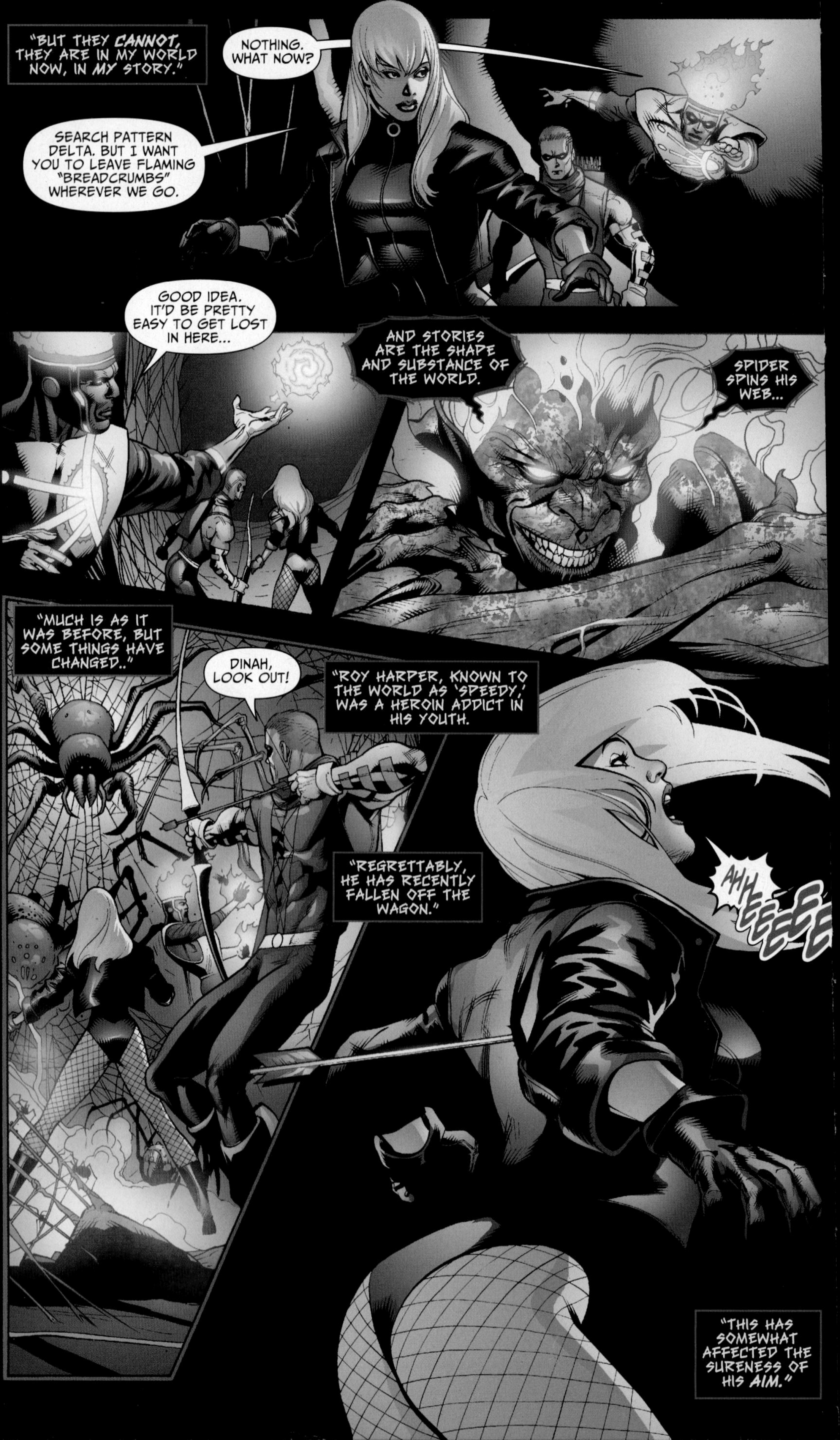
"BUT THEY CANNOT, THEY ARE IN MY WORLD NOW, IN MY STORY."
NOTHING. WHAT NOW?
SEARCH PATTERN DELTA. BUT I WANT YOU TO LEAVE FLAMING "BREADCRUMBS" WHEREVER WE GO.
GOOD IDEA. IT'D BE PRETTY EASY TO GET LOST IN HERE...
AND STORIES ARE THE SHAPE AND SUBSTANCE OF THE WORLD.
SPIDER SPINS HIS WEB...
"MUCH IS AS IT WAS BEFORE, BUT SOME THINGS HAVE CHANGED.."
DINAH, LOOK OUT!
"ROY HARPER, KNOWN TO THE WORLD AS 'SPEEDY,' WAS A HEROIN ADDICT IN HIS YOUTH.
"REGRETTABLY, HE HAS RECENTLY FALLEN OFF THE WAGON."
AHHEEEEE
"THIS HAS SOMEWHAT AFFECTED THE SURENESS OF HIS AIM."

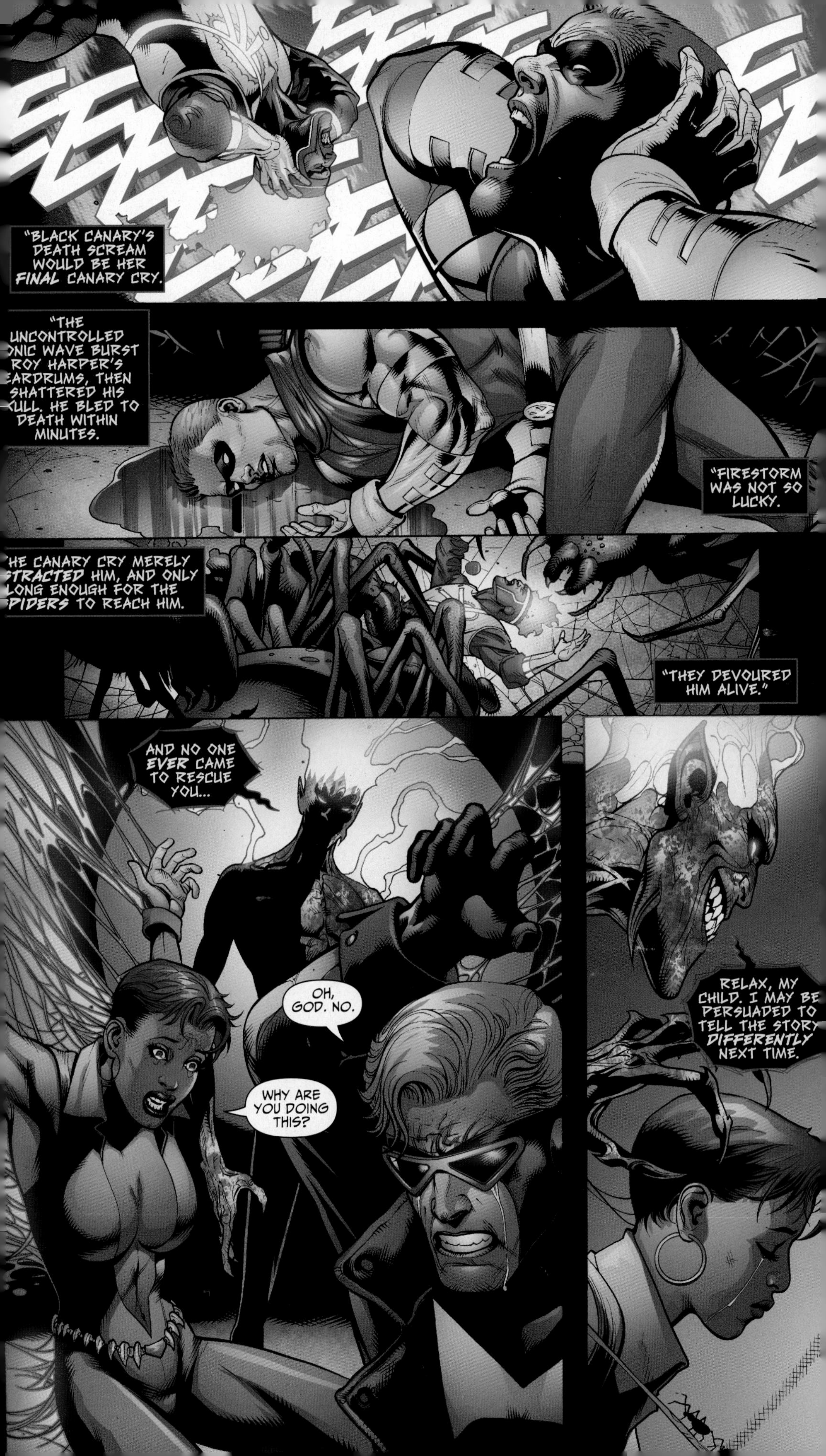
"BLACK CANARY'S DEATH SCREAM WOULD BE HER *FINAL* CANARY CRY.
"THE UNCONTROLLED ONIC WAVE BURST ROY HARPER'S EARDRUMS, THEN SHATTERED HIS KULL. HE BLED TO DEATH WITHIN MINUTES.
"FIRESTORM WAS NOT SO LUCKY.
HE CANARY CRY MERELY *STRACTED* HIM, AND ONLY LONG ENOUGH FOR THE *PIDERS* TO REACH HIM.
"THEY DEVOURED HIM ALIVE."
AND NO ONE *EVER* CAME TO RESCUE YOU...
OH, GOD. NO.
WHY ARE YOU DOING THIS?
RELAX, MY CHILD. I MAY BE PERSUADED TO TELL THE STORY *DIFFERENTLY* NEXT TIME.

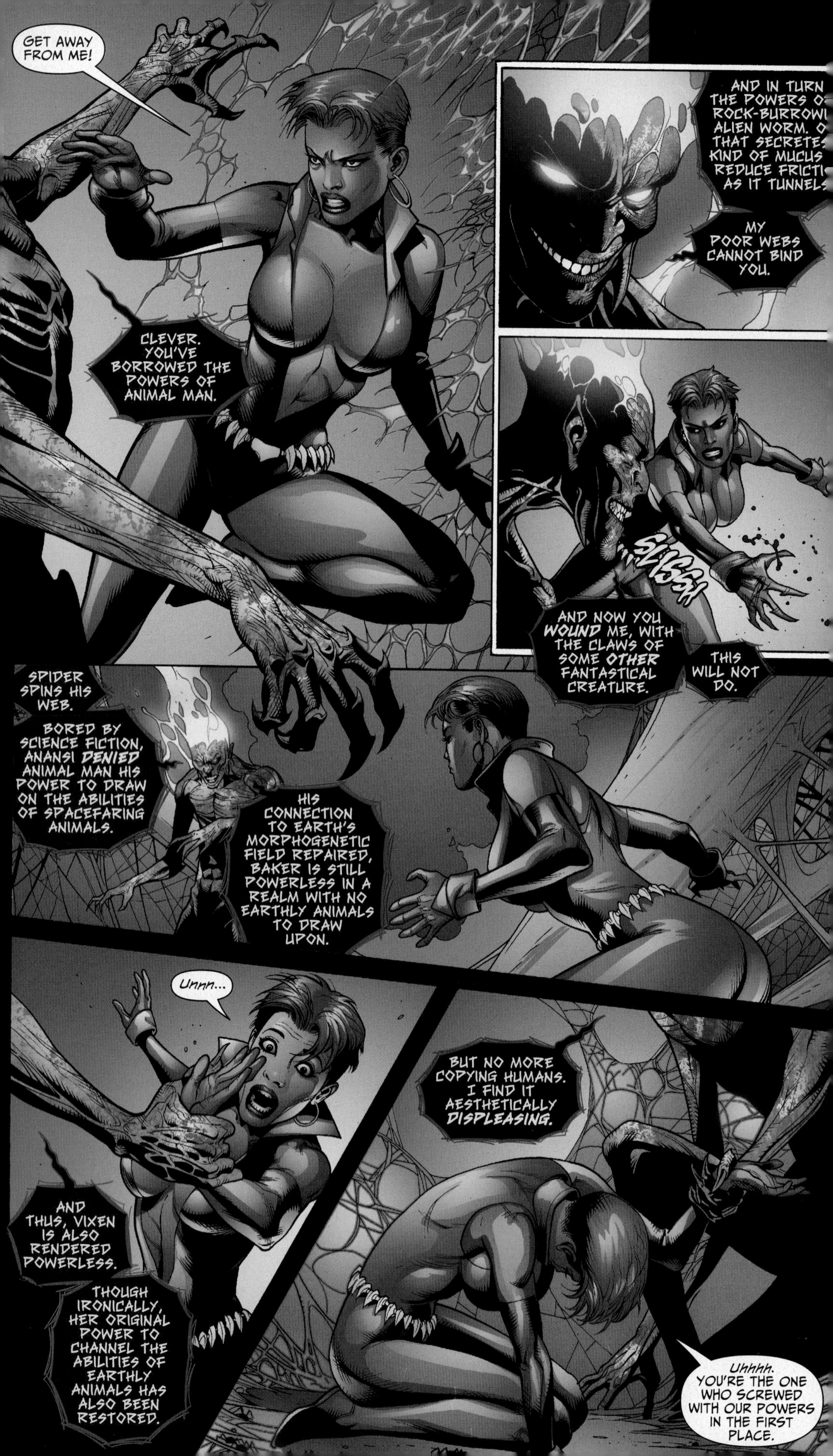
GET AWAY FROM ME!
CLEVER. YOU'VE BORROWED THE POWERS OF ANIMAL MAN.
AND IN TURN THE POWERS O ROCK-BURROWI ALIEN WORM. O THAT SECRETES KIND OF MUCUS REDUCE FRICTI AS IT TUNNELS
MY POOR WEBS CANNOT BIND YOU.
SLISSH
AND NOW YOU WOUND ME, WITH THE CLAWS OF SOME OTHER FANTASTICAL CREATURE.
THIS WILL NOT DO.
SPIDER SPINS HIS WEB.
BORED BY SCIENCE FICTION, ANANSI DENIED ANIMAL MAN HIS POWER TO DRAW ON THE ABILITIES OF SPACEFARING ANIMALS.
HIS CONNECTION TO EARTH'S MORPHOGENETIC FIELD REPAIRED, BAKER IS STILL POWERLESS IN A REALM WITH NO EARTHLY ANIMALS TO DRAW UPON.
Unnn...
AND THUS, VIXEN IS ALSO RENDERED POWERLESS.
THOUGH IRONICALLY, HER ORIGINAL POWER TO CHANNEL THE ABILITIES OF EARTHLY ANIMALS HAS ALSO BEEN RESTORED.
BUT NO MORE COPYING HUMANS. I FIND IT AESTHETICALLY DISPLEASING.
Uhhhh. YOU'RE THE ONE WHO SCREWED WITH OUR POWERS IN THE FIRST PLACE.

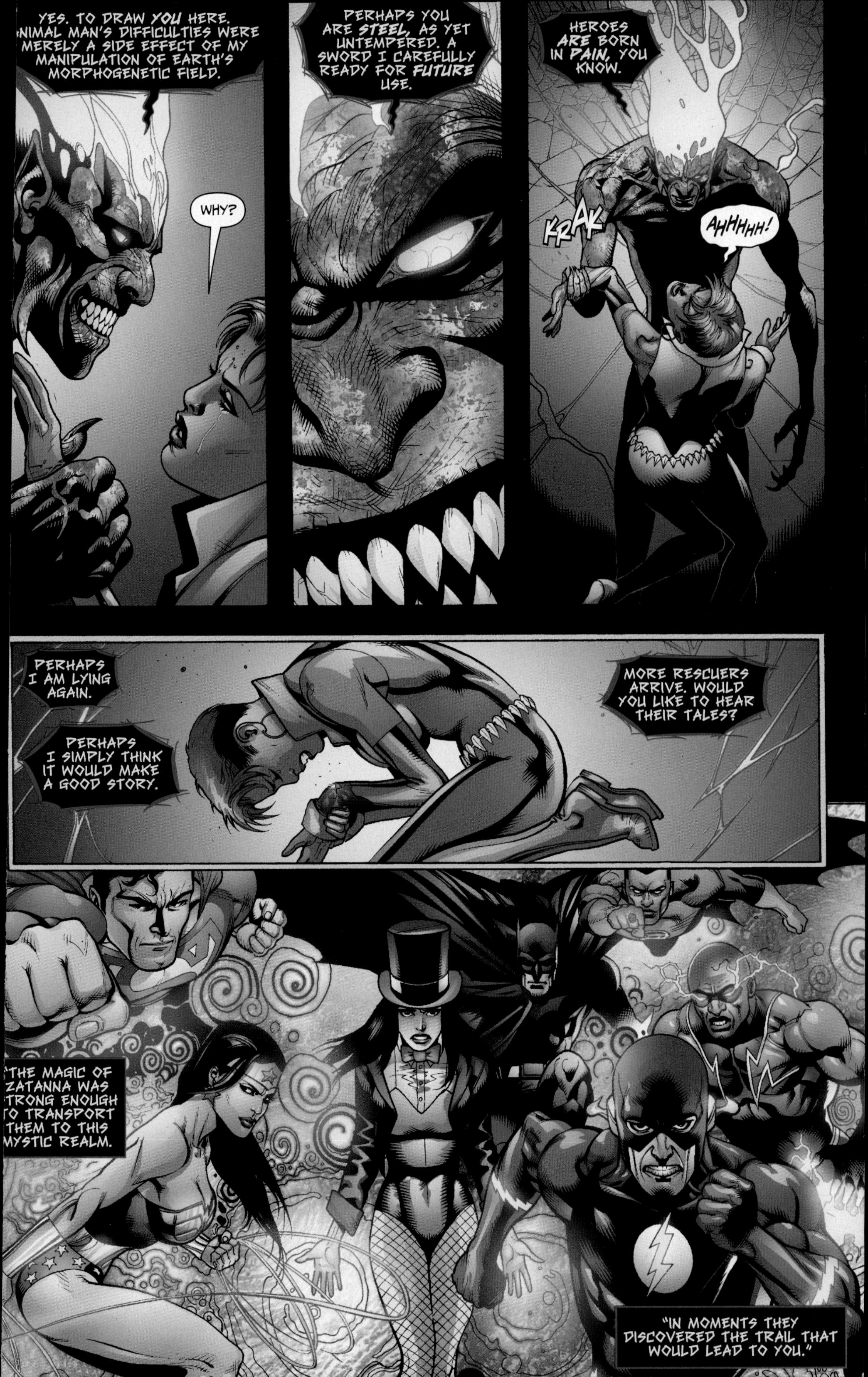
YES. TO DRAW YOU HERE. ANIMAL MAN'S DIFFICULTIES WERE MERELY A SIDE EFFECT OF MY MANIPULATION OF EARTH'S MORPHOGENETIC FIELD.
WHY?
PERHAPS YOU ARE STEEL, AS YET UNTEMPERED. A SWORD I CAREFULLY READY FOR FUTURE USE.
HEROES ARE BORN IN PAIN, YOU KNOW.
KRAK
AHHHHH!
PERHAPS I AM LYING AGAIN.
PERHAPS I SIMPLY THINK IT WOULD MAKE A GOOD STORY.
MORE RESCUERS ARRIVE. WOULD YOU LIKE TO HEAR THEIR TALES?
"THE MAGIC OF ZATANNA WAS STRONG ENOUGH TO TRANSPORT THEM TO THIS MYSTIC REALM.
"IN MOMENTS THEY DISCOVERED THE TRAIL THAT WOULD LEAD TO YOU."

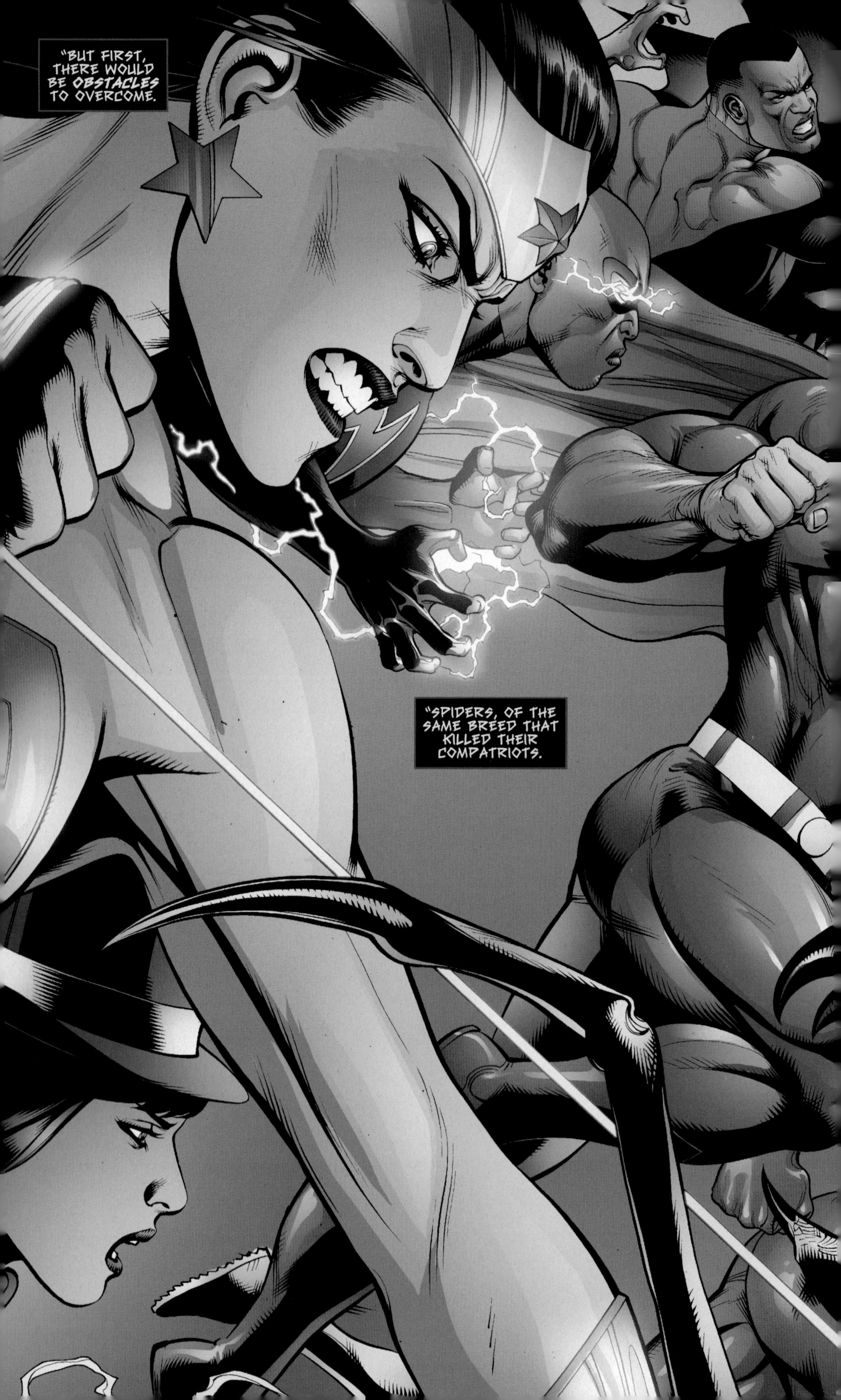
"BUT FIRST, THERE WOULD BE OBSTACLES TO OVERCOME.
"SPIDERS, OF THE SAME BREED THAT KILLED THEIR COMPATRIOTS.

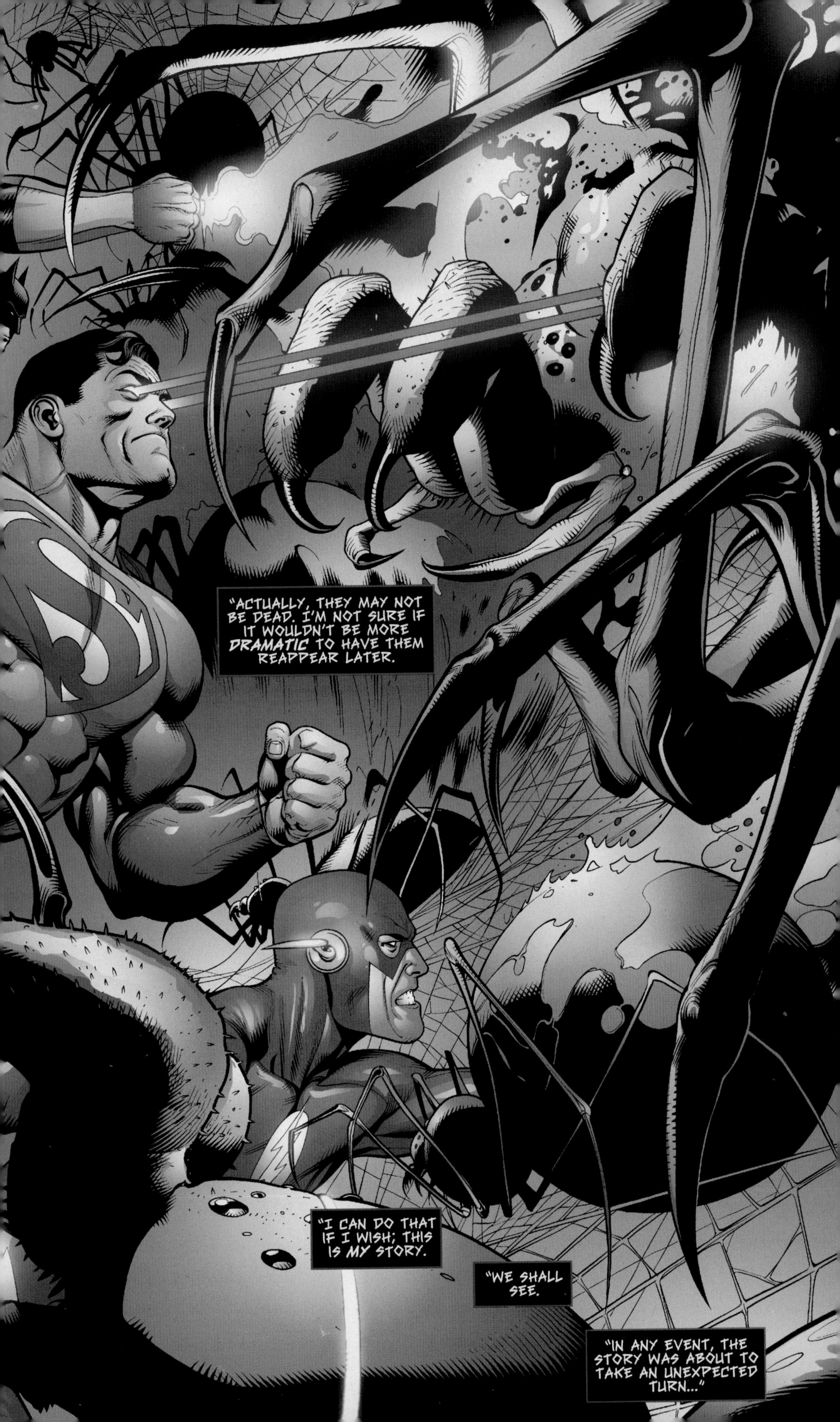
"ACTUALLY, THEY MAY NOT BE DEAD. I'M NOT SURE IF IT WOULDN'T BE MORE DRAMATIC TO HAVE THEM REAPPEAR LATER.
"I CAN DO THAT IF I WISH; THIS IS MY STORY.
"WE SHALL SEE.
"IN ANY EVENT, THE STORY WAS ABOUT TO TAKE AN UNEXPECTED TURN..."

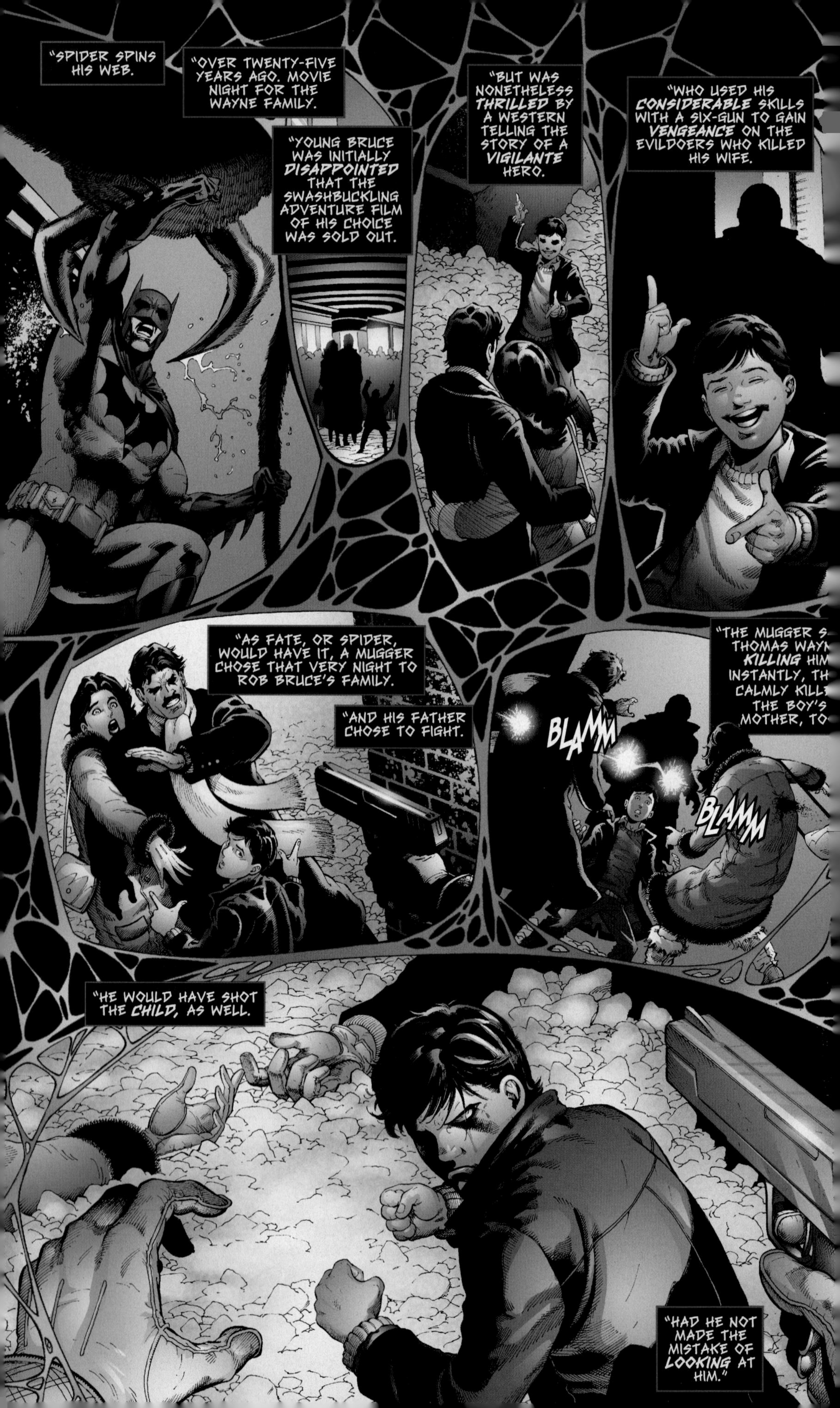

"SPIDER SPINS HIS WEB.
"OVER TWENTY-FIVE YEARS AGO. MOVIE NIGHT FOR THE WAYNE FAMILY.
"YOUNG BRUCE WAS INITIALLY *DISAPPOINTED* THAT THE SWASHBUCKLING ADVENTURE FILM OF HIS CHOICE WAS SOLD OUT.
"BUT WAS NONETHELESS *THRILLED* BY A WESTERN TELLING THE STORY OF A *VIGILANTE* HERO.
"WHO USED HIS *CONSIDERABLE* SKILLS WITH A SIX-GUN TO GAIN *VENGEANCE* ON THE EVILDOERS WHO KILLED HIS WIFE.
"AS FATE, OR SPIDER, WOULD HAVE IT, A MUGGER CHOSE THAT VERY NIGHT TO ROB BRUCE'S FAMILY.
"AND HIS FATHER CHOSE TO FIGHT.
"THE MUGGER S
THOMAS WAYN
KILLING HIM
INSTANTLY, TH
CALMLY KILL
THE BOY'S
MOTHER, TO
BLAMM
BLAMM
"HE WOULD HAVE SHOT THE *CHILD*, AS WELL.
"HAD HE NOT MADE THE MISTAKE OF *LOOKING* AT HIM."

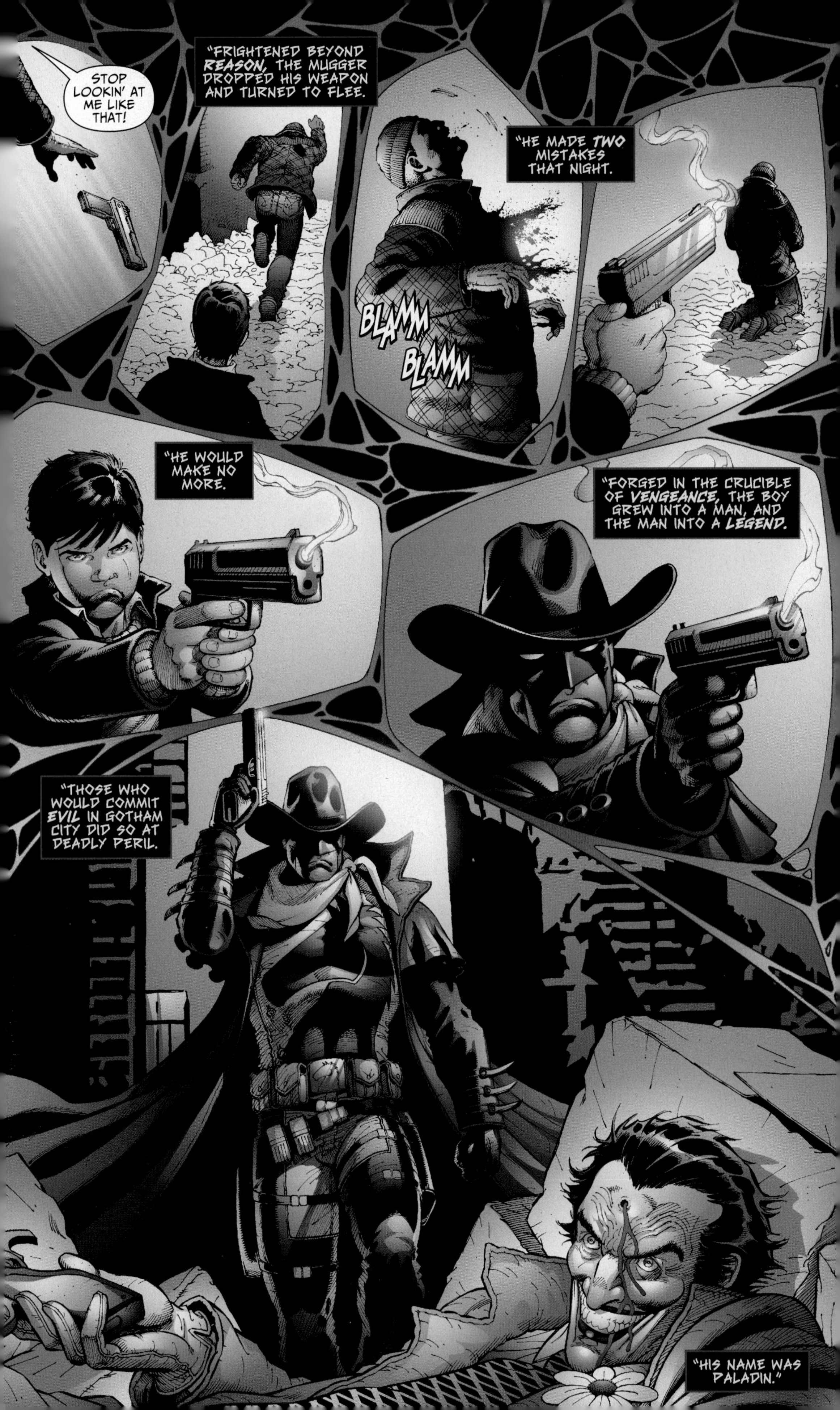
STOP LOOKIN' AT ME LIKE THAT!
"FRIGHTENED BEYOND REASON, THE MUGGER DROPPED HIS WEAPON AND TURNED TO FLEE.
"HE MADE TWO MISTAKES THAT NIGHT.
BLAMM
BLAMM
"HE WOULD MAKE NO MORE.
"FORGED IN THE CRUCIBLE OF VENGEANCE, THE BOY GREW INTO A MAN, AND THE MAN INTO A LEGEND.
"THOSE WHO WOULD COMMIT EVIL IN GOTHAM CITY DID SO AT DEADLY PERIL.
"HIS NAME WAS PALADIN."

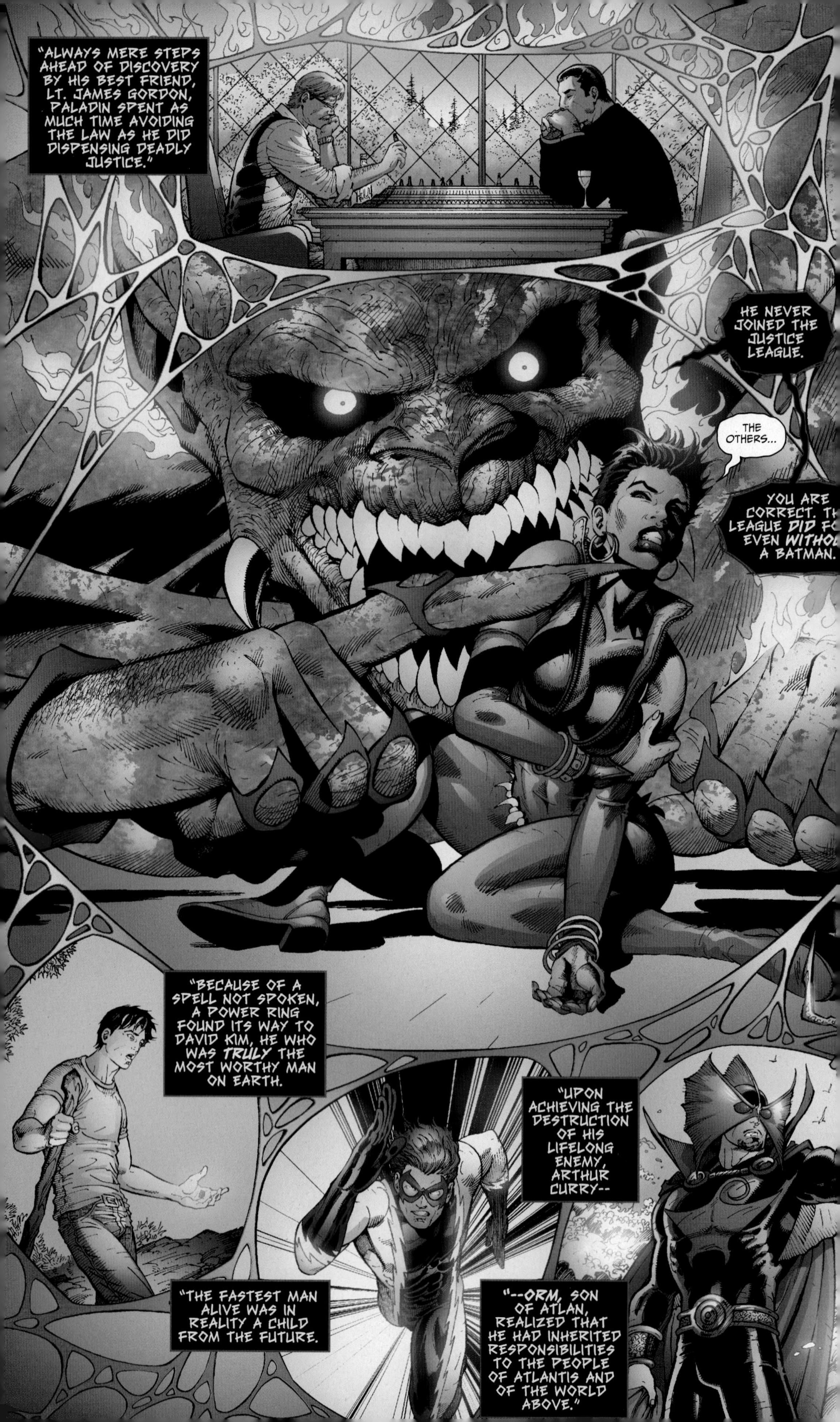
"ALWAYS MERE STEPS AHEAD OF DISCOVERY BY HIS BEST FRIEND, LT. JAMES GORDON, PALADIN SPENT AS MUCH TIME AVOIDING THE LAW AS HE DID DISPENSING DEADLY JUSTICE."
HE NEVER JOINED THE JUSTICE LEAGUE.
THE OTHERS...
YOU ARE CORRECT. TH LEAGUE *DID* FO EVEN *WITHOU* A BATMAN.
"BECAUSE OF A SPELL NOT SPOKEN, A POWER RING FOUND ITS WAY TO DAVID KIM, HE WHO WAS *TRULY* THE MOST WORTHY MAN ON EARTH.
"UPON ACHIEVING THE DESTRUCTION OF HIS LIFELONG ENEMY, ARTHUR CURRY--
"THE FASTEST MAN ALIVE WAS IN REALITY A CHILD FROM THE FUTURE.
"--*ORM*, SON OF ATLAN, REALIZED THAT HE HAD INHERITED RESPONSIBILITIES TO THE PEOPLE OF ATLANTIS AND OF THE WORLD ABOVE."

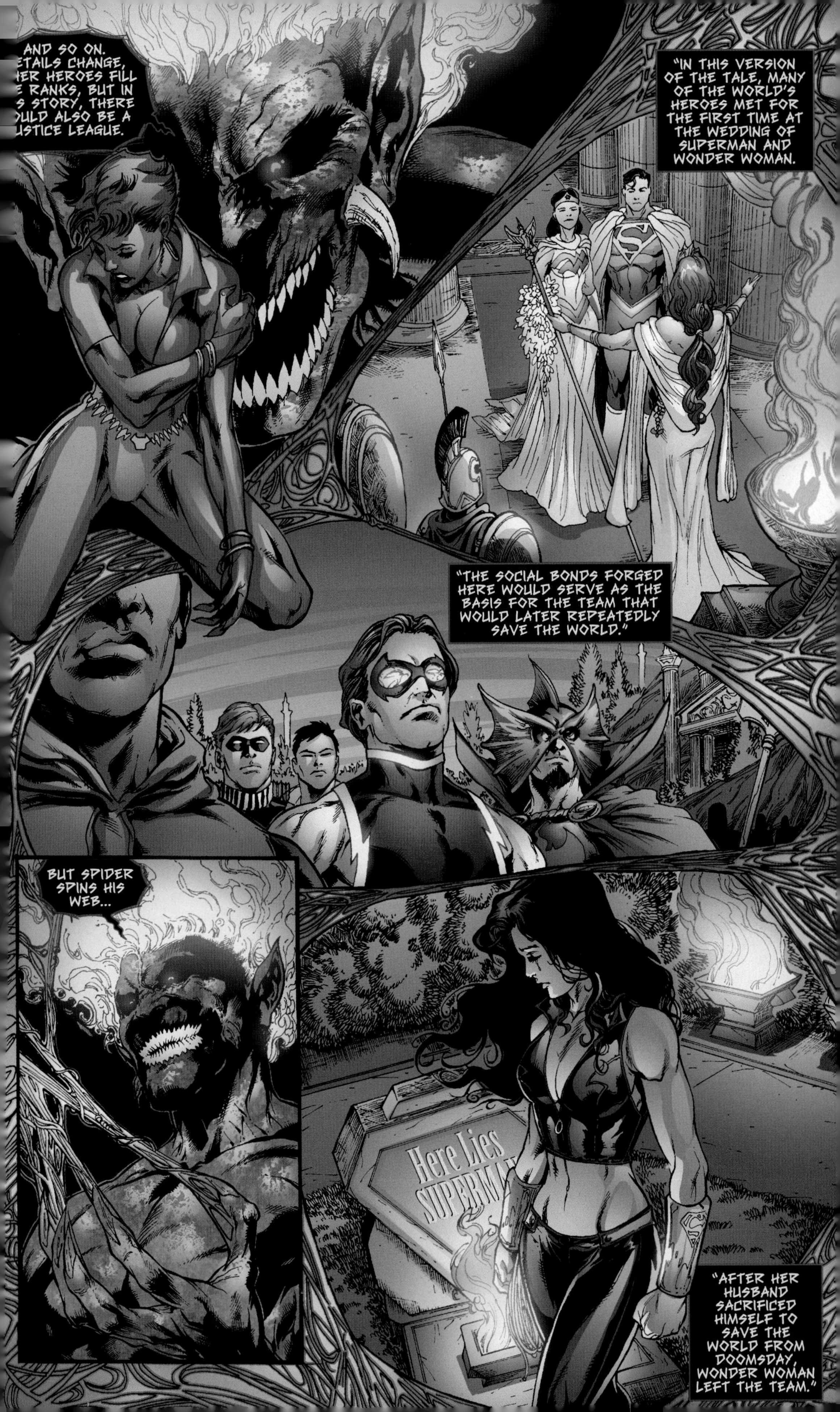
AND SO ON. ETAILS CHANGE, HER HEROES FILL E RANKS, BUT IN S STORY, THERE ULD ALSO BE A USTICE LEAGUE.
"IN THIS VERSION OF THE TALE, MANY OF THE WORLD'S HEROES MET FOR THE FIRST TIME AT THE WEDDING OF SUPERMAN AND WONDER WOMAN.
"THE SOCIAL BONDS FORGED HERE WOULD SERVE AS THE BASIS FOR THE TEAM THAT WOULD LATER REPEATEDLY SAVE THE WORLD."
BUT SPIDER SPINS HIS WEB...
Here Lies
"AFTER HER HUSBAND SACRIFICED HIMSELF TO SAVE THE WORLD FROM DOOMSDAY, WONDER WOMAN LEFT THE TEAM."

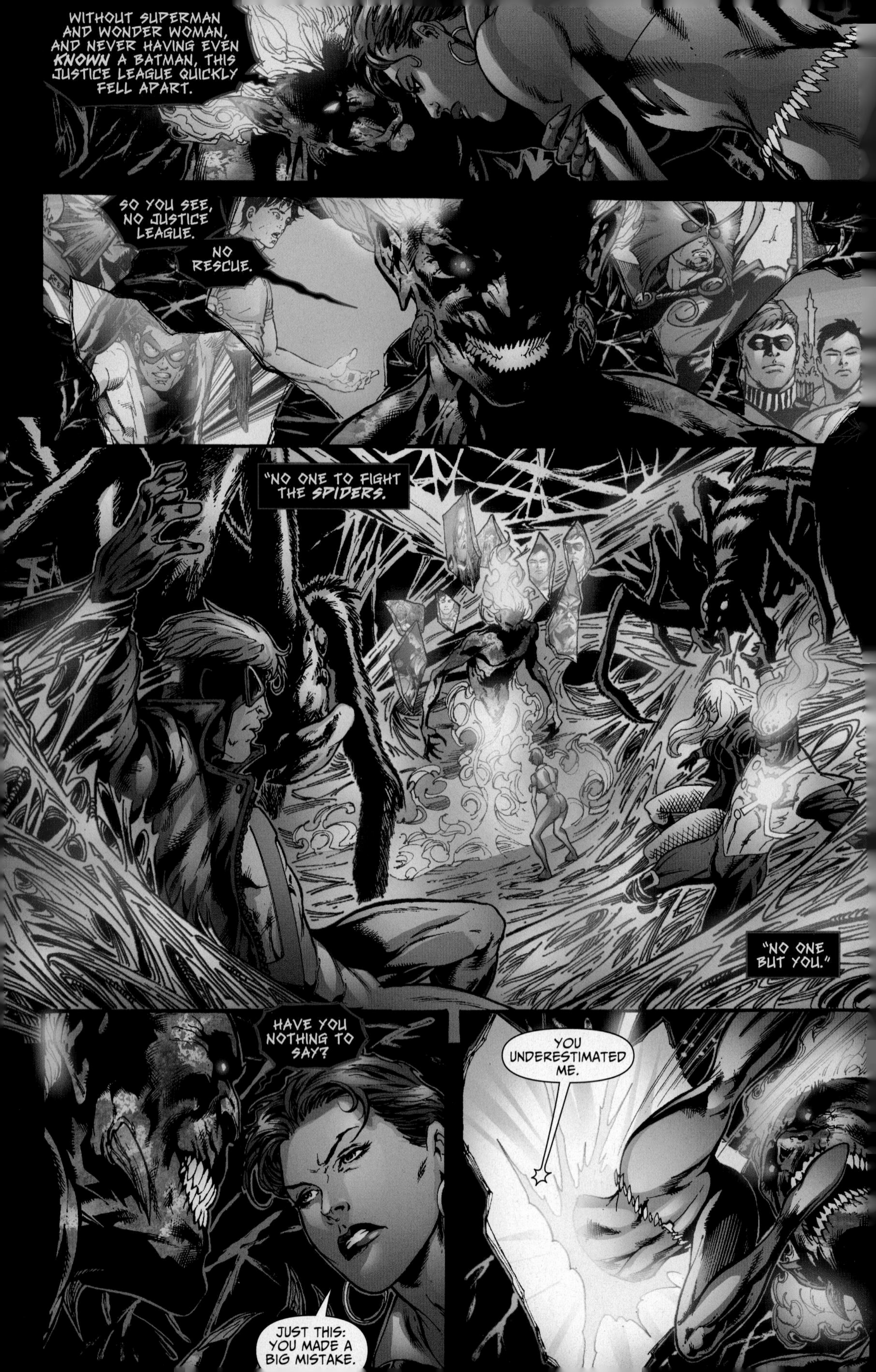
WITHOUT SUPERMAN AND WONDER WOMAN, AND NEVER HAVING EVEN KNOWN A BATMAN, THIS JUSTICE LEAGUE QUICKLY FELL APART.
SO YOU SEE, NO JUSTICE LEAGUE.
NO RESCUE.
"NO ONE TO FIGHT THE SPIDERS.
"NO ONE BUT YOU."
HAVE YOU NOTHING TO SAY?
JUST THIS: YOU MADE A BIG MISTAKE.
YOU UNDERESTIMATED ME.

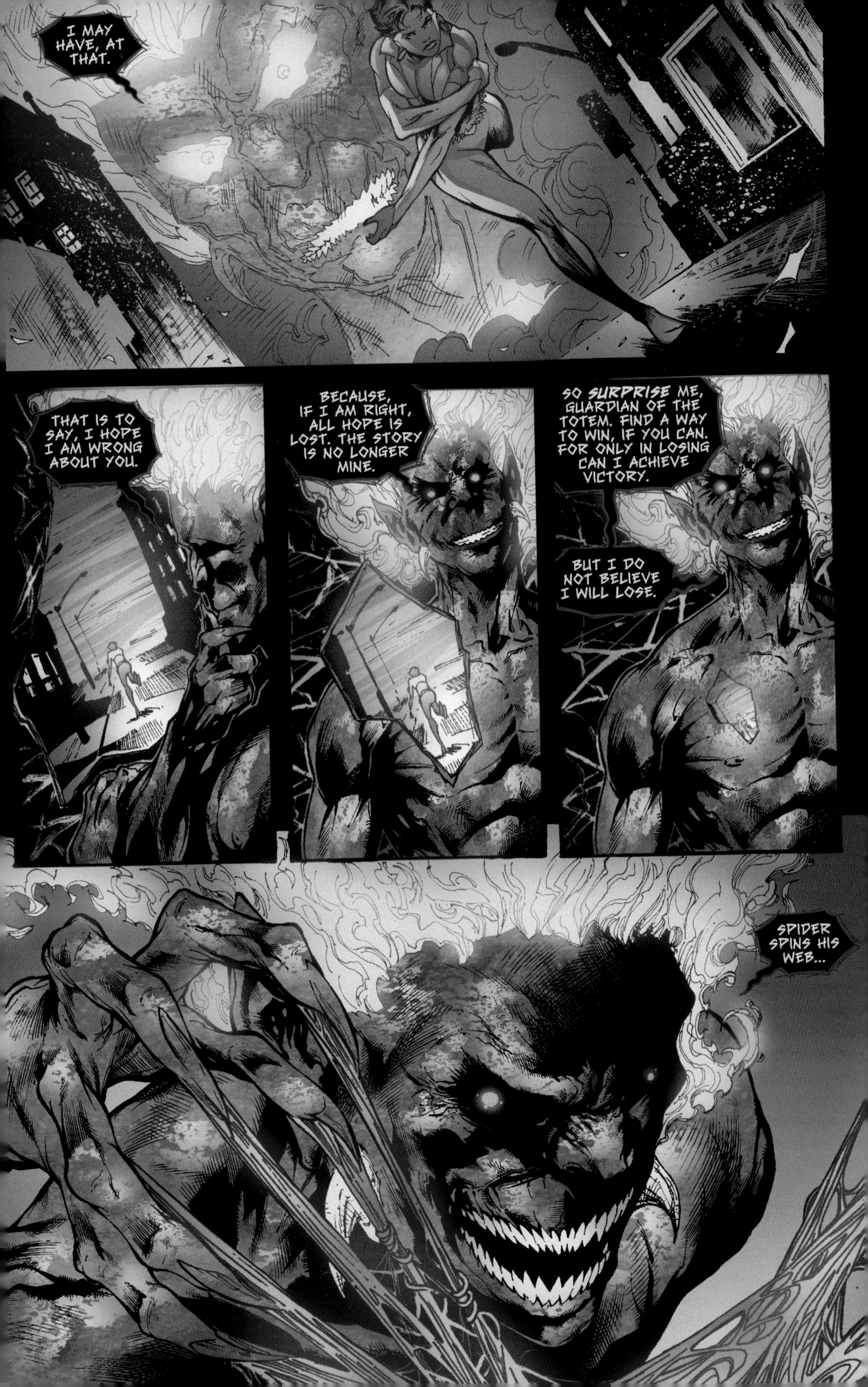
I MAY HAVE, AT THAT.
THAT IS TO SAY, I HOPE I AM WRONG ABOUT YOU.
BECAUSE, IF I AM RIGHT, ALL HOPE IS LOST. THE STORY IS NO LONGER MINE.
SO SURPRISE ME, GUARDIAN OF THE TOTEM. FIND A WAY TO WIN, IF YOU CAN. FOR ONLY IN LOSING CAN I ACHIEVE VICTORY.
BUT I DO NOT BELIEVE I WILL LOSE.
SPIDER SPINS HIS WEB...

JUSTICE LEAGUE of AMERICA

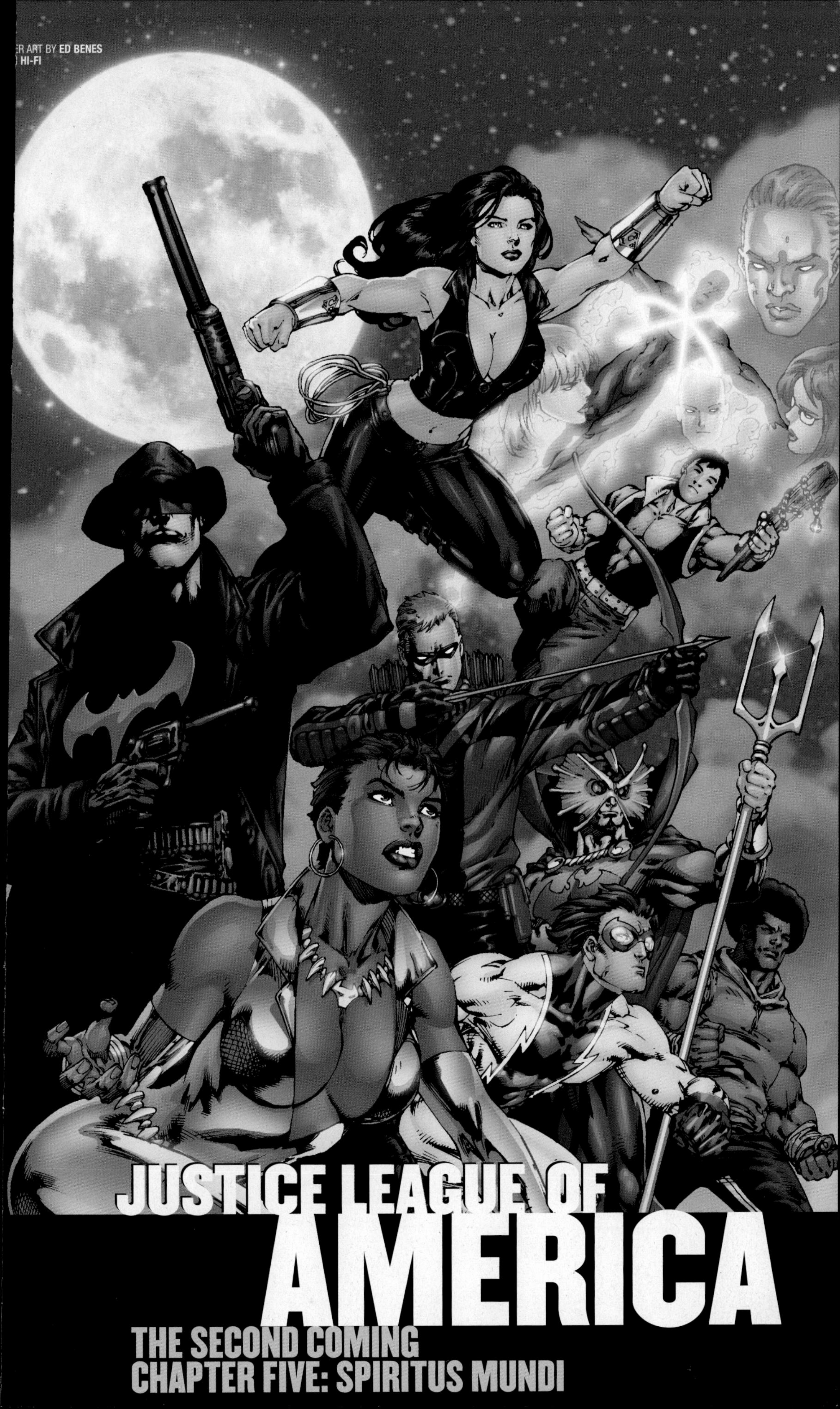
ER ART BY ED BENES
HI-FI
JUSTICE LEAGUE OF
AMERICA
THE SECOND COMING
CHAPTER FIVE: SPIRITUS MUNDI

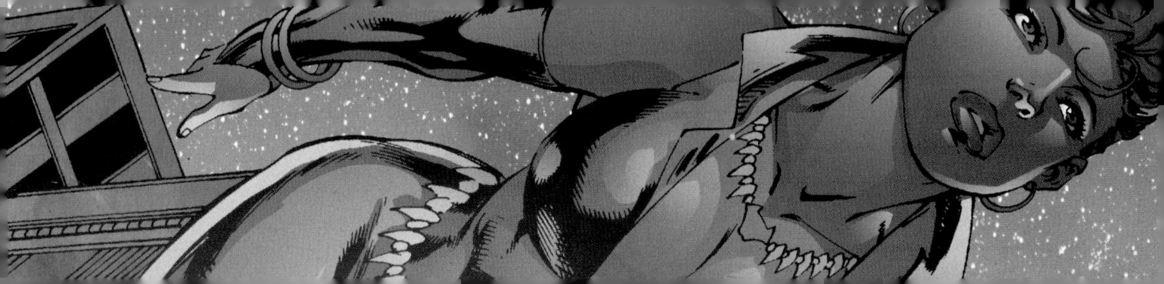

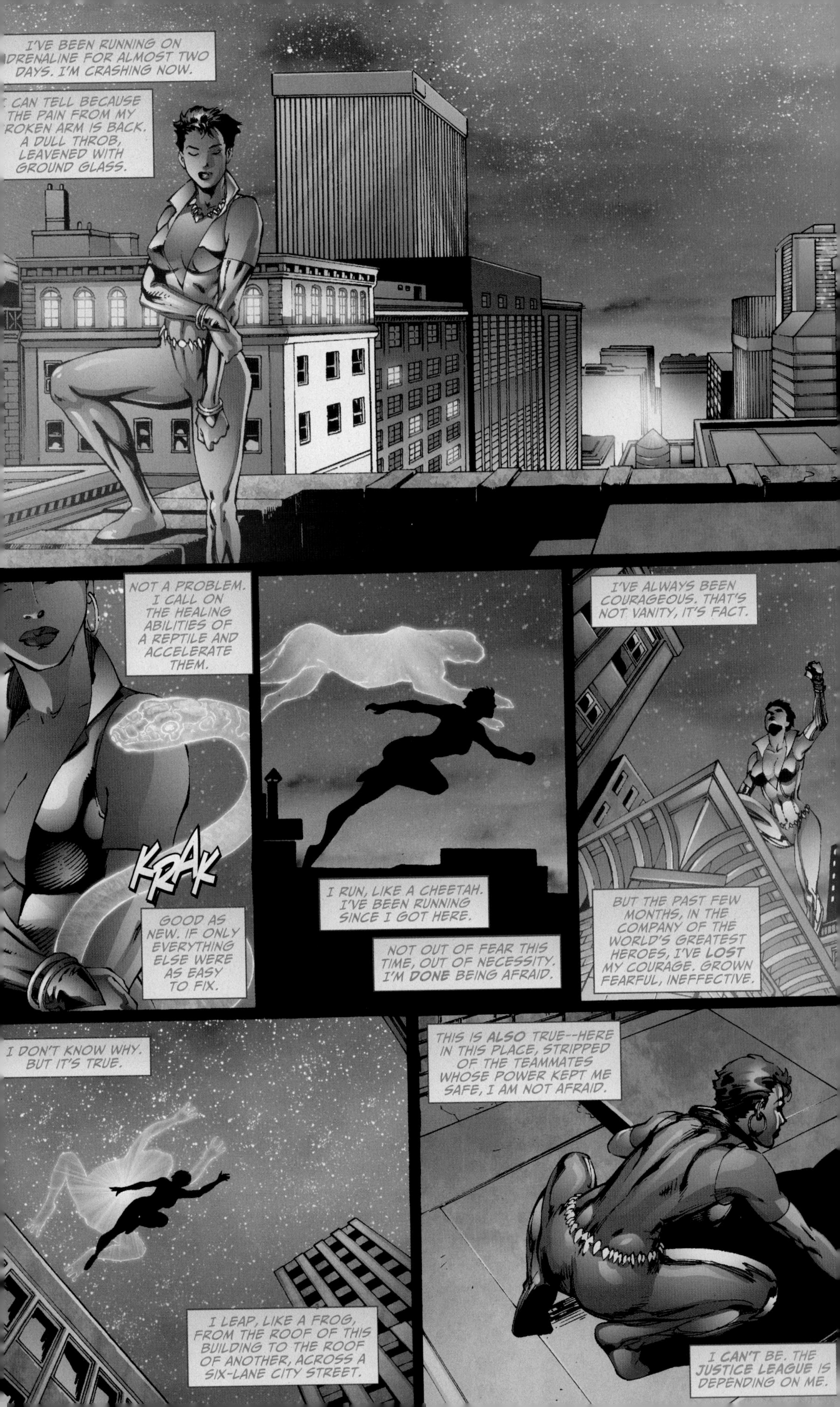
I'VE BEEN RUNNING ON ADRENALINE FOR ALMOST TWO DAYS. I'M CRASHING NOW.
I CAN TELL BECAUSE THE PAIN FROM MY BROKEN ARM IS BACK. A DULL THROB, LEAVENED WITH GROUND GLASS.
NOT A PROBLEM. I CALL ON THE HEALING ABILITIES OF A REPTILE AND ACCELERATE THEM.
KRAK
GOOD AS NEW. IF ONLY EVERYTHING ELSE WERE AS EASY TO FIX.
I RUN, LIKE A CHEETAH. I'VE BEEN RUNNING SINCE I GOT HERE.
NOT OUT OF FEAR THIS TIME, OUT OF NECESSITY. I'M DONE BEING AFRAID.
I'VE ALWAYS BEEN COURAGEOUS. THAT'S NOT VANITY, IT'S FACT.
BUT THE PAST FEW MONTHS, IN THE COMPANY OF THE WORLD'S GREATEST HEROES, I'VE LOST MY COURAGE. GROWN FEARFUL, INEFFECTIVE.
I DON'T KNOW WHY. BUT IT'S TRUE.
I LEAP, LIKE A FROG, FROM THE ROOF OF THIS BUILDING TO THE ROOF OF ANOTHER, ACROSS A SIX-LANE CITY STREET.
THIS IS ALSO TRUE--HERE IN THIS PLACE, STRIPPED OF THE TEAMMATES WHOSE POWER KEPT ME SAFE, I AM NOT AFRAID.
I CAN'T BE. THE JUSTICE LEAGUE IS DEPENDING ON ME.

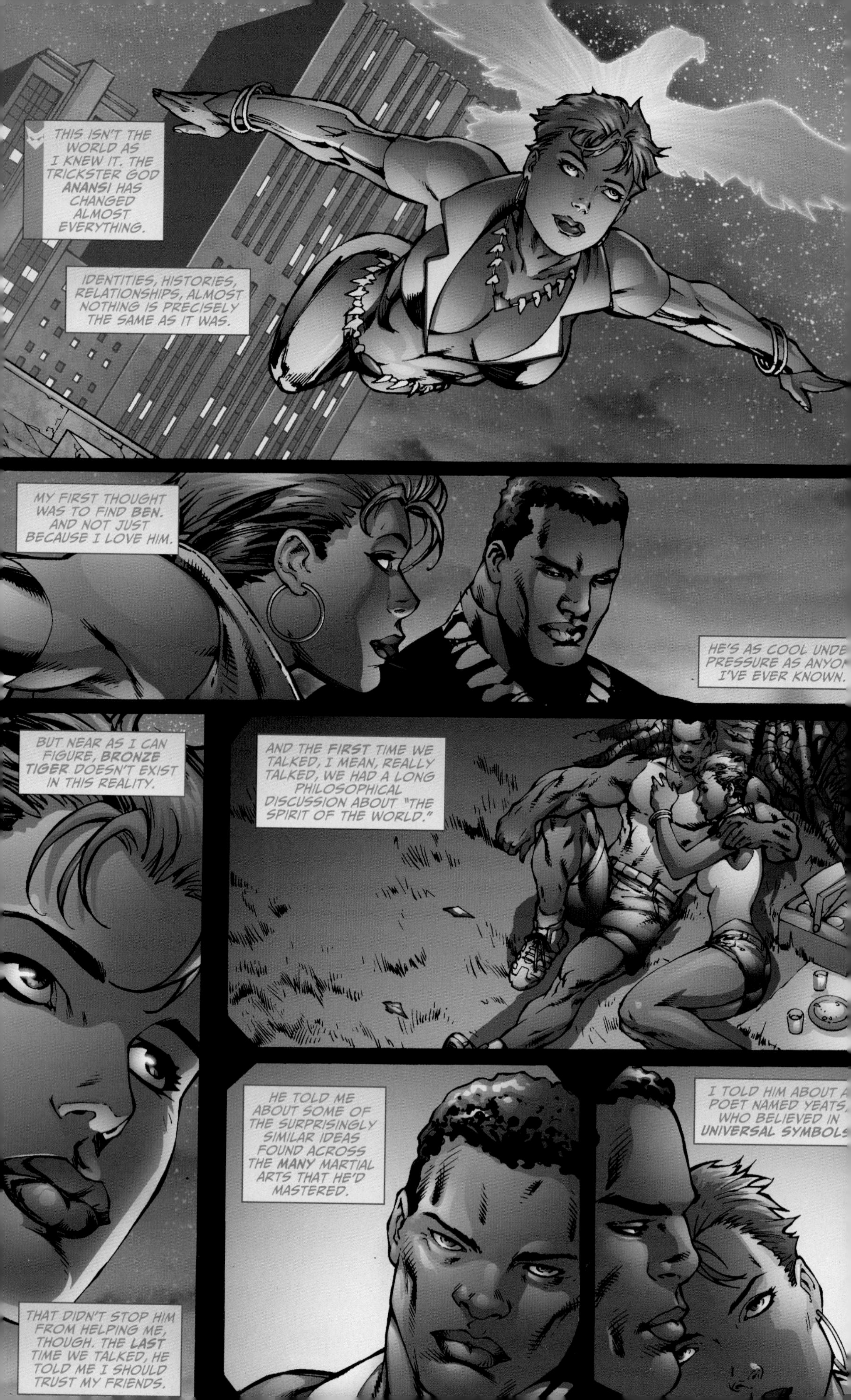
THIS ISN'T THE WORLD AS I KNEW IT. THE TRICKSTER GOD ANANSI HAS CHANGED ALMOST EVERYTHING.
IDENTITIES, HISTORIES, RELATIONSHIPS, ALMOST NOTHING IS PRECISELY THE SAME AS IT WAS.
MY FIRST THOUGHT WAS TO FIND BEN. AND NOT JUST BECAUSE I LOVE HIM.
HE'S AS COOL UNDE PRESSURE AS ANYO I'VE EVER KNOWN.
BUT NEAR AS I CAN FIGURE, BRONZE TIGER DOESN'T EXIST IN THIS REALITY.
AND THE FIRST TIME WE TALKED, I MEAN, REALLY TALKED, WE HAD A LONG PHILOSOPHICAL DISCUSSION ABOUT "THE SPIRIT OF THE WORLD."
HE TOLD ME ABOUT SOME OF THE SURPRISINGLY SIMILAR IDEAS FOUND ACROSS THE MANY MARTIAL ARTS THAT HE'D MASTERED.
I TOLD HIM ABOUT A POET NAMED YEATS, WHO BELIEVED IN UNIVERSAL SYMBOLS
THAT DIDN'T STOP HIM FROM HELPING ME, THOUGH. THE LAST TIME WE TALKED, HE TOLD ME I SHOULD TRUST MY FRIENDS.

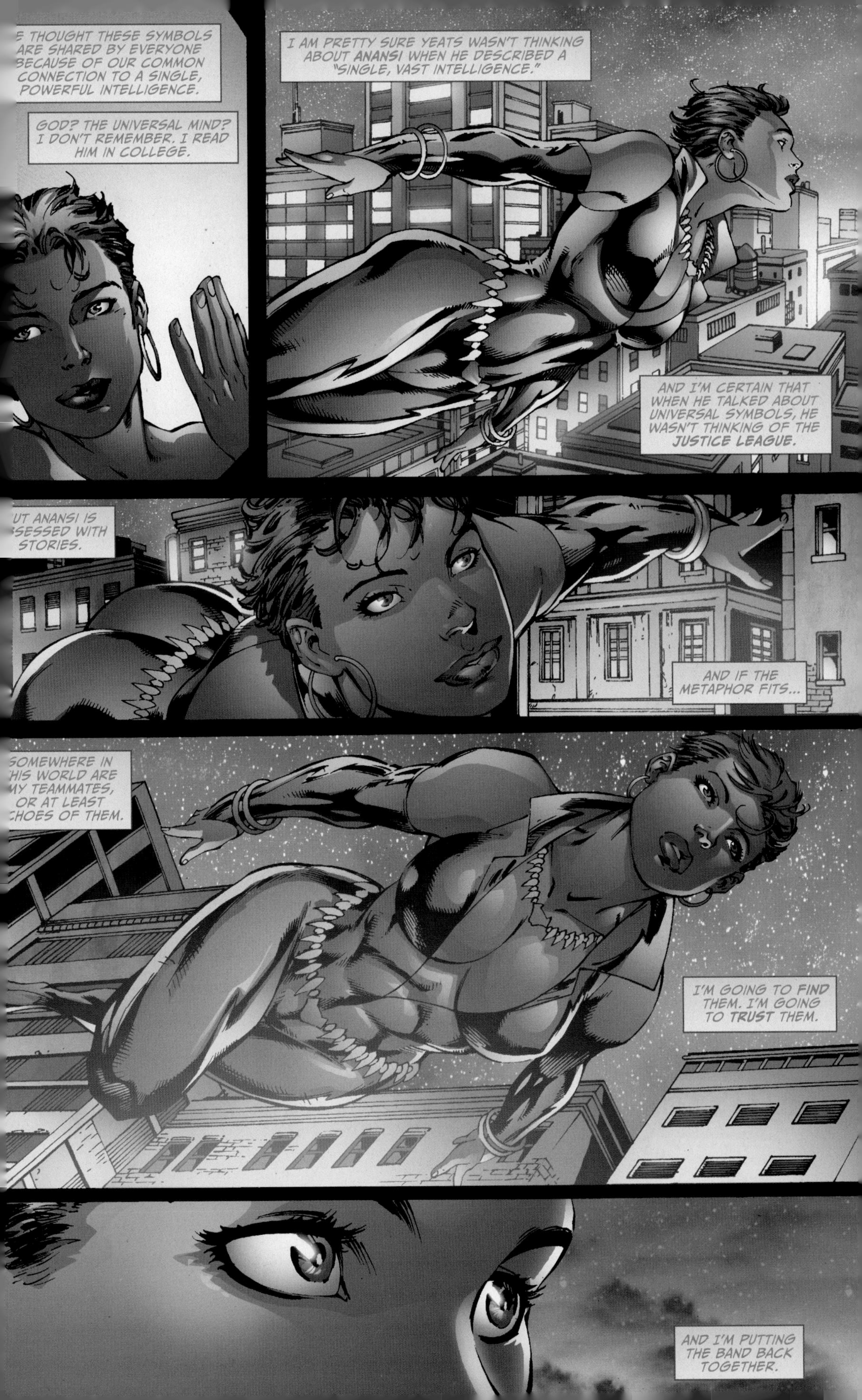
E THOUGHT THESE SYMBOLS ARE SHARED BY EVERYONE BECAUSE OF OUR COMMON CONNECTION TO A SINGLE, POWERFUL INTELLIGENCE.
GOD? THE UNIVERSAL MIND? I DON'T REMEMBER. I READ HIM IN COLLEGE.
I AM PRETTY SURE YEATS WASN'T THINKING ABOUT ANANSI WHEN HE DESCRIBED A "SINGLE, VAST INTELLIGENCE."
AND I'M CERTAIN THAT WHEN HE TALKED ABOUT UNIVERSAL SYMBOLS, HE WASN'T THINKING OF THE JUSTICE LEAGUE.
UT ANANSI IS SESSED WITH STORIES.
AND IF THE METAPHOR FITS...
SOMEWHERE IN HIS WORLD ARE MY TEAMMATES, OR AT LEAST CHOES OF THEM.
I'M GOING TO FIND THEM. I'M GOING TO TRUST THEM.
AND I'M PUTTING THE BAND BACK TOGETHER.

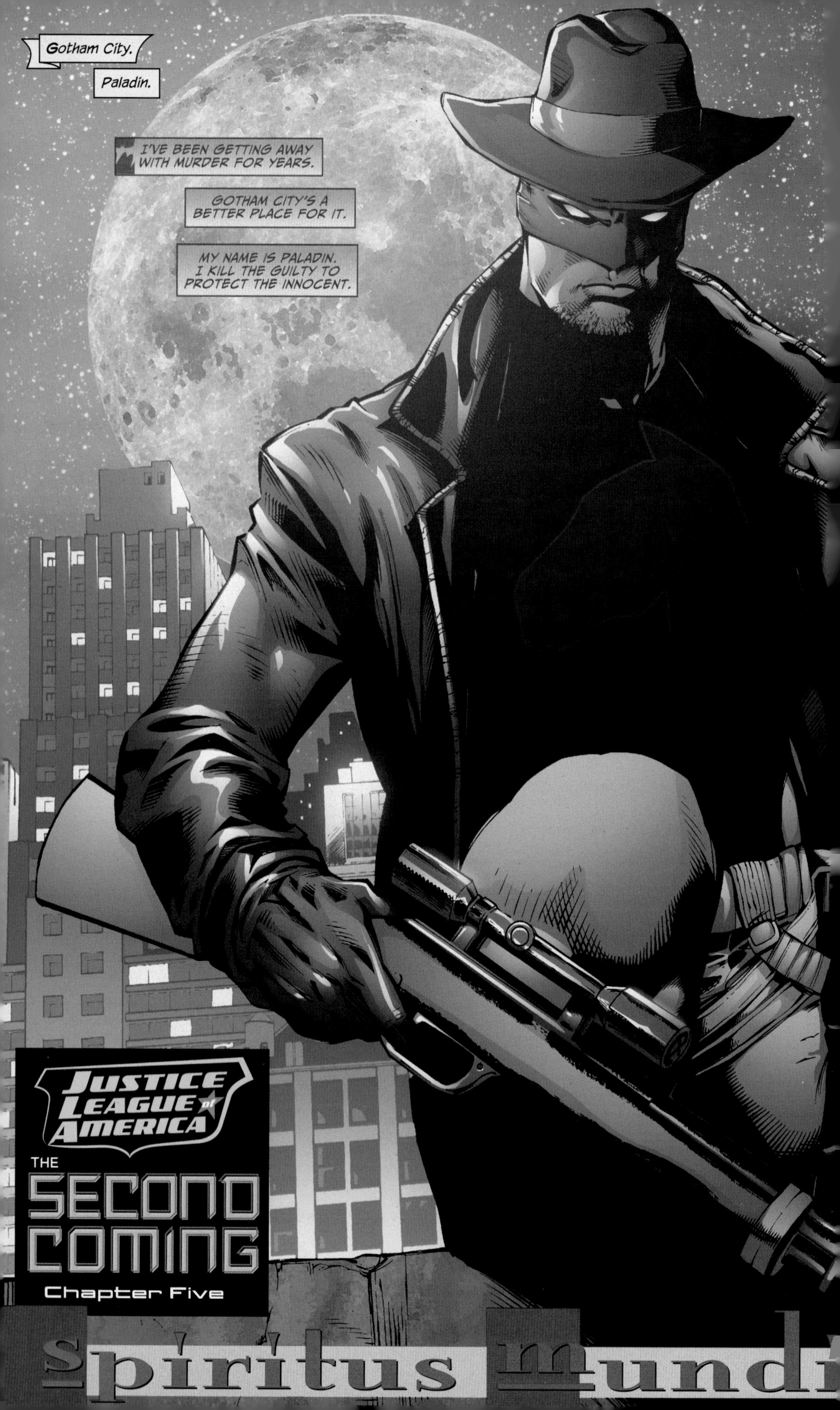
Gotham City.
Paladin.
I'VE BEEN GETTING AWAY WITH MURDER FOR YEARS.
GOTHAM CITY'S A BETTER PLACE FOR IT.
MY NAME IS PALADIN. I KILL THE GUILTY TO PROTECT THE INNOCENT.
JUSTICE LEAGUE of AMERICA
THE SECOND COMING
Chapter Five
Spiritus Mundi

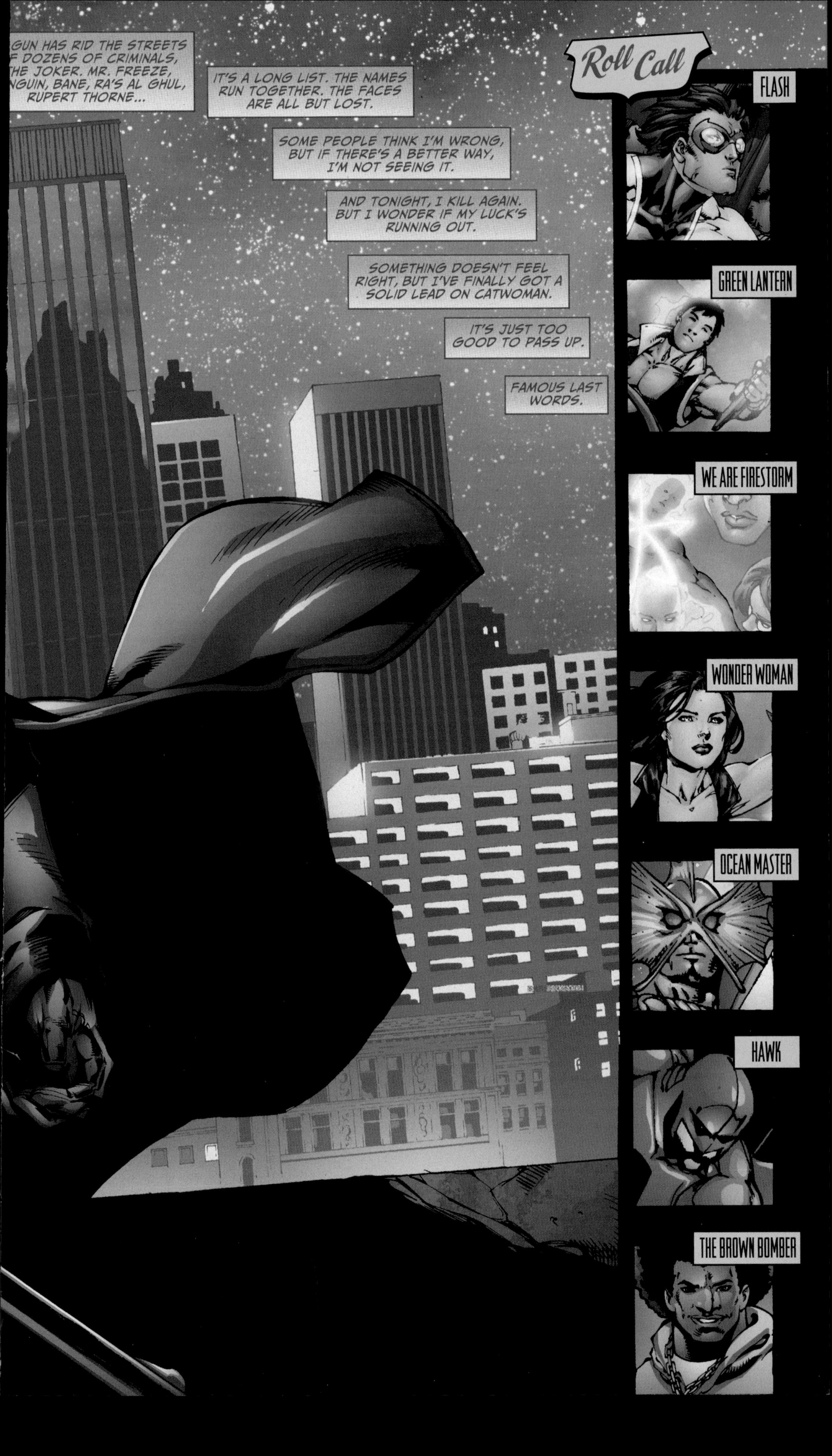
GUN HAS RID THE STREETS F DOZENS OF CRIMINALS, HE JOKER. MR. FREEZE, NGUIN, BANE, RA'S AL GHUL, RUPERT THORNE...
IT'S A LONG LIST. THE NAMES RUN TOGETHER. THE FACES ARE ALL BUT LOST.
SOME PEOPLE THINK I'M WRONG, BUT IF THERE'S A BETTER WAY, I'M NOT SEEING IT.
AND TONIGHT, I KILL AGAIN. BUT I WONDER IF MY LUCK'S RUNNING OUT.
SOMETHING DOESN'T FEEL RIGHT, BUT I'VE FINALLY GOT A SOLID LEAD ON CATWOMAN.
IT'S JUST TOO GOOD TO PASS UP.
FAMOUS LAST WORDS.
Roll Call
FLASH
GREEN LANTERN
WE ARE FIRESTORM
WONDER WOMAN
OCEAN MASTER
HAWK
THE BROWN BOMBER

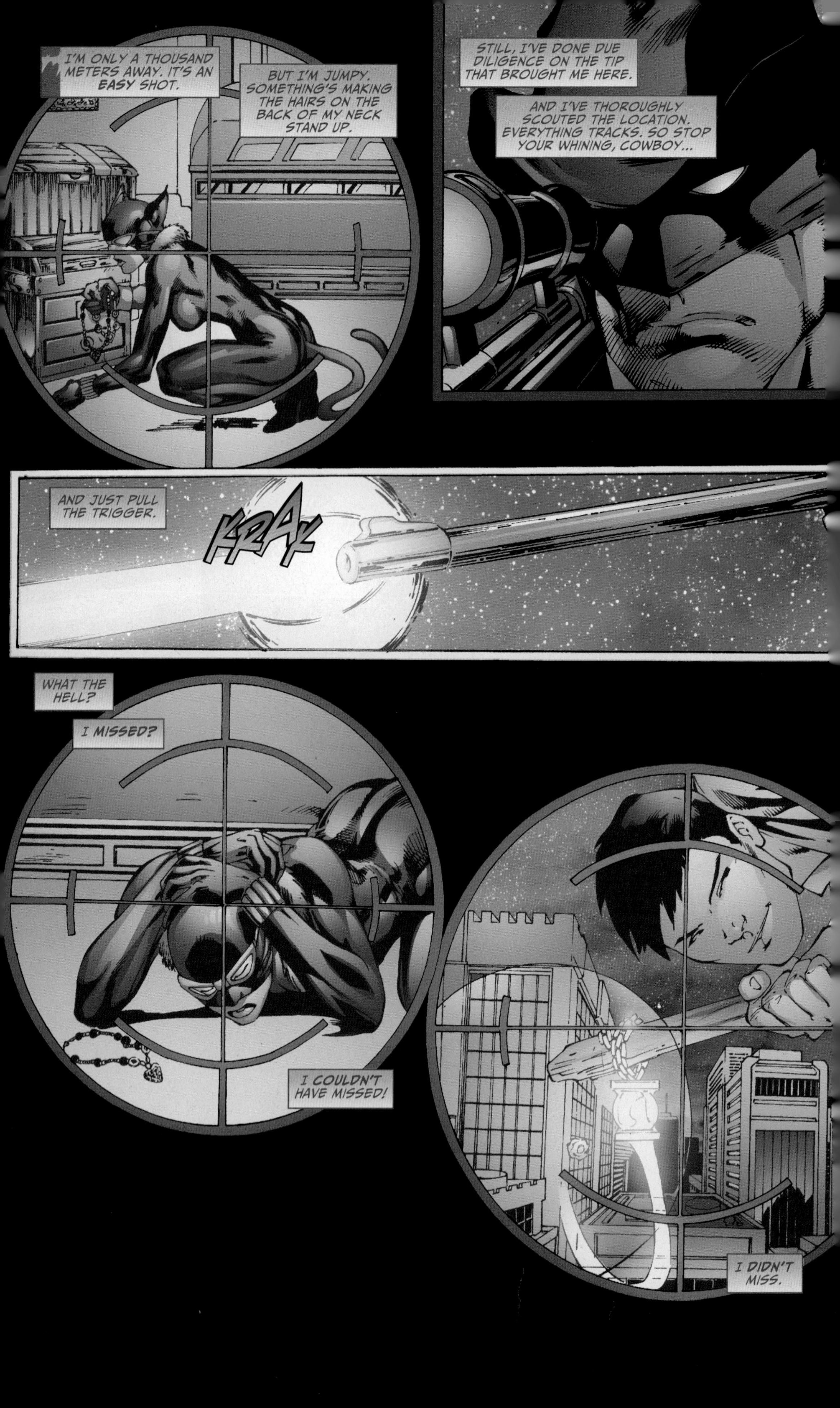
I'M ONLY A THOUSAND METERS AWAY. IT'S AN EASY SHOT.
BUT I'M JUMPY. SOMETHING'S MAKING THE HAIRS ON THE BACK OF MY NECK STAND UP.
STILL, I'VE DONE DUE DILIGENCE ON THE TIP THAT BROUGHT ME HERE.
AND I'VE THOROUGHLY SCOUTED THE LOCATION. EVERYTHING TRACKS. SO STOP YOUR WHINING, COWBOY...
AND JUST PULL THE TRIGGER.
KRAK
WHAT THE HELL?
I MISSED?
I COULDN'T HAVE MISSED!
I DIDN'T MISS.

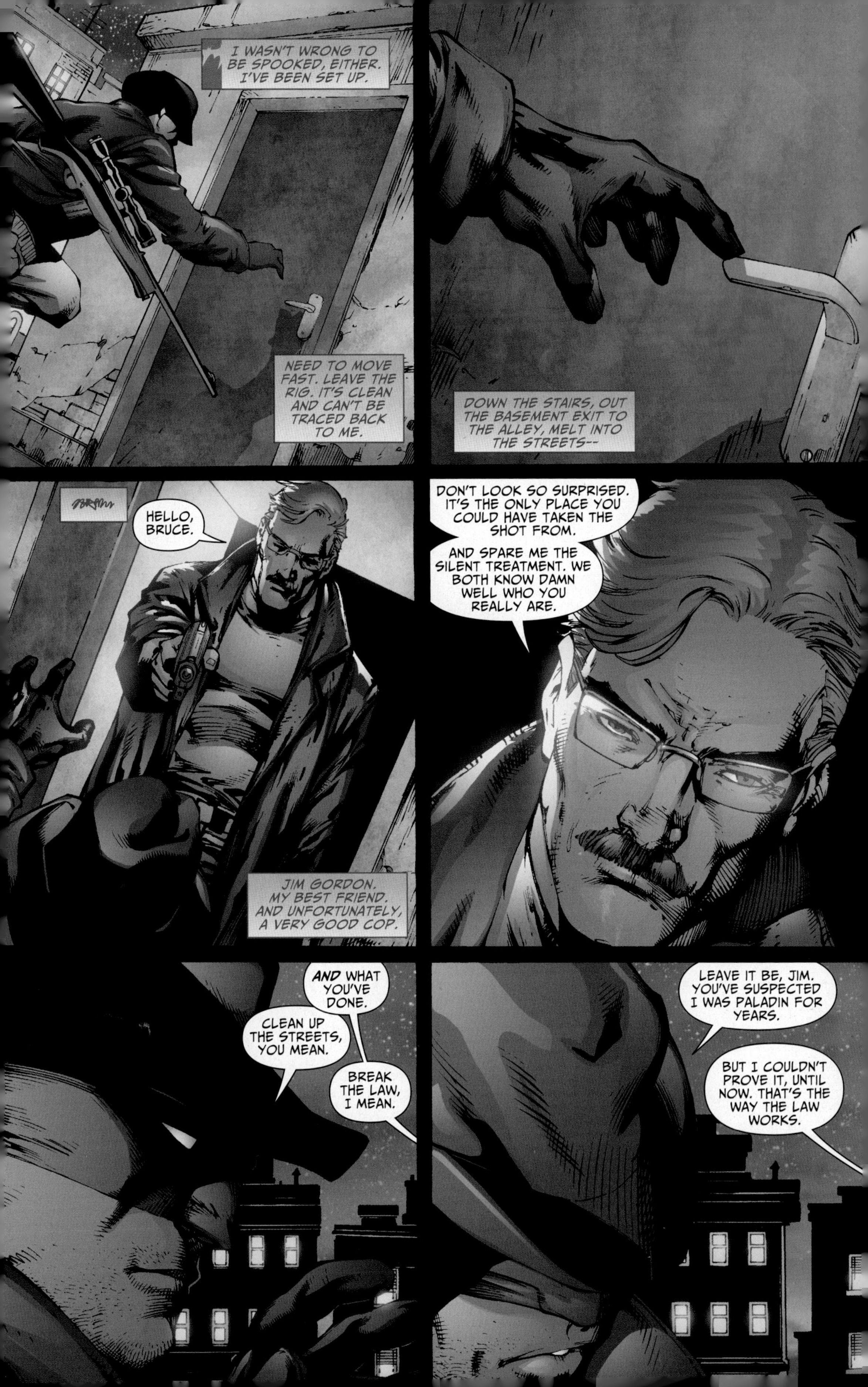
I WASN'T WRONG TO BE SPOOKED, EITHER. I'VE BEEN SET UP.
NEED TO MOVE FAST. LEAVE THE RIG. IT'S CLEAN AND CAN'T BE TRACED BACK TO ME.
DOWN THE STAIRS, OUT THE BASEMENT EXIT TO THE ALLEY, MELT INTO THE STREETS--
HELLO, BRUCE.
JIM GORDON. MY BEST FRIEND. AND UNFORTUNATELY, A VERY GOOD COP.
DON'T LOOK SO SURPRISED. IT'S THE ONLY PLACE YOU COULD HAVE TAKEN THE SHOT FROM.
AND SPARE ME THE SILENT TREATMENT. WE BOTH KNOW DAMN WELL WHO YOU REALLY ARE.
AND WHAT YOU'VE DONE.
CLEAN UP THE STREETS, YOU MEAN.
BREAK THE LAW, I MEAN.
LEAVE IT BE, JIM. YOU'VE SUSPECTED I WAS PALADIN FOR YEARS.
BUT I COULDN'T PROVE IT, UNTIL NOW. THAT'S THE WAY THE LAW WORKS.

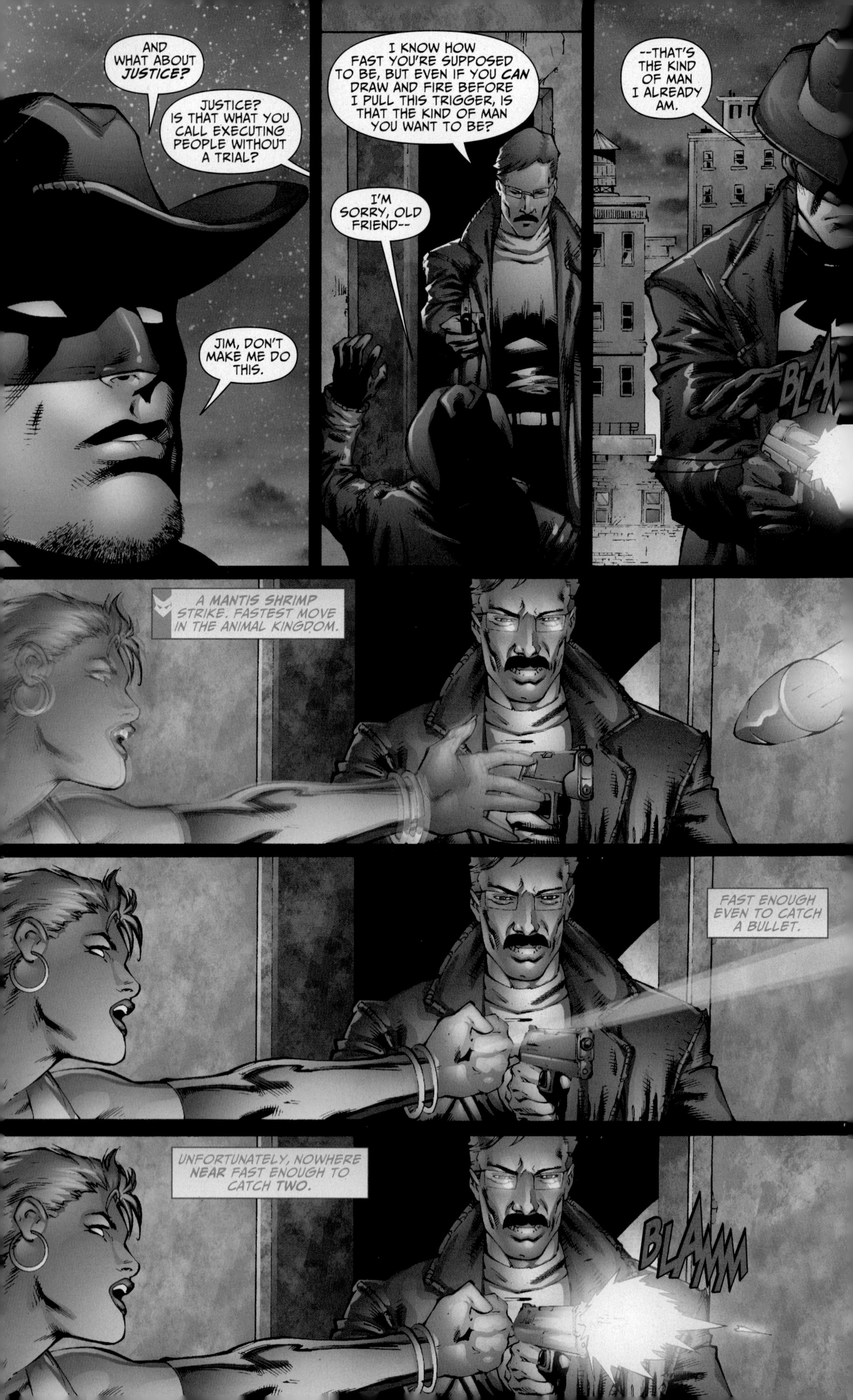
AND WHAT ABOUT JUSTICE?
JUSTICE? IS THAT WHAT YOU CALL EXECUTING PEOPLE WITHOUT A TRIAL?
JIM, DON'T MAKE ME DO THIS.
I KNOW HOW FAST YOU'RE SUPPOSED TO BE, BUT EVEN IF YOU CAN DRAW AND FIRE BEFORE I PULL THIS TRIGGER, IS THAT THE KIND OF MAN YOU WANT TO BE?
I'M SORRY, OLD FRIEND--
--THAT'S THE KIND OF MAN I ALREADY AM.
BLAM
A MANTIS SHRIMP STRIKE. FASTEST MOVE IN THE ANIMAL KINGDOM.
FAST ENOUGH EVEN TO CATCH A BULLET.
UNFORTUNATELY, NOWHERE NEAR FAST ENOUGH TO CATCH TWO.
BLAMM

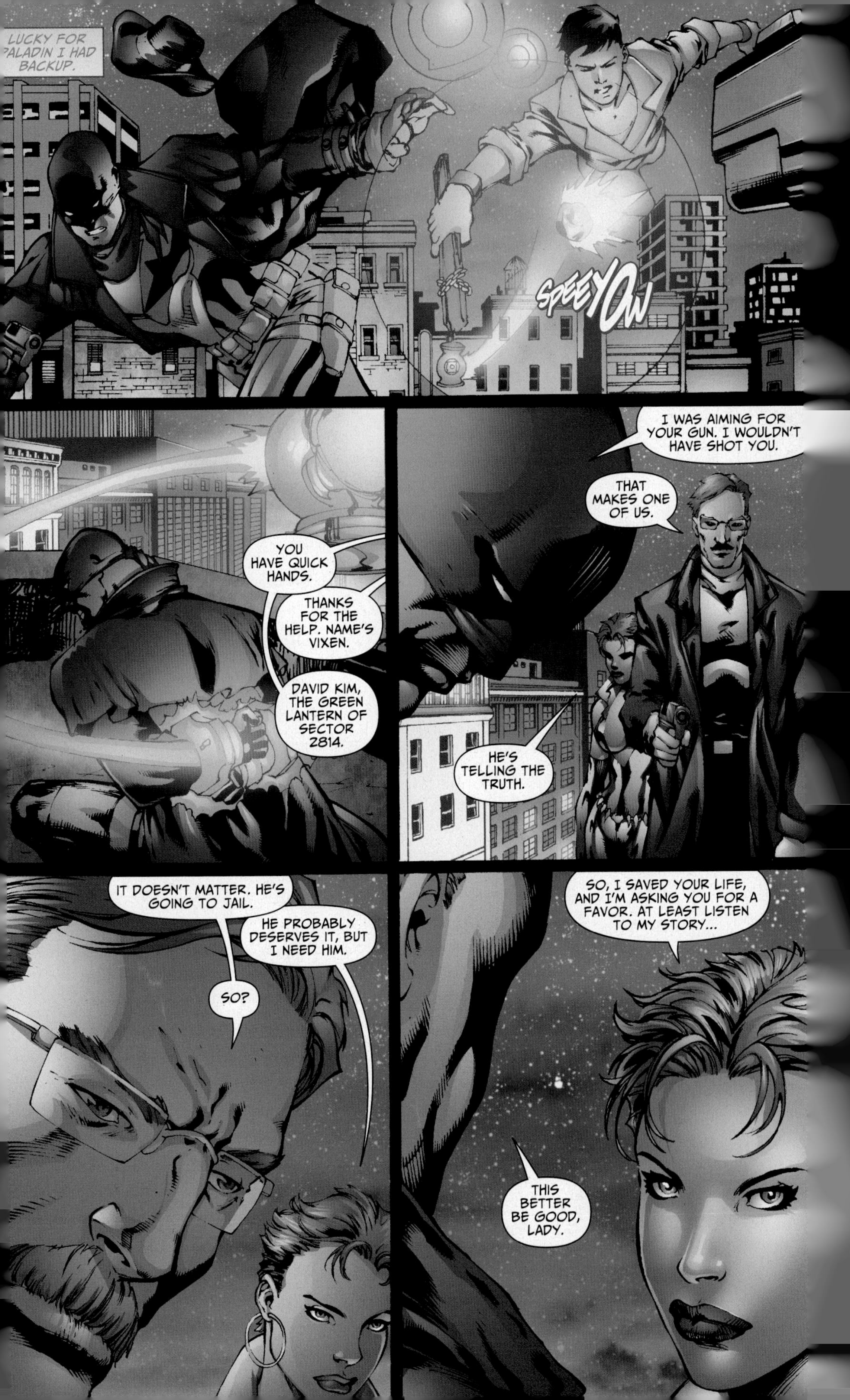

LUCKY FOR PALADIN I HAD BACKUP.
SPEEYOW
YOU HAVE QUICK HANDS.
THANKS FOR THE HELP. NAME'S VIXEN.
DAVID KIM, THE GREEN LANTERN OF SECTOR 2814.
I WAS AIMING FOR YOUR GUN. I WOULDN'T HAVE SHOT YOU.
THAT MAKES ONE OF US.
HE'S TELLING THE TRUTH.
IT DOESN'T MATTER. HE'S GOING TO JAIL.
HE PROBABLY DESERVES IT, BUT I NEED HIM.
SO?
SO, I SAVED YOUR LIFE, AND I'M ASKING YOU FOR A FAVOR. AT LEAST LISTEN TO MY STORY...
THIS BETTER BE GOOD, LADY.

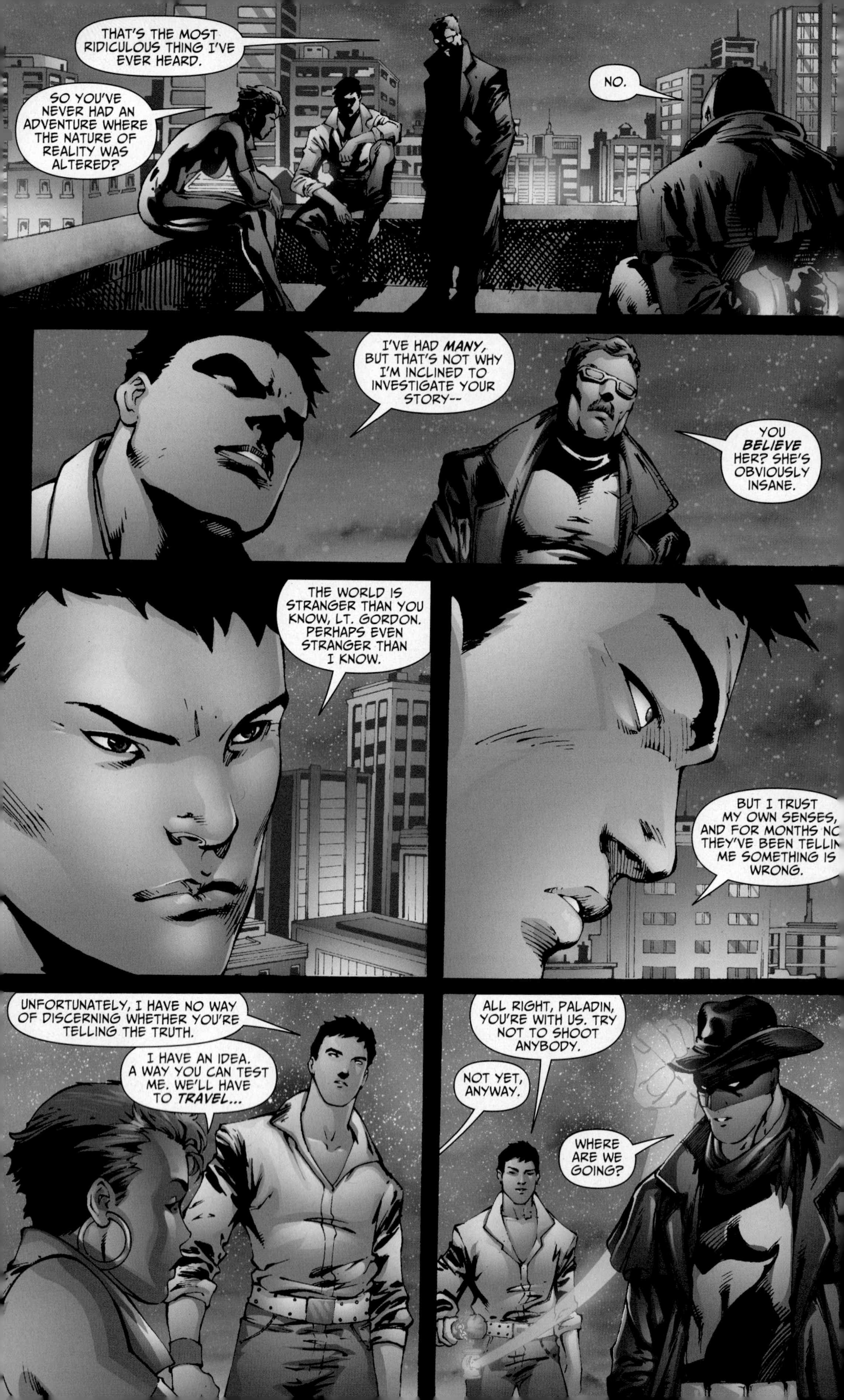
THAT'S THE MOST RIDICULOUS THING I'VE EVER HEARD.
SO YOU'VE NEVER HAD AN ADVENTURE WHERE THE NATURE OF REALITY WAS ALTERED?
NO.
I'VE HAD MANY, BUT THAT'S NOT WHY I'M INCLINED TO INVESTIGATE YOUR STORY--
YOU BELIEVE HER? SHE'S OBVIOUSLY INSANE.
THE WORLD IS STRANGER THAN YOU KNOW, LT. GORDON. PERHAPS EVEN STRANGER THAN I KNOW.
BUT I TRUST MY OWN SENSES, AND FOR MONTHS NO THEY'VE BEEN TELLING ME SOMETHING IS WRONG.
UNFORTUNATELY, I HAVE NO WAY OF DISCERNING WHETHER YOU'RE TELLING THE TRUTH.
I HAVE AN IDEA. A WAY YOU CAN TEST ME. WE'LL HAVE TO TRAVEL...
ALL RIGHT, PALADIN, YOU'RE WITH US. TRY NOT TO SHOOT ANYBODY.
NOT YET, ANYWAY.
WHERE ARE WE GOING?

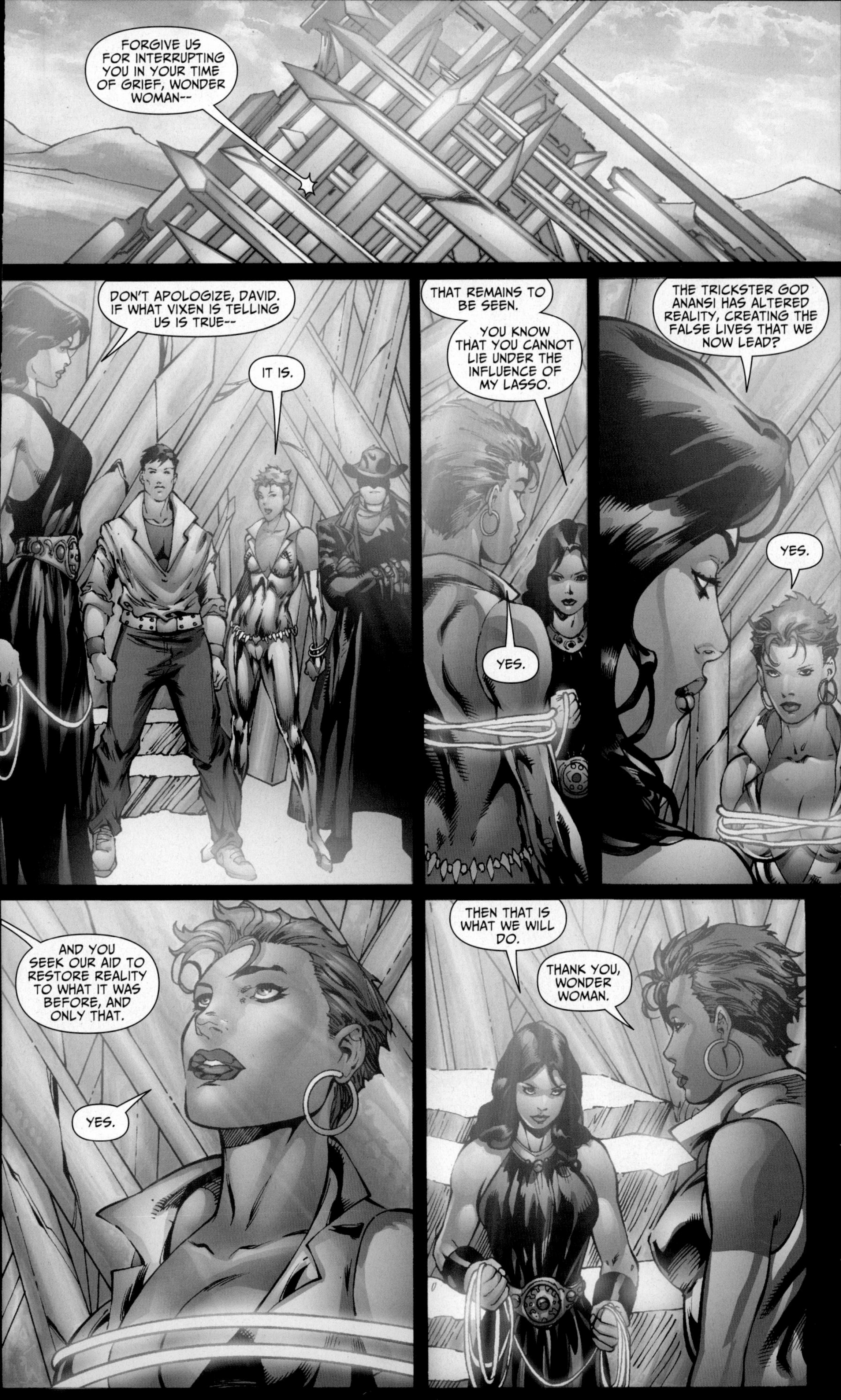
FORGIVE US FOR INTERRUPTING YOU IN YOUR TIME OF GRIEF, WONDER WOMAN--
DON'T APOLOGIZE, DAVID. IF WHAT VIXEN IS TELLING US IS TRUE--
IT IS.
THAT REMAINS TO BE SEEN.
YOU KNOW THAT YOU CANNOT LIE UNDER THE INFLUENCE OF MY LASSO.
YES.
THE TRICKSTER GOD ANANSI HAS ALTERED REALITY, CREATING THE FALSE LIVES THAT WE NOW LEAD?
YES.
AND YOU SEEK OUR AID TO RESTORE REALITY TO WHAT IT WAS BEFORE, AND ONLY THAT.
YES.
THEN THAT IS WHAT WE WILL DO.
THANK YOU, WONDER WOMAN.

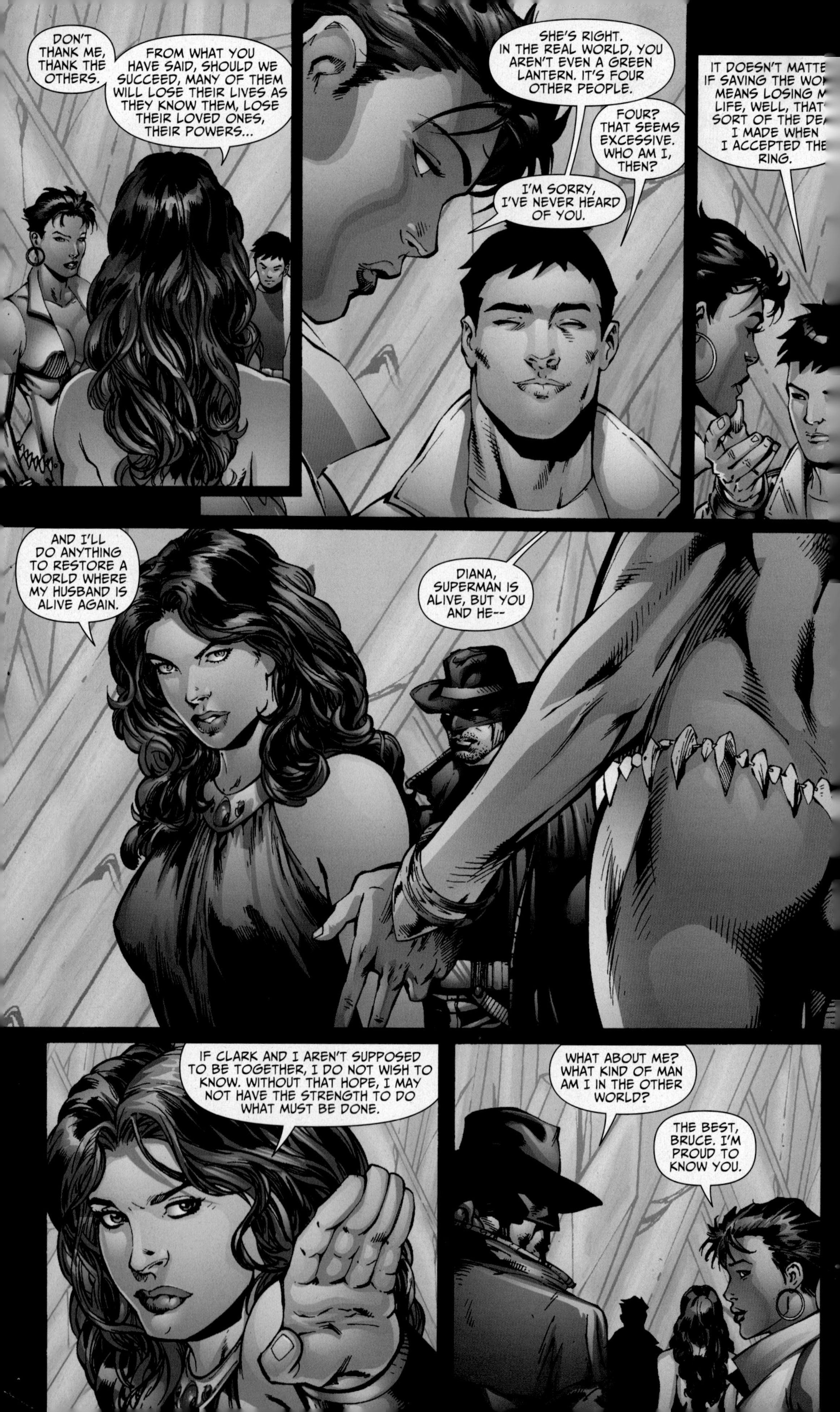

DON'T THANK ME, THANK THE OTHERS.
FROM WHAT YOU HAVE SAID, SHOULD WE SUCCEED, MANY OF THEM WILL LOSE THEIR LIVES AS THEY KNOW THEM, LOSE THEIR LOVED ONES, THEIR POWERS...
SHE'S RIGHT. IN THE REAL WORLD, YOU AREN'T EVEN A GREEN LANTERN. IT'S FOUR OTHER PEOPLE.
FOUR? THAT SEEMS EXCESSIVE. WHO AM I, THEN?
I'M SORRY, I'VE NEVER HEARD OF YOU.
IT DOESN'T MATTE IF SAVING THE WO MEANS LOSING M LIFE, WELL, THAT SORT OF THE DEA I MADE WHEN I ACCEPTED THE RING.
AND I'LL DO ANYTHING TO RESTORE A WORLD WHERE MY HUSBAND IS ALIVE AGAIN.
DIANA, SUPERMAN IS ALIVE, BUT YOU AND HE--
IF CLARK AND I AREN'T SUPPOSED TO BE TOGETHER, I DO NOT WISH TO KNOW. WITHOUT THAT HOPE, I MAY NOT HAVE THE STRENGTH TO DO WHAT MUST BE DONE.
WHAT ABOUT ME? WHAT KIND OF MAN AM I IN THE OTHER WORLD?
THE BEST, BRUCE. I'M PROUD TO KNOW YOU.

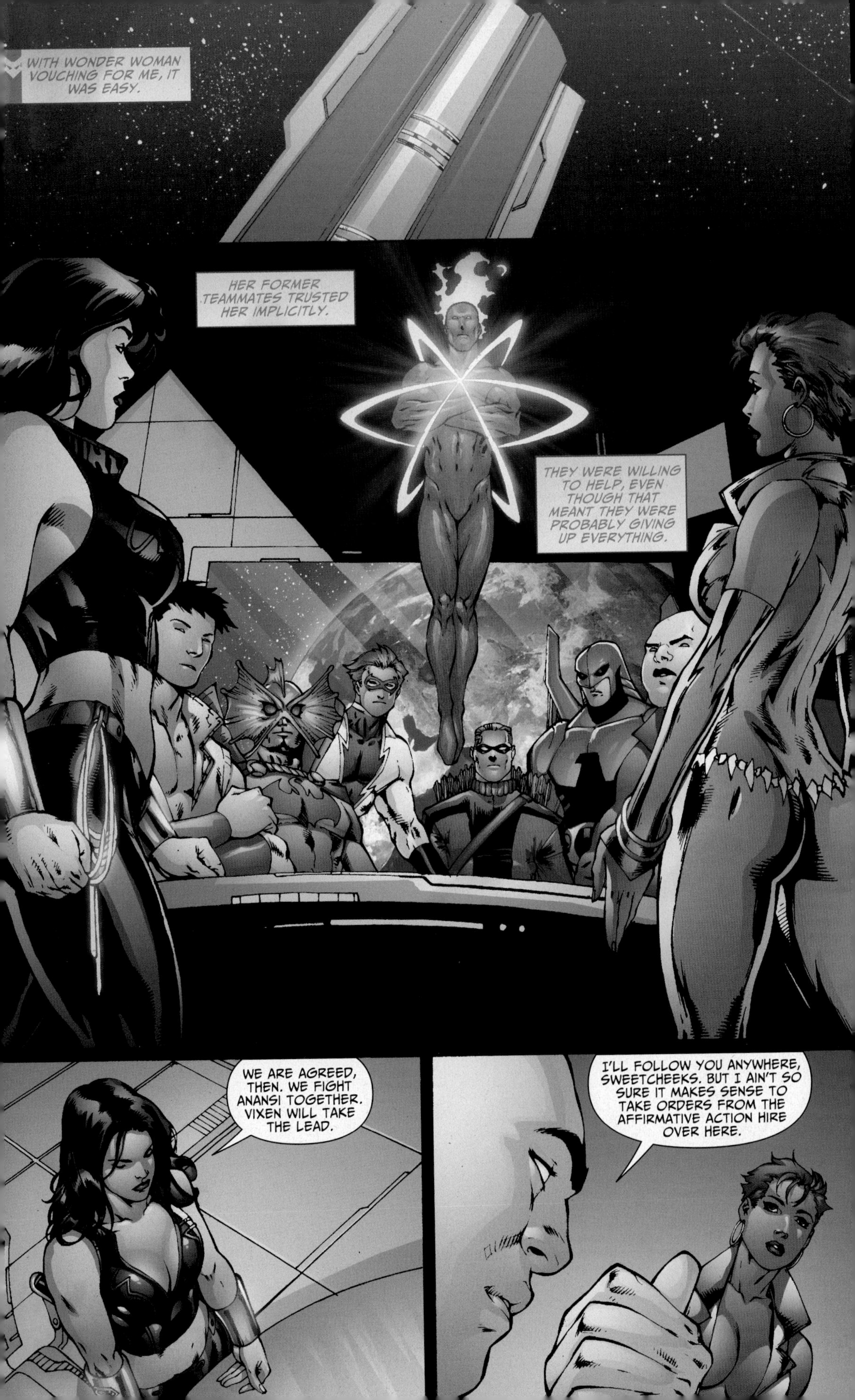
WITH WONDER WOMAN VOUCHING FOR ME, IT WAS EASY.
HER FORMER TEAMMATES TRUSTED HER IMPLICITLY.
THEY WERE WILLING TO HELP, EVEN THOUGH THAT MEANT THEY WERE PROBABLY GIVING UP EVERYTHING.
WE ARE AGREED, THEN. WE FIGHT ANANSI TOGETHER. VIXEN WILL TAKE THE LEAD.
I'LL FOLLOW YOU ANYWHERE, SWEETCHEEKS. BUT I AIN'T SO SURE IT MAKES SENSE TO TAKE ORDERS FROM THE AFFIRMATIVE ACTION HIRE OVER HERE.

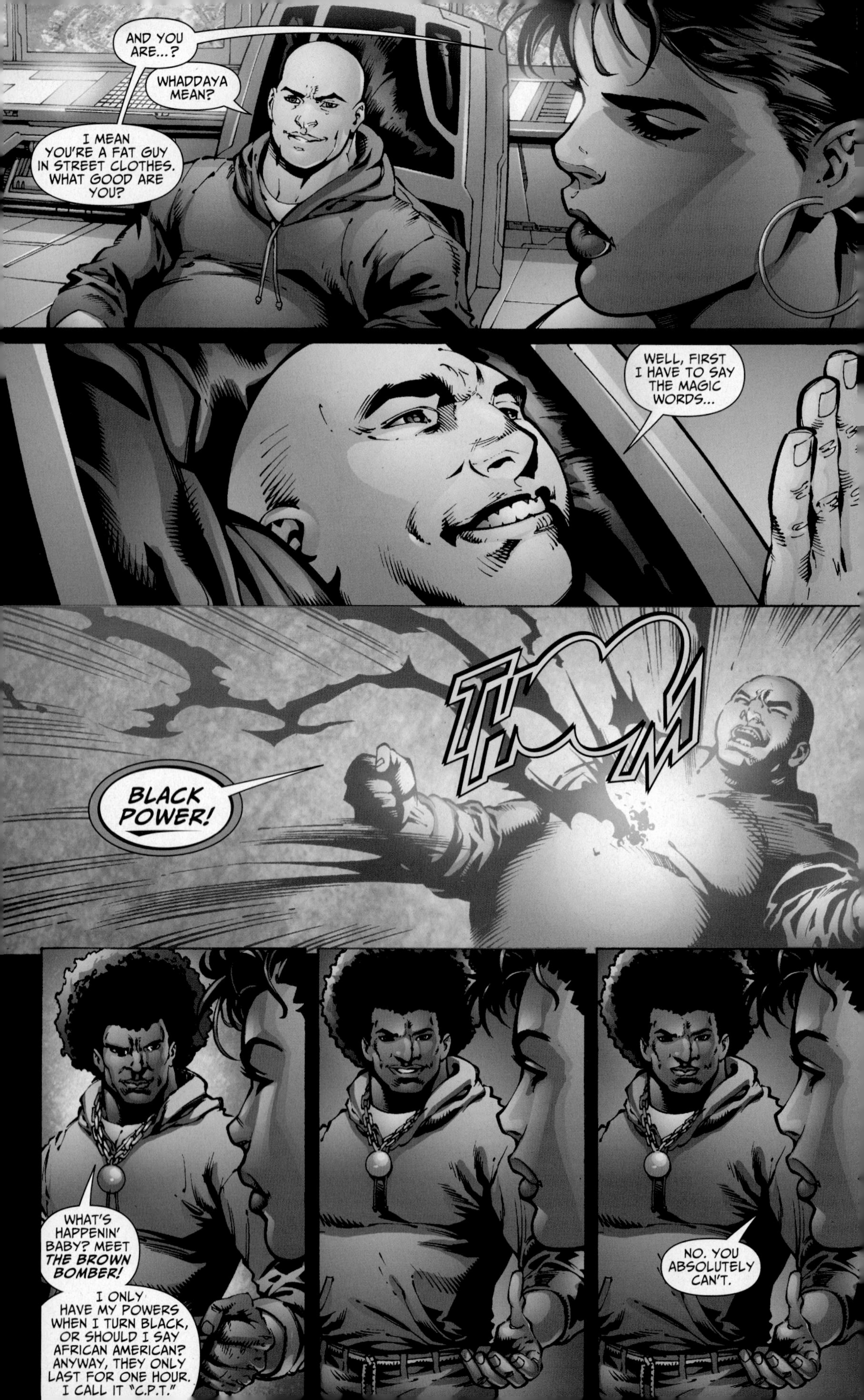
AND YOU ARE...?
WHADDAYA MEAN?
I MEAN YOU'RE A FAT GUY IN STREET CLOTHES. WHAT GOOD ARE YOU?
WELL, FIRST I HAVE TO SAY THE MAGIC WORDS...
BLACK POWER!
THOOM
WHAT'S HAPPENIN' BABY? MEET THE BROWN BOMBER!
I ONLY HAVE MY POWERS WHEN I TURN BLACK, OR SHOULD I SAY AFRICAN AMERICAN? ANYWAY, THEY ONLY LAST FOR ONE HOUR. I CALL IT "C.P.T."
NO. YOU ABSOLUTELY CAN'T.

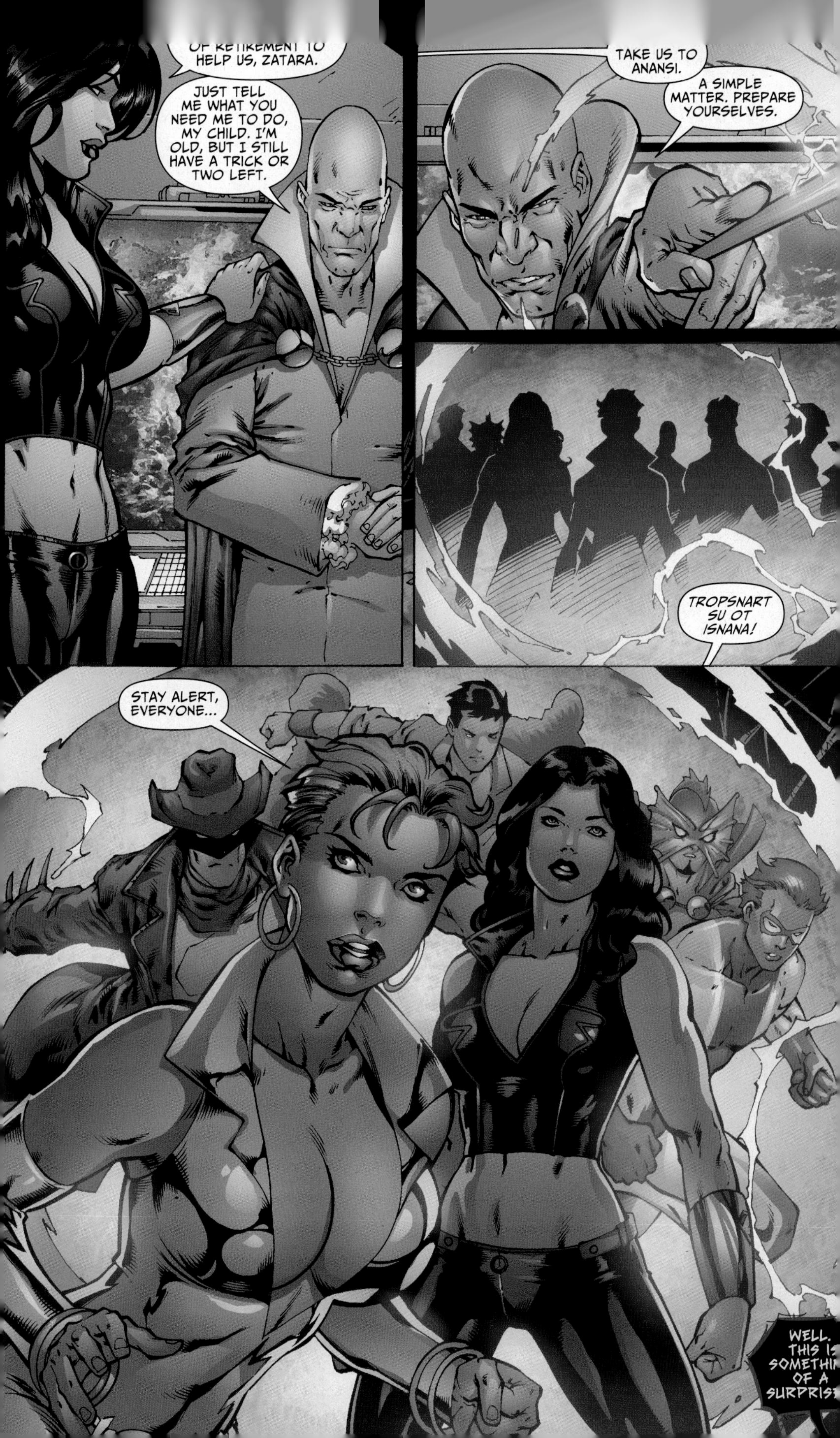
OF RETIREMENT TO HELP US, ZATARA.
JUST TELL ME WHAT YOU NEED ME TO DO, MY CHILD. I'M OLD, BUT I STILL HAVE A TRICK OR TWO LEFT.
TAKE US TO ANANSI.
A SIMPLE MATTER. PREPARE YOURSELVES.
TROPSNART SU OT ISNANA!
STAY ALERT, EVERYONE...
WELL. THIS I SOMETHIN OF A SURPRIS

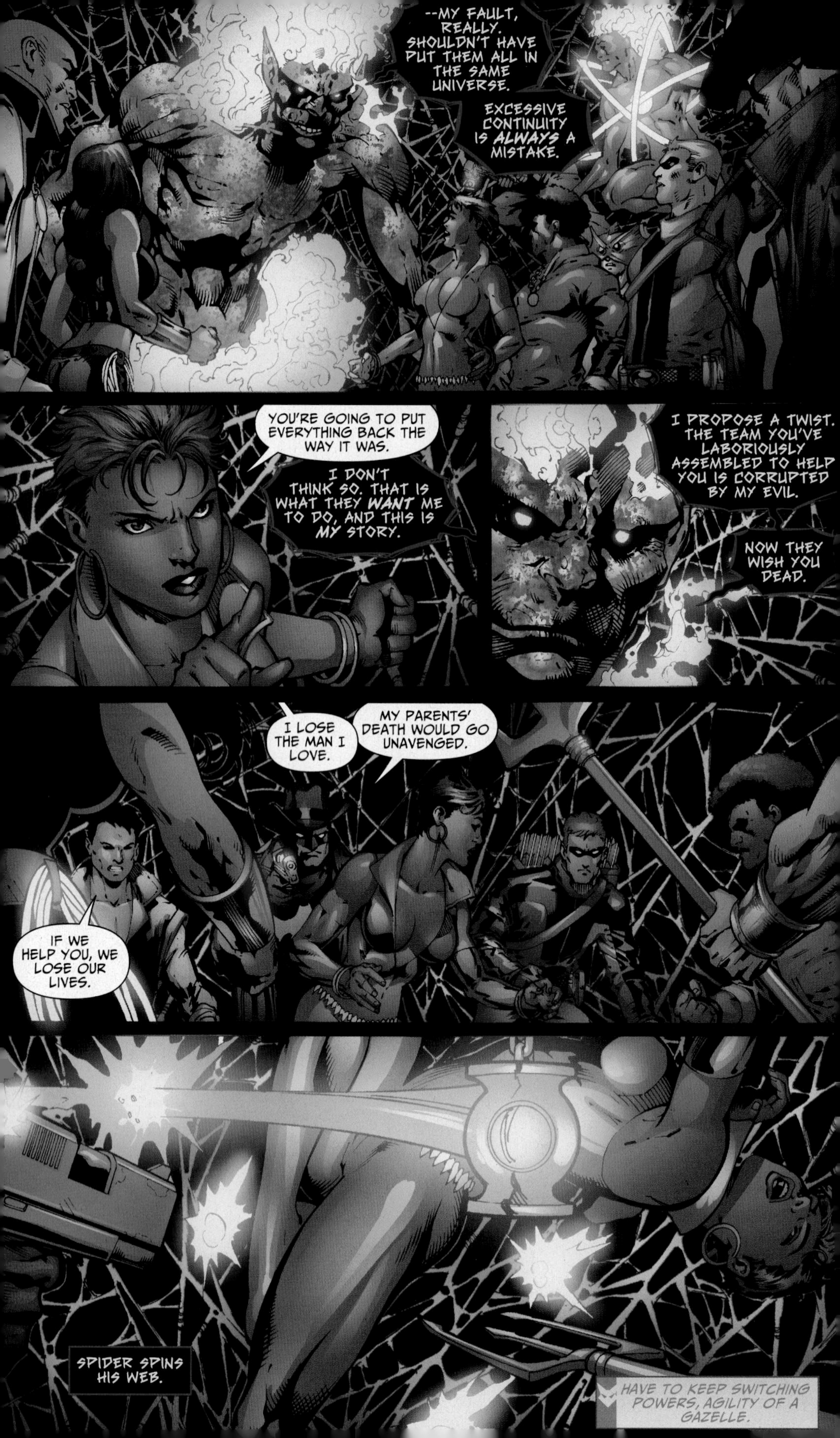
--MY FAULT, REALLY. SHOULDN'T HAVE PUT THEM ALL IN THE SAME UNIVERSE.
EXCESSIVE CONTINUITY IS ALWAYS A MISTAKE.
YOU'RE GOING TO PUT EVERYTHING BACK THE WAY IT WAS.
I DON'T THINK SO. THAT IS WHAT THEY WANT ME TO DO, AND THIS IS MY STORY.
I PROPOSE A TWIST. THE TEAM YOU'VE LABORIOUSLY ASSEMBLED TO HELP YOU IS CORRUPTED BY MY EVIL.
NOW THEY WISH YOU DEAD.
I LOSE THE MAN I LOVE.
MY PARENTS' DEATH WOULD GO UNAVENGED.
IF WE HELP YOU, WE LOSE OUR LIVES.
SPIDER SPINS HIS WEB.
HAVE TO KEEP SWITCHING POWERS, AGILITY OF A GAZELLE.

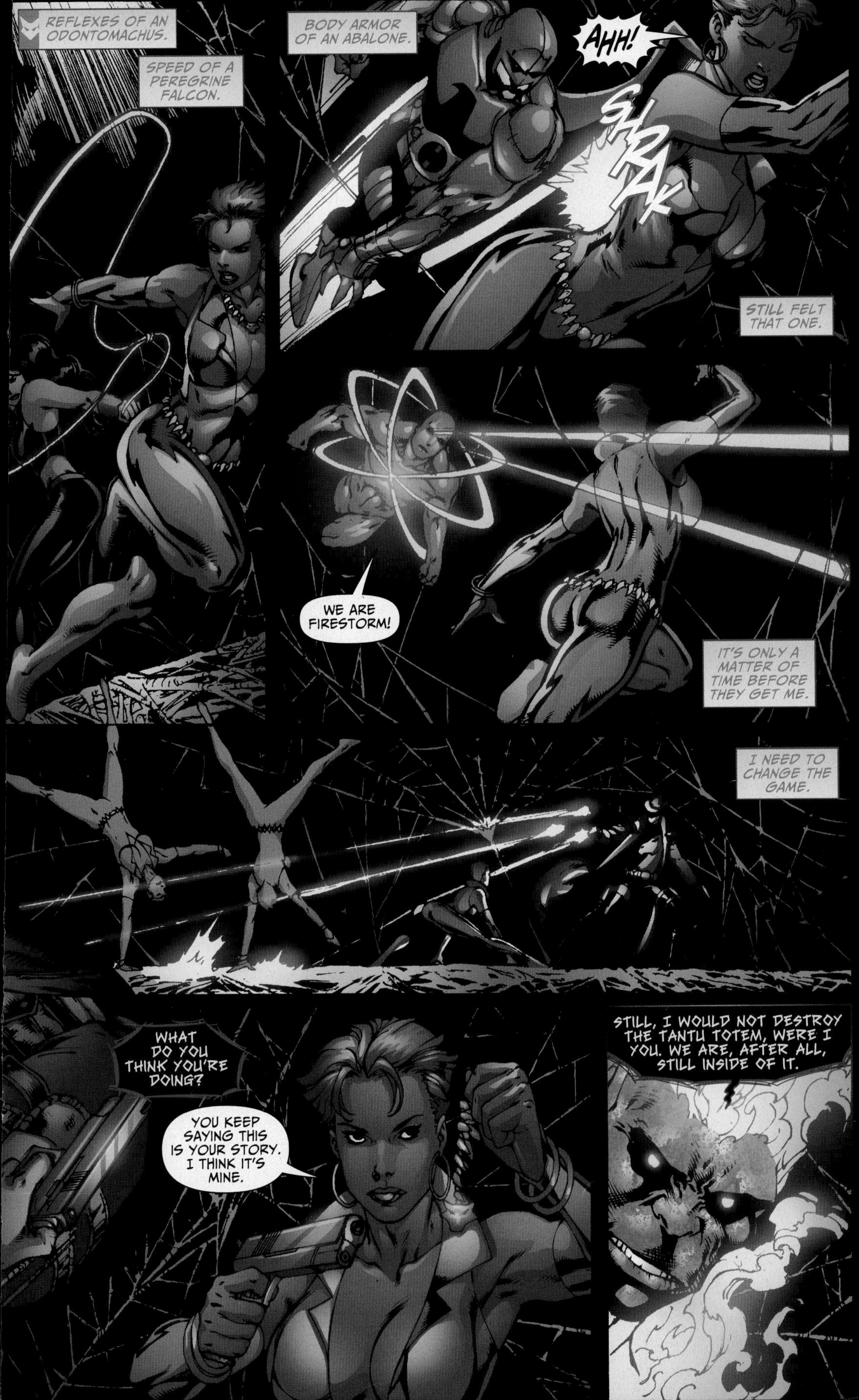
REFLEXES OF AN ODONTOMACHUS.
SPEED OF A PEREGRINE FALCON.
BODY ARMOR OF AN ABALONE.
AHH!
SHRAK
STILL FELT THAT ONE.
WE ARE FIRESTORM!
IT'S ONLY A MATTER OF TIME BEFORE THEY GET ME.
I NEED TO CHANGE THE GAME.
WHAT DO YOU THINK YOU'RE DOING?
YOU KEEP SAYING THIS IS YOUR STORY. I THINK IT'S MINE.
STILL, I WOULD NOT DESTROY THE TANTU TOTEM, WERE I YOU. WE ARE, AFTER ALL, STILL INSIDE OF IT.

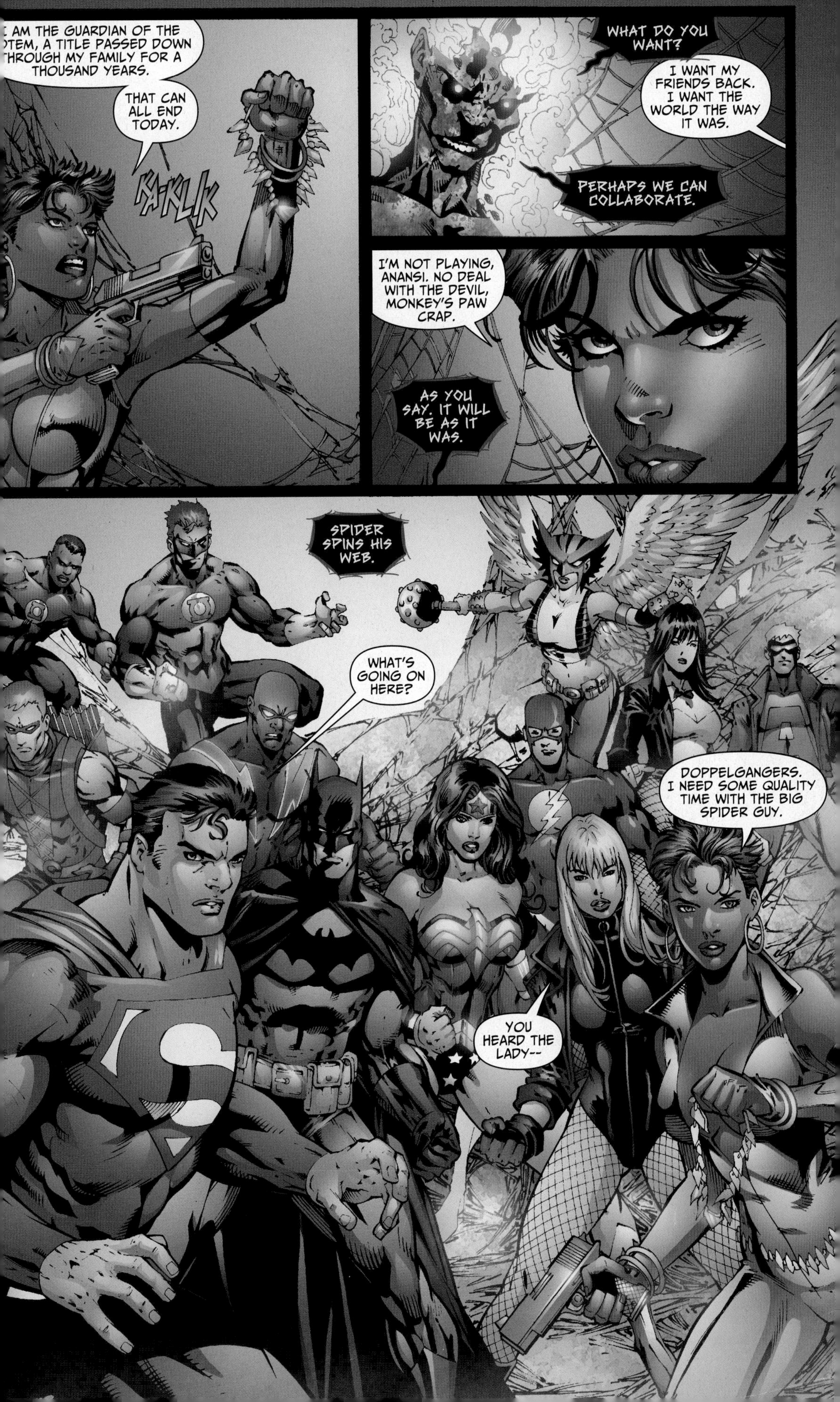
I AM THE GUARDIAN OF THE
OTEM, A TITLE PASSED DOWN
THROUGH MY FAMILY FOR A
THOUSAND YEARS.
THAT CAN ALL END TODAY.
KA-KLIK
WHAT DO YOU WANT?
I WANT MY FRIENDS BACK. I WANT THE WORLD THE WAY IT WAS.
PERHAPS WE CAN COLLABORATE.
I'M NOT PLAYING, ANANSI. NO DEAL WITH THE DEVIL, MONKEY'S PAW CRAP.
AS YOU SAY. IT WILL BE AS IT WAS.
SPIDER SPINS HIS WEB.
WHAT'S GOING ON HERE?
DOPPELGANGERS. I NEED SOME QUALITY TIME WITH THE BIG SPIDER GUY.
YOU HEARD THE LADY--

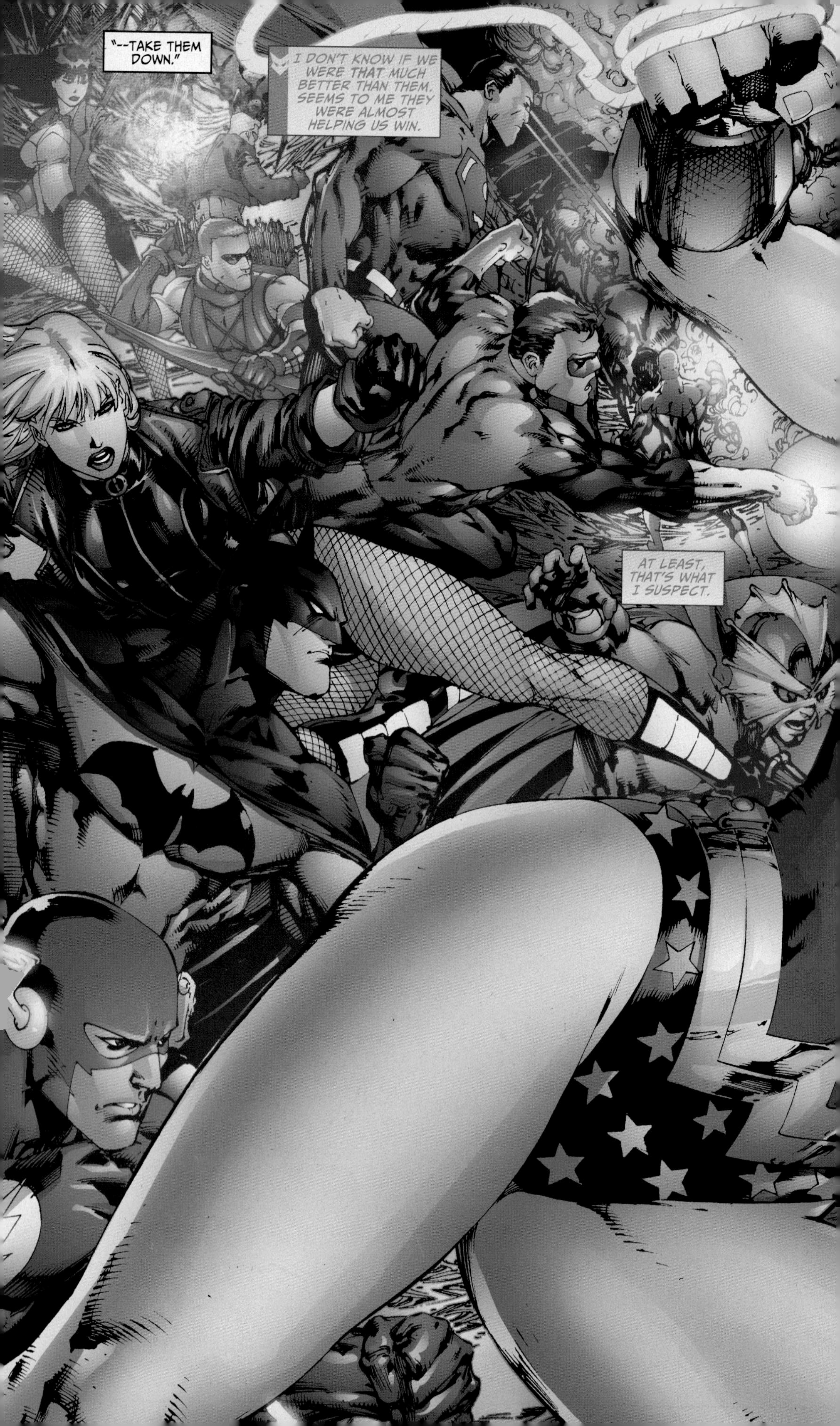
"--TAKE THEM DOWN."
I DON'T KNOW IF WE WERE THAT MUCH BETTER THAN THEM. SEEMS TO ME THEY WERE ALMOST HELPING US WIN.
AT LEAST, THAT'S WHAT I SUSPECT.

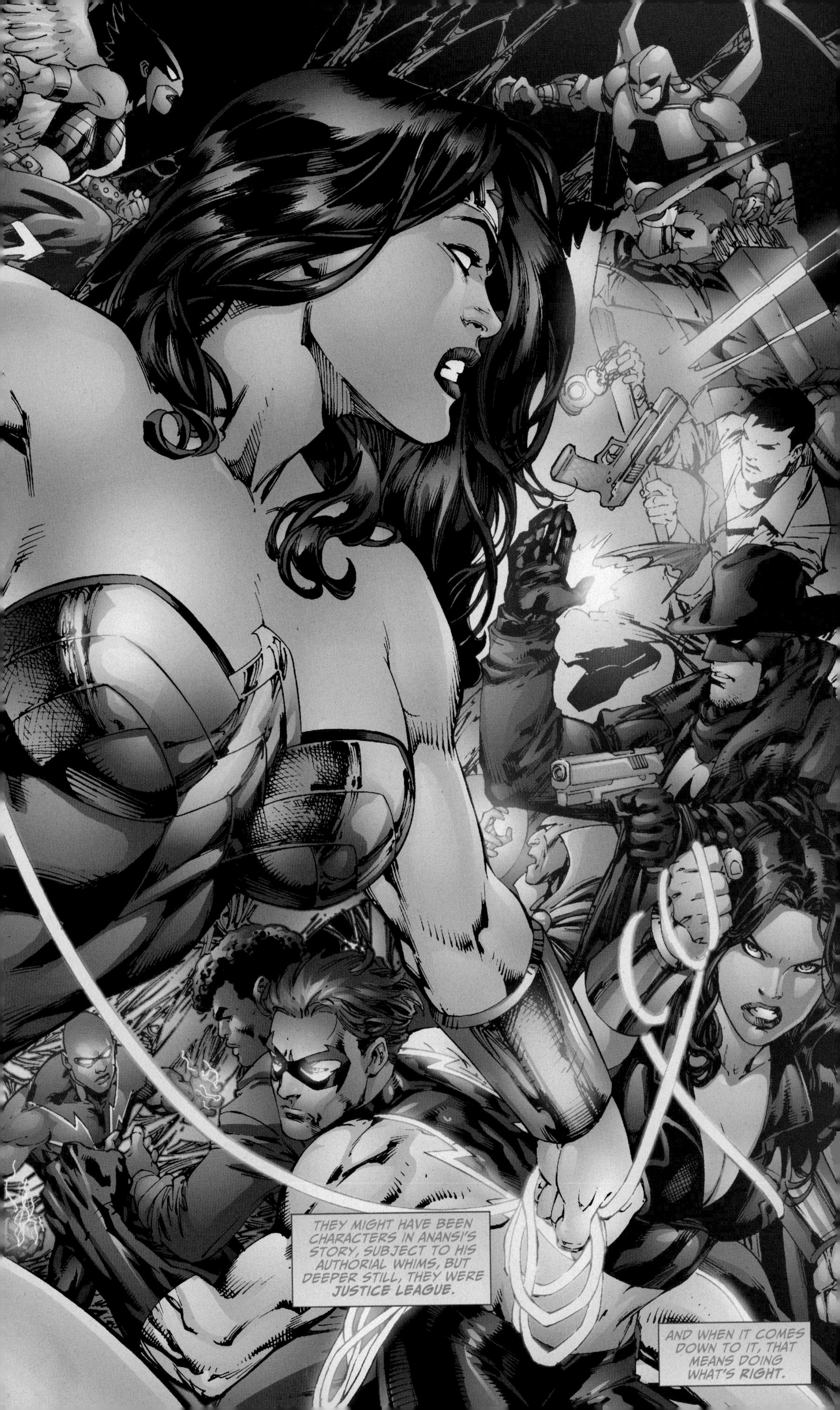
THEY MIGHT HAVE BEEN CHARACTERS IN ANANSI'S STORY, SUBJECT TO HIS AUTHORIAL WHIMS, BUT DEEPER STILL, THEY WERE JUSTICE LEAGUE.
AND WHEN IT COMES DOWN TO IT, THAT MEANS DOING WHAT'S RIGHT.

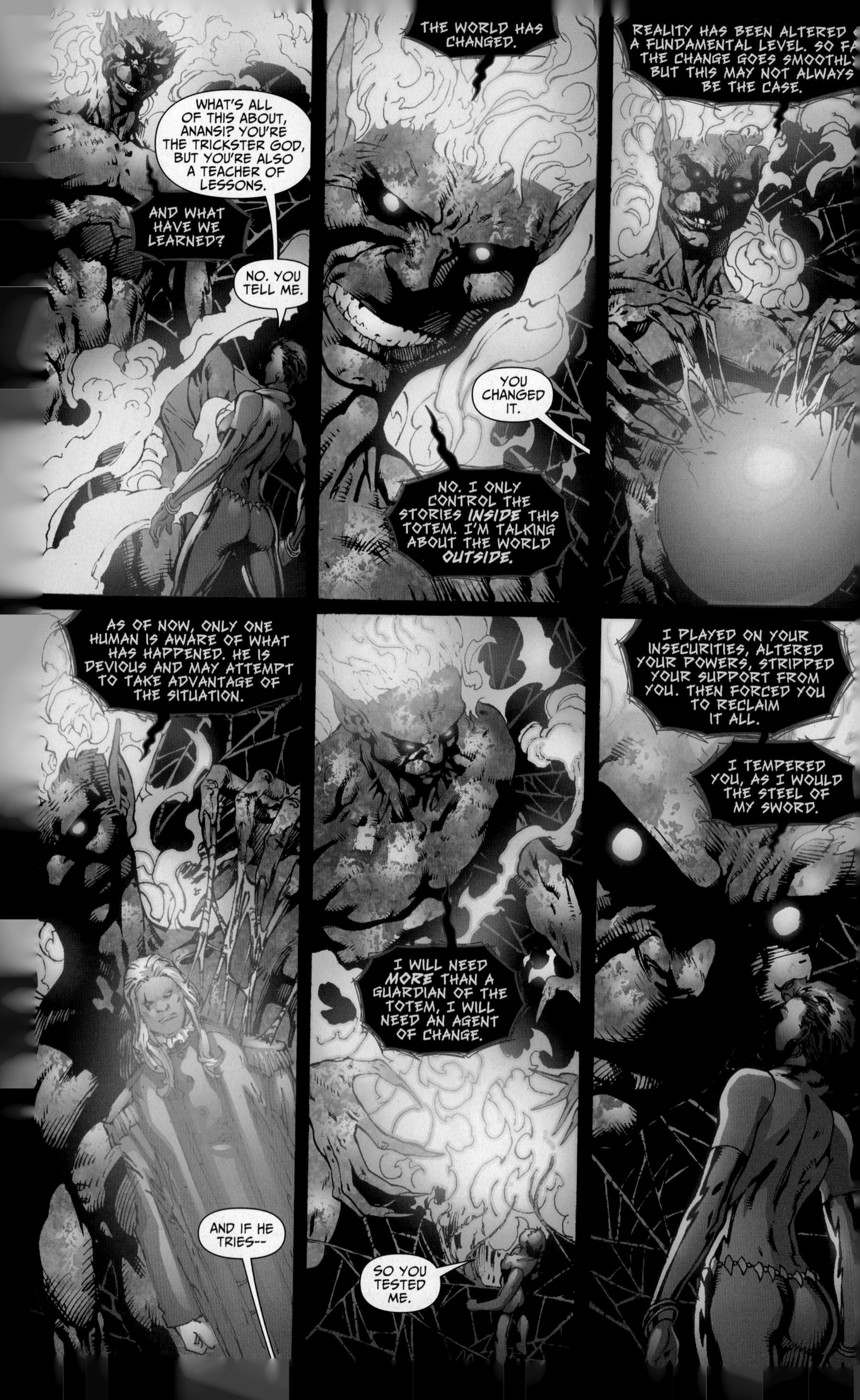
WHAT'S ALL OF THIS ABOUT, ANANSI? YOU'RE THE TRICKSTER GOD, BUT YOU'RE ALSO A TEACHER OF LESSONS.
AND WHAT HAVE WE LEARNED?
NO. YOU TELL ME.
THE WORLD HAS CHANGED.
YOU CHANGED IT.
NO. I ONLY CONTROL THE STORIES INSIDE THIS TOTEM. I'M TALKING ABOUT THE WORLD OUTSIDE.
AS OF NOW, ONLY ONE HUMAN IS AWARE OF WHAT HAS HAPPENED. HE IS DEVIOUS AND MAY ATTEMPT TO TAKE ADVANTAGE OF THE SITUATION.
AND IF HE TRIES--
I WILL NEED MORE THAN A GUARDIAN OF THE TOTEM, I WILL NEED AN AGENT OF CHANGE.
SO YOU TESTED ME.
I PLAYED ON YOUR INSECURITIES, ALTERED YOUR POWERS, STRIPPED YOUR SUPPORT FROM YOU. THEN FORCED YOU TO RECLAIM IT ALL.
I TEMPERED YOU, AS I WOULD THE STEEL OF MY SWORD.

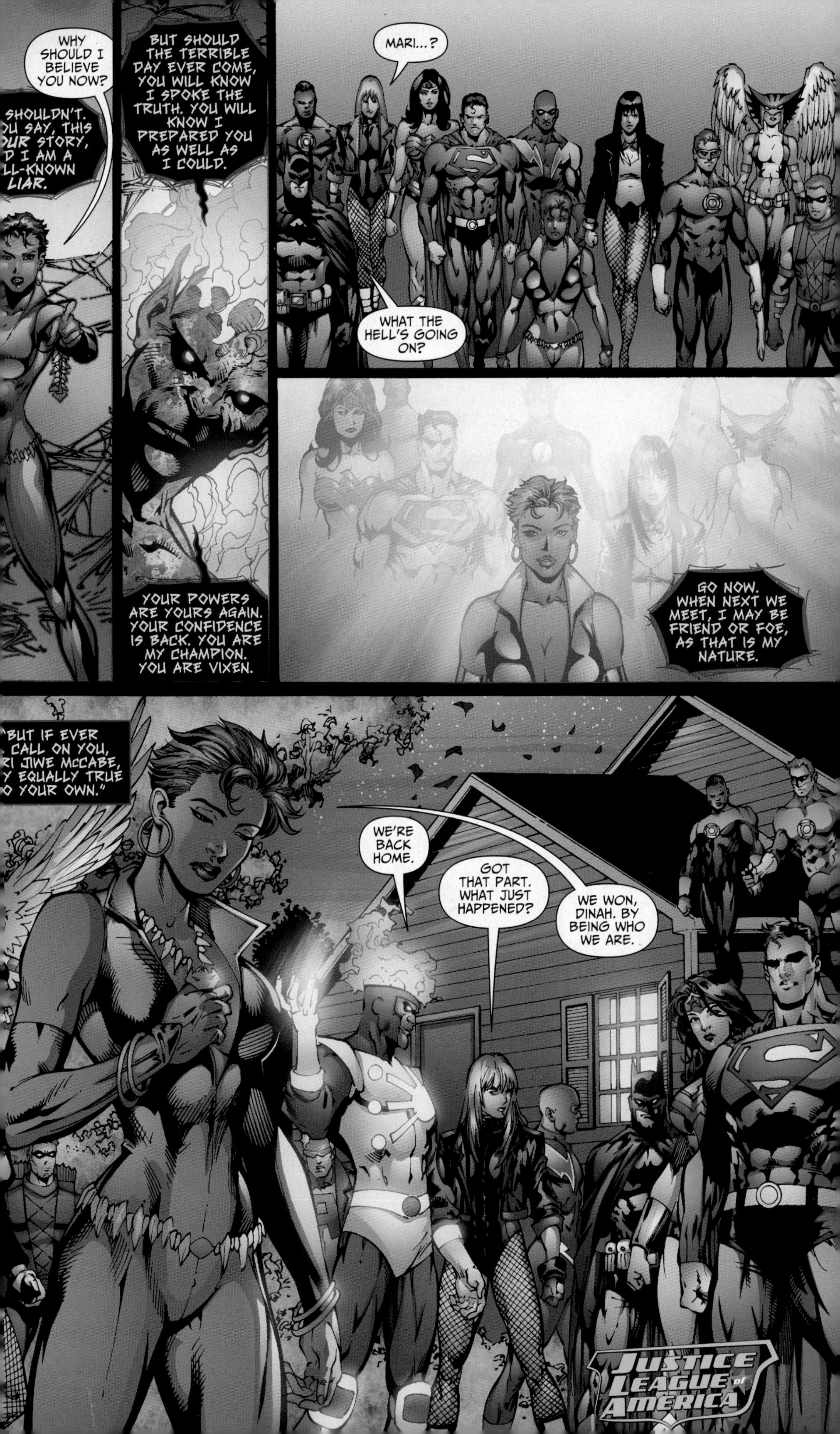
WHY SHOULD I BELIEVE YOU NOW?
SHOULDN'T. OU SAY, THIS OUR STORY, D I AM A LL-KNOWN LIAR.
BUT SHOULD THE TERRIBLE DAY EVER COME, YOU WILL KNOW I SPOKE THE TRUTH. YOU WILL KNOW I PREPARED YOU AS WELL AS I COULD.
YOUR POWERS ARE YOURS AGAIN. YOUR CONFIDENCE IS BACK. YOU ARE MY CHAMPION. YOU ARE VIXEN.
MARI...?
WHAT THE HELL'S GOING ON?
GO NOW. WHEN NEXT WE MEET, I MAY BE FRIEND OR FOE, AS THAT IS MY NATURE.
"BUT IF EVER CALL ON YOU, RI JIWE McCABE, Y EQUALLY TRUE O YOUR OWN."
WE'RE BACK HOME.
GOT THAT PART. WHAT JUST HAPPENED?
WE WON, DINAH. BY BEING WHO WE ARE.
JUSTICE LEAGUE of AMERICA